RURAL DEVELOPMENT IN ACTION
*The Comprehensive Experiment at Comilla,
East Pakistan*

RURAL DEVELOPMENT IN ACTION

The Comprehensive Experiment at Comilla, East Pakistan

By ARTHUR F. RAPER

ASSISTED BY

HARRY L. CASE, RICHARD O. NIEHOFF,
WILLIAM T. ROSS, AND EDGAR A. SCHULER

Cornell University Press

ITHACA AND LONDON

Copyright © 1970 by Cornell University

All rights reserved. Except for brief quotations in a review, this book, or parts thereof, must not be reproduced in any form without permission in writing from the publisher. For information address Cornell University Press, 124 Roberts Place, Ithaca, New York 14850.

First published 1970

Standard Book Number 8014-0570-x
Library of Congress Catalog Card Number 73-111605

PRINTED IN THE UNITED STATES OF AMERICA
BY KINGSPORT PRESS, INC.

Foreword

For the last ten years a sustained and impressive effort has been made to bring radical change to a rural area in East Pakistan. This book is a report on that effort. It is an interim report, for the effort is continuing, and the story is far from ended. But enough has occurred to shed much illumination on a baffling problem of great importance in the developing countries: how to help rural families who live at the ragged edge of survival to acquire power—the power of knowledge and of organization—to lift themselves toward a better life.

The scene of this particular effort is Comilla *thana*, a county-size rural area of about one hundred square miles, named for and centering on the small city of Comilla. The thana lies at the eastern edge of the delta of the mighty Brahmaputra River, 80 miles north of the Bay of Bengal. This is rice-growing country, green, hot, cut up by waterways, in the rainy season soggily wet. About a quarter of a million people live there. They are Bengalis, small, shrewd, inured over centuries to the overpowering vagaries of natural disasters in the form of floods, typhoons, epidemics. The land is beautiful, and the Bengalis add to its beauty with their graceful boats and their lyrical songs. But their life is excruciatingly hard.

Statistics can convey only dimly what it means to live as a rural Bengali family. The average farmer in Comilla thana owns or leases about 1.7 acres of land, broken up into several parcels of half an acre or less. But he does not keep all of his small harvest; if he is a landowner, 40 per cent of the crop, on the average, goes to the moneylender; if he is a tenant, half goes to the landlord. The family house has a mud floor, woven bamboo walls, and for roofing, thatch, or—if they are lucky—corrugated sheet iron. Their light, if any, is a kerosene lamp. The parents have had little or no schooling, although the children probably have access to a primary school in their own village or one nearby. Modern medical services and communications are virtually unknown to them.

The conditions in Comilla thana are not at all unique. These are the conditions of hundreds of millions of people in many countries around the world. The problem of development is to change those conditions, and many good men have poured their energies into fruitless efforts to accomplish this.

The efforts being made in Comilla thana are plainly not fruitless. It is too soon to claim great success, but not too soon to assess what has worked and what has not worked at Comilla, and to think about what lessons may be learned for application in other places. That is the purpose of this book.

The Comilla story is important partly because it records some success, more because the hard and imaginative work that has been done has been consistently documented, tested, and appraised. The result is a more carefully organized set of data about rural change—more scientific information, if you will—than is generally available.

The Comilla story centers in a sense around an institution, the East Pakistan Academy for Rural Development, established in the late 1950's, along with a second Academy in West Pakistan, to conduct research and to offer training to government officials concerned with rural problems. The Academy at Comilla has been assisted since the early planning stages by advisers from Michigan State University, financed by the Ford Foundation.

The Comilla story centers in a more important sense around a man—a remarkable man—Akhter Hameed Khan, who except for a brief interlude has been director of the Academy since its inception and is the prime cause of its success. Akhter Hameed Khan was a brilliant young government official who in 1944 retired from the Indian Civil Service to devote himself to what would now be called development work in rural areas. At the time the Academy in East Pakistan was conceived, he was principal of a small college in Comilla, and the Academy was located at Comilla, a rather obscure place, in order that he could be persuaded to become its director.

The choice could not have been wiser, for it was he who brought to the Academy its central concept, which had grown out of his own direct experience in rural areas. This central concept, which may well be the most important lesson taught by this book, is that anyone who seeks to assist Bengali villagers must approach them ready to listen and learn, not to talk and instruct. The outsider can offer no prescription for assured progress; he cannot know in advance what will bring successful change in any one area, such as Comilla. An outsider can bring ideas, seeds, implements, organizational concepts, all derived from scientific and practical experience elsewhere. They may or may not work in Comilla. Only careful experimentation will tell. And the key experimenters must be the Bengalis themselves, who know little about science or the outside world—but they do know what has worked in Comilla in the past, and they have survived.

The central concept of the Academy from its beginning therefore has been to regard Comilla thana as a laboratory for social and economic research, and to enlist the people of the thana, the staff of the Academy, and the local officers of government in a joint program of research and experimentation. And the staff members of the Academy—Pakistani and foreign alike—had to start by listening to the villagers, because that was the only way to find out where the process of change had to begin, and—furthermore—the only way to persuade the villagers that the people from the Academy might be worth listening to.

Over these ten years many things have been tried, and, painfully, by trial and error, some beachheads of success have been established. This book documents again and again how agonizingly slow any progress must be when initial circumstances are so difficult. But it also shows the beginnings of the self-reinforcing, upward spiral of change that can come when new ideas begin to pay off in the form of higher incomes, which in turn permit larger investments in more new ideas—and when new organizations having held together under initial stresses begin to produce stronger leadership and rising confidence among their members.

And above all, the Comilla experience demonstrates that the typical withdrawn and fatalistic attitude of the rural people in countries with very low incomes can be overcome —that the traditional apathy of the villagers disappears as soon as they are convinced of the possibility of significant improvement in their standard of living.

Anyone who doubts this need only visit Comilla, as I have done. Let him visit the new cooperative cold-storage plant, look at the meticulously kept books of the village cooperative societies, inspect the cooperative machine shop, and talk with villagers who headed up the public works projects. Like everyone who goes to Comilla, I came away a believer. The cumulative process of economic and social change has begun, and the system seems strong enough to carry on.

Will the Comilla pattern work elsewhere? No one yet knows. Akhter Hameed Khan has been asked by the Pakistan government to spread it to pilot thanas throughout East Pakistan, and the evidence should become available over the next few years. Does the Comilla experience depend too much on this one man? Perhaps. But surely the job of development anywhere is largely that of finding leaders and supporting them as they grope for answers, teach what they learn, and inspire others.

In any event, Comilla is there to be seen. Like Thanjavur and Ludhiana districts in India, like Laguna province in the Philippines, like Taiwan, Comilla thana is evidence that rapid rural development in Asia can be achieved—with hard work but without miracles—and that the average Asian villager, far from being indifferent to change as he is often portrayed, given quite feasible conditions—of incentives, knowledge, organization, and supplies—is a canny and hard-driving entrepreneur, ready for swift innovation.

For bringing us this full and careful account of the Comilla experience, all of us interested in rural development owe much to Arthur Raper and his colleagues at Michigan State University.

DAVID E. BELL
Vice President
The Ford Foundation

New York City
April 25, 1968

Preface

This book is a documentation of the Academy for Rural Development at Comilla in East Pakistan, and the outreach of its work. There is a second Academy at Peshawar in West Pakistan. Their origins are treated together in the early part of Chapter 2, but otherwise this book is limited to programs centering at Comilla. The Peshawar Academy operates in a different setting and with different leadership, and so developed in other directions.

To no small degree, it was the self-awareness of the development effort at Comilla that made this volume possible. The academy there decided at the outset to keep a full record of all its operations and field experiments. The files at Michigan State University also cover the whole of the project, from the first discussions about it in the mid-1950's to the present.

Most citations are from Academy publications and documents. Two types of spelling will be encountered: the American and the British, the latter limited to direct quotations. When a Bengali term is first used, it is italicized. The glossary defines Bengali words. A list of abbreviations precedes the text.

For the development of the manuscript, a wide range of documentation was available. After some months of close study, the files at the Academy and at Michigan State University yielded an action diary of more than 200 pages—and another document of similar size when the entries were grouped by subject matter. Here was a myriad of facts that needed to be fitted into a balanced statement.

Equally important were the personal resources available. On the Michigan State University campus when the draft manuscript was being written were: William T. Ross, the university's first resident advisor in Pakistan, and later the campus coordinator of the project; Richard O. Niehoff, the campus coordinator of the project since 1962, and for two years before that the resident chief advisor in Pakistan; Edgar A. Schuler, the first senior advisor at Comilla; myself, who was the second; and Robert D. Stevens, who was the third. All were interested in the project and contributed to the work on the manuscript. Helpful, too, have been Wilbur B. Brookover, first campus coordinator of the project (1957–1960) and a member of the Michigan State University planning teams that went to Pakistan in the summers of 1956 and 1957; Floyd W. Reeves, chief of party for both teams; Cole S. Brembeck, member of the first team and involved in planning for the training of the Academy faculties; Albert E. Levak, in charge of the staff training operations (1958–1959); Harvey M. Choldin, former research associate at the Academy for the Population Council, Inc.; and Florence E. McCarthy, a graduate student from Michigan State University who has recently returned from more than a year in Comilla, where she made observations on village women innovators, and who earlier as a Peace Corps Volunteer was actively involved in the women's work there.

Also on the university campus—working on their doctorates—were two of the original members of the Comilla

Academy faculty: Abdul Muyeed, instructor in communications and education, and S. A. Rahim, research specialist, who also assisted in updating the program statistics for 1968. Each helped keep the record straight. Available on campus, too, for nearly two months in the fall of 1966 was Akhter Hameed Khan, director of the Academy; he read an early version of the manuscript and made many helpful suggestions.

Yet other help came from a study of the reports sent to Michigan State University by advisors Henry W. Fairchild, Delvin W. Martens, Robert D. Havener, and Nicolaas G. M. Luykx, II, the resident senior advisor from early 1966 to mid-1968. A special debt is owed to Sol Tax, anthropologist, University of Chicago, who read an early draft of the manuscript and made basic recommendations on the presentation of materials.

In late 1966 I went back to Comilla to update quantitative data and check further on my own impressions. While I was there each chapter was read by the staff member immediately responsible. Also while there, information was secured from A. Musa S. Ahmad, then secretary of the Department of Basic Democracies and Local Government, about the provincial public works program, including the rate at which thana training and development centers were being established, and from Richard H. Patten, consultant to the International Bank for Reconstruction and Development, and earlier with the Harvard University Advisory Group to the Planning and Development Department at Dacca, about the various other ongoing development programs in East Pakistan.

Financial support for the preparation of this manuscript was supplied by the Asian Studies Center of Michigan State University, with the costs for the last half of 1966, including my return to Comilla, taken care of by a grant from the Midwest Universities Consortium for International Activities, Inc. The secretaries who assisted at one time and another—Cheri Whan, Marjorie Lang, Jean Van Douser, and Catherine Burt—were patient and resourceful in moving the manuscript forward. Martha J. Raper, even though not well, gave a critical reading to one draft after another, and contributed insights gained from her two years as editorial associate at the Academy.

Much help was received from many quarters, and all of it was appreciated. The result was a voluminous manuscript, expertly reduced to small-book length by Harry L. Case, of the Institute for International Studies in Education, Michigan State University, and formerly a representative of the Ford Foundation in Pakistan. Richard O. Niehoff added updated materials, and he and Harry Case collaborated with me in putting the manuscript into final form for publication.

ARTHUR F. RAPER

Oakton, Virginia
June 1969

Contents

Foreword, by David E. Bell	v
Preface	xi
Abbreviations	xix
1 The Setting, and Operating Assumptions	1
2 Origins and Institutional Development	21
3 A New Village-based Cooperative System	45
4 Changing Concepts of Local Government	98
5 Irrigation and Rural Electrification	135
6 The Women's and Family Planning Programs	157
7 Some Experiments in Rural Education	186
8 Research and Communications	210
9 The Impact of the Academy	232
10 Reflections	266

Appendixes

I "A Light in the Darkness"	279
II Principal Personnel Associated with the Academy	289
III Curriculum Vitae of Akhter Hameed Khan, Director of the Academy	292
IV Acknowledgment of Assistance Received by the Academy	294
V Foreign Personnel Associated with the Academy	298
VI Statistical Tables	302
VII Principal Sources of Financial Support	315

VIII A Brief Chronology of the History of the
　　　Academy　　　　　　　　　　　　　　　318

Glossary　　　　　　　　　　　　　　　　　333
Bibliography　　　　　　　　　　　　　　　336
Index　　　　　　　　　　　　　　　　　　345

Illustrations

Plates follow page 74

Maps

1	East Pakistan, population density by districts, 1961	6
2	Comilla Kotwali thana, the agricultural cooperative societies, by years, 1959–1966	62
3	Comilla Kotwali thana, villages with women's programs, mid-1966	170
4	East Pakistan, thanas with Comilla-type programs, mid-1966	237

Charts

1	Structural and functional dimensions of Comilla cooperative system, 1968	64
2	An organizational chart for a thana training and development center	129

Abbreviations

ACF	Agricultural Cooperatives Federation; this organization provides training and supervision of the village-based agricultural societies in Comilla thana. ACF is a unit of the KTCCA.
ADC	Agricultural Development Corporation is a government agency set up to accelerate agricultural production.
AID	United States Agency for International Development, the principal foreign aid-giving agency of the United States government since 1962. It was preceded by the United States International Cooperation Administration (ICA).
CARE	Committee on American Relief Everywhere.
EPWAPDA	East Pakistan Water and Power Development Authority.
FAO	Food and Agriculture Organization of the United Nations.
ICA	United States International Cooperation Administration; predecessor to United States Agency for International Development (AID).

	Abbreviations
IRRI	International Rice Research Institute, located in Los Baños, Philippines.
IUD	Intrauterine device—a contraceptive device.
KTCCA	Kotwali Thana Central Cooperative Association.
MSU	Michigan State University, East Lansing, Michigan.
NDO	National Development Organization, an agency set up to integrate V-AID (below) and Department of Basic Democracies and Local Government.
PARD and PAVD	Pakistan Academy for Rural Development; name changed from Pakistan Academy for Village Development in October 1962.
PL-480	United States Public Law No. 480, which makes surplus farm products available for overseas use through intergovernment arrangements.
TTDC	Thana Training and Development Center.
UNICEF	United Nations International Children's Emergency Fund.
USIS	United States Information Service, the country unit of the United States Information Agency (USIA).
V-AID	Village Agricultural and Industrial Development, a community development program which operated in Pakistan from 1953 to 1961. Village-level workers in the V-AID program usually served five or so villages, functioning as multipurpose liaison between the villagers and the various provincial representatives located at the headquarters of the V-AID development area.

RURAL DEVELOPMENT IN ACTION
*The Comprehensive Experiment at Comilla,
East Pakistan*

1. The Setting, and Operating Assumptions

The Comilla story relates to the large part of the world where most of the people are poor in worldly goods, ill fed, often suffering from disease, and see little prospect of improving their lot; where people fear change lest their tenuous hold on what little they have be broken.

These are the problems of East Pakistan, where Comilla is located. The programs here to be discussed are designed to alleviate the problems, and the results to date are hopeful. The programs are elemental, as they have to be in order to be relevant. Even modest achievements are important in an area so fraught with concern for survival. Answers found to the needs in this area are proving helpful elsewhere in Pakistan and may be found useful, with adaptations, in other developing countries.

The Physical and Cultural Setting in East Pakistan

The terrain and the climate provide a harsh setting for the people of Comilla. The area is part of a great deltaic plain no more than 30 feet above sea level a hundred miles inland; it floods each year. To be above the floodwater, every house has to be built on the highest available ground, much of which is man-made in the process of excavating for a tank (pond) which serves as an all-purpose water supply, and fish-rearing pool. Every village path and road must be a causeway. The silt-laden meandering rivers—the largest of which are the Brahmaputra, Megna, Ganges, and Triputanes—are forever changing their courses. The annual flood is followed by the dry season. But a few weeks after the flooding, the soil is too dry and hard for farming unless irrigation water is provided, which requires more organization and capital than the villagers have had.

Then there are the recurring storms—the nor'westers in April and May, and cyclones, hurricanes, and an occasional tidal bore in October and November. The nor'westers, shot through with electrical activity and packing galelike winds and cloudburst rains, usher in the monsoon, and the cyclonic weather ushers it out. Ninety per cent of the annual rainfall (60–175 inches) occurs from May to November.

The summer, which extends over more than half of the year, is hot and humid; ideal for hydroponic rice varieties, water hyacinth, ferns, mildew, and termites. The remainder of the year is made up of a short, hardly distinguishable fall and spring, and between them several weeks of "wintry weather," clear, cool, crisp, invigorating for the well-dressed in good houses, but often a time of real discomfort for undernourished people in bamboo huts with few or no wool clothes or blankets.

Food is often in short supply, especially toward the end of the dry season. The main dishes are rice, pumpkins and gourds, beans and pulses, with now and then some fish or beef, often in small bits as flavoring for the rice. Practically all cooked dishes are highly spiced. Clothing, too, is scarce and made of cotton, most of which is imported.

Illness is common, with numerous cases of cholera, ty-

The Setting, and Operating Assumptions 3

phoid, malaria, tuberculosis, dysentery, and worm infections. Modern medical care is nearly unknown in rural areas. Life expectancy at birth is around 48 years.

Village dwellings are small. Most of them have woven bamboo walls, thinly plastered, and roofs of thatch which has to be replaced every few seasons. The better houses have mud walls and are covered with galvanized iron sheets, rusty except when new. Household furnishings are minimal.

Villages are often isolated for lack of local roads during the annual monsoon flood, and for lack of navigable waterways before the end of the dry season. Community life is patterned in general by the Islamic annual cycle. There are the month of *Ramadan*[1] with its requirements and prohibitions, *Eid* festivals, and holy days, the weekly time of worship at the mosque, the value put on brotherhood and on community consensus. The men sell most of their surplus commodities and buy provisions at the local markets (*hāts*) once or twice a week. They enjoy visiting at the numerous tea stalls which also sell matches and other small household necessities and more recently family planning supplies. The women are virtually housebound by *purdah*, which is practiced above the age of around twelve. When they do go out they are covered from the head down with the *burqa*, an all-covering outer garment with peepholes for seeing through.

The physical and psychological isolation of the villagers has resulted in a tightly knit social structure. The individual's economic and psychological margins of security are so small that he dares not deviate much from established

[1] See Glossary. Bengali words will be italicized the first time used.

norms lest he jeopardize his good standing in the village, a fact which has important implications for those concerned with rural development.

In the rural areas there is about one school for every three villages. The village schools reflect the social and economic disintegration that has characterized the rural areas of East Pakistan in recent decades. The schoolhouses are for the most part poorly constructed, poorly equipped, and poorly maintained. This situation obtains alike for the public schools, which have continued more or less along the lines of those established by the British in Bengal in the 1830's, and for the *madrassa* or religious schools, which are mainly concerned with teaching the *Quran*.

The teachers of both types of schools have had little training, receive low pay, and in general are indifferent about their work. Because of the low allowance provided, even such in-service training as has been arranged for the teachers is often regarded as a burden. The curriculum is largely unrelated to the lives of the children; instruction is primarily by the rote method.

A large majority of rural men and almost all women are illiterate. As of 1961, nearly half of the children age five to fourteen had never been to school at all, and most of those who had attended dropped out after a year or two. Less than 30 per cent of the children then in school were girls. In fact, unless a parent or guardian hoped for his child or ward to leave the village, he saw little reason to send him to school. Yet in Bengal the man who can write poetry and songs is deeply appreciated; the learned man who can read the sayings of the Buddha is looked up to, and the man who can recite extensive portions of the Quran is revered. The printed page is sacred even to the unlettered villagers. Despite the poor schools and high illiteracy rates, there is an

The Setting, and Operating Assumptions 5

appreciation of the past glories of Islamic and Persian and Buddhist scholars and poets. But of modern knowledge there has been little appreciation. The numerous madrassa schools are still teaching the twelfth- and thirteenth-century Greek concepts of anatomy, astronomy, physics, and chemistry that were brought into Bengal in translations from the Arabic.

Weekly newspaper distribution is meager; telephone and telegraphic connections are limited almost wholly to the cities and larger towns and to government headquarters. Recently, however, transistor radios have begun to appear in the villages.

The population of East Pakistan is somewhat more than 50 million. This number represents slightly over half of the total population of the nation, living on approximately 15 per cent of the nation's area. Population density is one of the highest in the world, with approximately 1,600 people to the square mile, with more than four-fifths of them rural. Roughly four-fifths embrace the Muslim faith. The remainder are Hindus, except about one per cent who are Christians, Buddhists, and other faiths. Practically all speak Bengali. Nine-tenths of the men are engaged in agriculture, about which most village life revolves, though there is an occasional village of craftsmen, usually weavers or potters. Scattered through the village population are carpenters, and bamboo and cane workers, and a few blacksmiths, shoe menders, mechanics, fishnet makers, and other artisans.

The cities and larger towns have a somewhat wider range of opportunities for livelihood—from household industries (furniture making, for example), rickshaw pedaling, to modern, semiautomatic manufacturing plants. But factories are rare, for that part of Bengal which became East Pakistan contained but few industrial enterprises. Em-

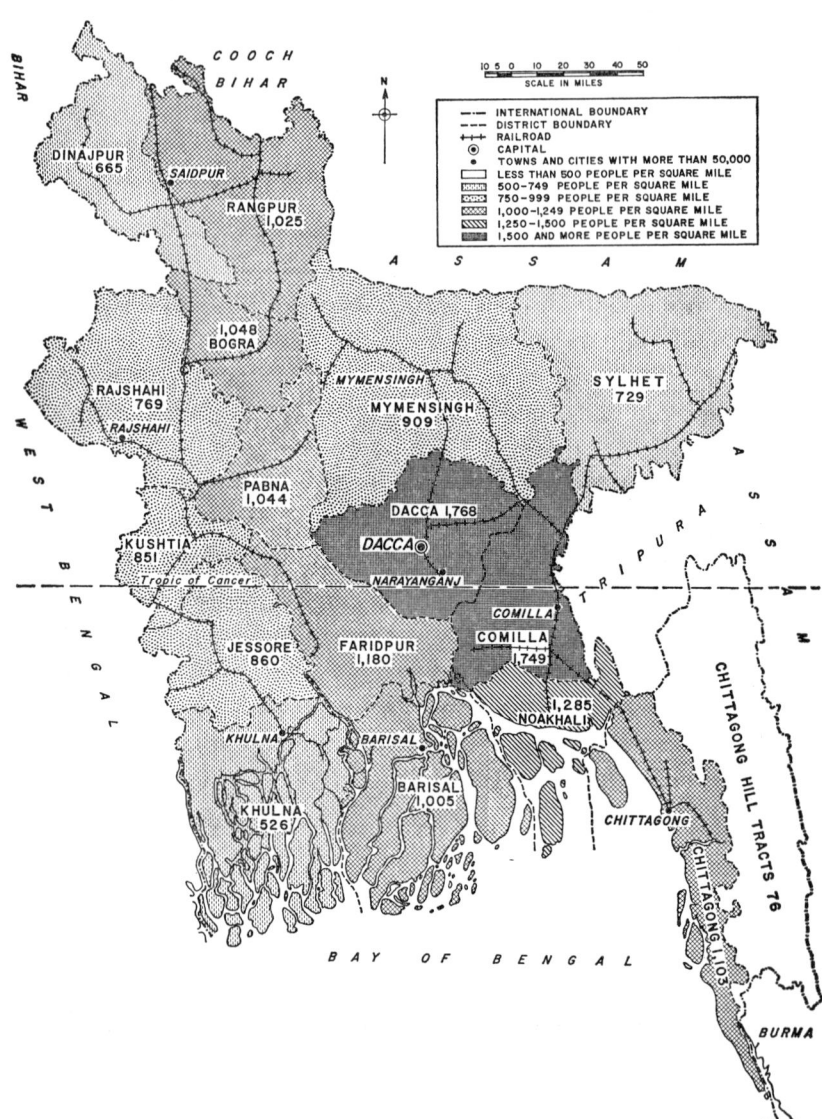

Map. 1. East Pakistan, population density by districts, 1961. Based on data from the Pakistan Census of Population, 1961, Karachi, Government of Pakistan. Drawn by M. A. Quddus, PARD, December 1966.

The Setting, and Operating Assumptions 7

ployment opportunities for white-collar workers are concentrated in government offices and government-operated enterprises.

Farms in East Pakistan average 3.7 acres in size (1960 census), and roughly a tenth of the would-be farming families, as reported by the census, have no land to farm. As a result of inheritance practices, practically all of the holdings of small farmers are made up of scattered fields. Clear land titles are rare, as a consequence of the breakdown of the *zamindari* system after 1900, the movement out of the area of many Hindu landlords after Partition (1947), and the great backlog of unfinished work in the Land Settlement Office, where the determinations are made on disposition of the erstwhile zamindar's acreage. Meanwhile most farmers operate on a traditional cultivation right, protected by the 1950 East Bengal State Acquisition and Tenancy Act. Thus in the Comilla area, as in most of East Bengal, there has occurred a generally effective, if highly confused, land reform. Most farm families "own" the land they cultivate, that is, their claim to it through use is more valid than the claim of anyone else. So, while the Land Settlement Office is completing administrative work on the titles, they pay the taxes and use the land as their own. And woe be to anyone who challenges these arrangements.

The tools and implements of the farmers are few and simple. The most common are the short-handled hoe-shovel, heavy-bladed knife, hand scythe, wooden-wheeled cart, metal-pointed wooden plow to stir the soil, split-bamboo ladder to level off the submerged land, and the puddler to prepare the soggy soil for the transplanting of rice seedlings. Bullocks supplement manpower; most of the animals are small, ill fed, and weak.

Both the dry and the wet seasons present special problems, but each has its advantages too. In the monsoon some types of vegetation grow rapidly, especially the *aus* and *amon* paddy crops, and jute. During the dry season there is continuous sunshine. Then the amon crop can be readily dried and winnowed, and the straw prepared for rope- or mat-making or for cattle feed. If watered, a wide range of vegetables can be grown, as can also *boro* paddy. The plans for widespread irrigation described later have greatly improved the prospects for farming under controlled conditions, adding a third crop and increasing the variety of agricultural products.

Until recently only one farmer in 25 used commercial fertilizers, and only half of the farmers in the province put manure on their fields—use of manure as a fertilizer is limited because it serves also as a household fuel. Improved seeds were rarely planted, and cultural practices employed were generally primitive. Accordingly, yields were extremely low and per capita income less than *Rupees* 300[2] a year ($60).

Under the prevailing system of credit, loans were secured by the sale of parcels of land to the moneylenders; the borrowing farmer then paid rent to the new owner for the use of the land. Annual carrying charges have ranged between 60 and 90 per cent of the loan. Hence most of the farmers were deeply in debt to the moneylenders.

Furthermore, farmers have been doubly penalized by their marketing and purchasing practices. They have sold their small surpluses at harvest time at depressed prices, and purchased their supplies at high prices.

[2] The exchange rate, through the period of this study, has been Rs. 4.76 to the dollar. Thus, to convert rupees into dollars a rough formula is to divide by five. In this text all financial data are presented in rupees, except where the amount is actually a dollar figure.

The Comilla Area

The preceding discussion of life in East Pakistan is also a description of life in the area in and around Comilla, except that, by and large, Comilla is below the average standard of living for East Pakistan. Population densities in Comilla district and Comilla *thana*[3] are well above the density for the province, the farms are smaller, and the proportions of rural dwellers without land are greater. Thus in 1961 the population density was approximately 1,600 per square mile for East Pakistan; 1,693 for Comilla district; and 2,031 for Comilla thana; the average size of farms was 3.7 acres, 1.8 acres, and 1.7 acres respectively; and the proportions of rural families unable to arrange for any land to farm was about 10 per cent, 18 per cent, and 20 per cent. Comilla district had a population of 4,388,906, all but 1.8 per cent of whom were born within the district. More than 99.5 per cent of the population spoke Bengali, and 85 per cent were Muslim. The characteristics of Comilla thana's population, more than 200,000, were much the same.

Flood conditions in the Comilla area are complicated by the 300-year-old levee system on the Gumti River that flows through it from the hills of India to the east. The river passes close to Comilla town; it is referred to in the 1961 Pakistan population census as "Comilla's Sorrow." Nearly every year there are breaches of its levees, resulting in great damage to crops, roads, and village structures. The level of the land inside the levees rises year by year from

---

[3] Pronounced "t'ana"—ä as in father, the thana is a unit of police administration in East Pakistan; it is roughly comparable to a county in the United States, and is, in Pakistan, the smallest unit of civil administration. Most government departments have official representatives at this level. There are 411 thanas in the province.

siltation, and so the river, once the levee breaks, rushes downhill into the surrounding country. The economy of the Comilla area still suffers from the location of the eastern demarcation line, made at Partition, between Pakistan and India along the outer edge of the flood plain, five miles east of Comilla town. Creation of this international boundary disrupted the long-established commerce between the plain and the hill country—mostly exchange of rice and fish from the delta for bamboo and thatch from the hills.

On the other hand, the city of Comilla has some advantages. The railroad between Dacca and Chittagong passes through it, as does the main highway. It has over the years been something of a business and cultural center, with banks, business establishments, two colleges, and significant activity in music and other arts.

The villagers in Comilla thana, as in East Pakistan generally, have over the decades been adjusting their standard of living downward in response to conditions beyond their control—rising costs, increased population pressure, further division of land holdings, disruption of the traditional plains-hills economy, and increasing indebtedness. Within this situation it has been the small farm operators—the majority of the villagers—who have become increasingly uneasy about what the future holds for them and their children. These transmitters of the traditional virtues were becoming convinced that living conditions were making it harder and harder for them to maintain self-sufficient family units. Common sayings among the farmers in the Comilla area in 1959, when the Academy was being started, were: "Things can't go on like this much longer. . . ." "There's got to be a change."

The government of Pakistan for a long time had been

The Setting, and Operating Assumptions 11

generally aware of these deteriorating conditions of agriculture and rural life, and over the years had undertaken various programs of amelioration—without substantial success, however. In 1953, with assistance from the United States International Cooperation Administration (ICA) and the Ford Foundation, the government established a special program for rural development—the Village Agricultural and Industrial Development program (V-AID). This program was set up outside the Ministry of Agriculture and other ministries connected with development. No doubt for this reason, among other administrative defects, the V-AID program floundered, as had earlier efforts at rural rehabilitation. By 1955 the need for some new initiatives in rural development was apparent, and out of the recognition of this need arose the Academy for Village Development.[4]

Planning and Organization of the Academy

The Comilla Academy for Rural Development was conceived initially by the government as a training center for public officials responsible for rural development programs, with the primary objective of helping the government officials put to more productive use the administrative and technical skills they already had, and of aiding them in the acquisition of new skills needed in rural development pro-

[4] Initially called "Academies of Administration and Community Development" and "Village-AID Academies." Later they were named "Academies for Village Development" and were officially so gazetted; this name remained until 1962 when the governance was decentralized to a board for each Academy in East and West Pakistan, and the name was changed to "Academies for Rural Development." Prior to October 1962, the term PAVD (Pakistan Academy for Village Development) is used; since then PARD (Pakistan Academy for Rural Development).

grams. Especially needed was increased understanding of village life and competence in the techniques of guiding constructive change. The overall plan for the Academy was developed around the needs of Pakistan public administration as identified by government officials, with major advisory assistance from a team of social scientists from Michigan State University (MSU). The Academy was set up to operate as a semiautonomous institution under a board of governors made up of ranking government officials, whose responsibilities included various aspects of rural development.

As initially planned, the Academy faculty was composed of a director and approximately ten social scientists with advanced training beyond the master's level. Other faculty members, trained in agriculture and other technical subjects, were to be added as needed. The initial faculty members were given a year's special training at Michigan State University before the Academy opened.

PROGRAM ASSUMPTIONS

The Academy has from the beginning and throughout its life been a government institution concerned with public administration. Its policies are established by a board of governors made up of government officials; most of the capital and recurring costs are covered by the government; the director and the faculty are government employees; most of the trainees (except the participating villagers) are governmental employees; and the findings of the experimental-demonstration work of the Academy are made available directly and immediately to the government for policy and operational uses. Fortunately, the board of governors has clearly sensed the value of providing the director and faculty with sufficient program latitude and adminis-

The Setting, and Operating Assumptions 13

trative flexibility to carry on novel and creative rural development work, which has come to be the distinctive contribution of the Comilla Academy to rural development in Pakistan.

But what could be done at a new training institution that would make any difference? What knowledge did the director and staff members then have that was relevant to the situation? What were the kinds of information and insights that were needed, and how could they be secured? What could be learned by firsthand observations in the villages? What from visits with the officials on duty in the area?

There was clearly need for a reorientation of attitude and purpose, for new methods of stimulating participation in the developmental process rather than securing mere acquiescence, and for the adoption of new modernizing methods to replace conventional methods which were not very useful in achieving the new goals. These were the tentative conclusions of the government, and they were reinforced by the team of consultants from Michigan State University.

The director and staff of the Academy early began to realize that if the Academy was to fulfill its basic function of training provincial officials for developmental activities, the trainers themselves had to learn the realities of what villagers were up against, and that this could best be done by themselves being actively involved in developmental work. They decided therefore that they must begin by making close and systematic observations of village conditions, and by encouraging and guiding experiments on the Academy farm and with villagers in selected areas near the Academy. They also decided that they must keep from the outset full records of events as they took place at the

Academy and in the field activities. It was early realized that these records would form some of the primary materials for realistic training, and be the basis for later meaningful research and evaluation.

Before the Academy was a half-year old, it arranged with the provincial government to use the hundred-square mile Comilla thana in which it was located as a laboratory area for experiments in local government and in economic development. In less than two years the Comilla thana council was reorganized to function as a local planning and development agency, involving collaboration between Academy staff and thana agricultural and other officers responsible for nation building. In less than four years the private sector in the form of new cooperatives joined with the public sector (thana council) to form the Comilla Thana Training and Development Center (TTDC).

With the creation of the Thana Training and Development Center all of the thana representatives of the various government departments concerned with development were brought together in one location for the first time, on the Academy campus. This association of the officials with the Academy staff led to a changing attitude on the part of the government officials; they began to be concerned with teaching better methods of rural development as well as with regulation.

VILLAGE ORGANIZATION AND LEADERSHIP

The Academy made the assumption that progress in rural modernization would depend initially on the willingness of villagers to try something new, and that this in turn would require on their part, particularly in the early stages, faith and trust in their own local leaders and in the Academy staff. At later stages when the fruits of change had been experienced and validated, knowledge and experience could take the place of faith. Thus the attitudes and priorities of the village leaders were the first concern of the development strategists.

Because of the extremely small land holdings of East Pakistan villagers and the lack of any apparent basis for establishing credit worthiness, adoption of changes by scattered individuals could have little effect on development. For this reason and because the village was a potent force in the control of behavior, the village had to be approached as the unit through which modernization could be introduced. Individual villagers, to be sure, had to be persuaded to change, but enough of them in any one village had to act together to achieve the benefits of modernization. Furthermore the nature of the initial changes had to be small enough to be within their means, for example, line sowing, composting, and seed selection, but effective enough to be convincing. The process of adopting small changes and finding them effective would lead to an appetite for larger, more complicated and costly changes.

This initial strategy—first applied to elementary innovation in agriculture—was applied later to more extensive changes, for example, to investments in commercial fertilizer and mechanization, including irrigation, and to the inclusion of other programs: experiments and demonstrations in local public works, in the emancipation of village women, family planning, home sanitation, rural youth and adult education. One after another of these activities, which became mutually supportive, emerged as new needs became visible.

In order to reach large numbers of villagers quickly and economically, it was decided that those farmers in each village electing to participate in the program would select one of their number to serve as the "organizer" for that village. He would be the intermediary between the village group and the Academy. He would come to the Academy for training each week. The training received at the Academy would be communicated to the participating villagers at a weekly meeting in the village, with relevant reactions being taken back to the Academy. The organizer would also serve as the fiscal agent to collect the savings of the individual villagers for deposit to the credit of the village group for later investment in joint purchases, use of machinery, and other centrally provided services. Another feature of the program was the use of "model farmers," selected by the village groups for their success in farming and for their literacy and leadership qualities. Thus through the organizers and the model farmers a new concept of "extension" was developed which utilized existing resources and leadership.

In addition to the organizers and the model farmers, other villagers were to come to the Academy for shortcourse training in specific skills, such as the operation of irrigation pumps and farm tractors, or to help implement some new activity such as the thana public works program.

Previous efforts to pursue a development strategy based on some of the above principles—in Pakistan, in V-AID—faltered in part because too much was attempted in too large a geographical area—the whole of the provinces of East and West Pakistan. The Comilla Academy avoided this mistake, in part, by concentrating its efforts in a limited laboratory area. The concentration of effort in an area of reasonable size made it possible to design and administer experimental programs in such a manner that the results could be closely evaluated before being applied to other areas. Through this process, validated experience formed

The Setting, and Operating Assumptions 17

the basis for expansion rather than for purely theoretical formulations, and premature extrapolation was avoided.

COOPERATIVES

The decision was taken at the very beginning that the major tenets of cooperative organization would be adopted, in spite of a history of dismal failure of cooperatives in this part of the world. But capital could be formed, it was believed, through the savings of the villagers themselves, even though villagers were heavily burdened with debts, and money incomes were almost nonexistent. Weekly savings, credited to individual savers but aggregated in the name of the voluntary village group, became the means of capital formation and the discipline which tested the willingness of the villagers to engage in an extensive bootstrap-lifting operation. Thus it became possible to rely upon village credit-worthiness as collateral for loans; for the villagers to agree upon joint planning for the use of tractors and pumps; and later to develop a whole array of more sophisticated central services such as cold-storage plants, rice mills, central dairy operation and other services, all set up on a cooperative basis.

RESEARCH, EVALUATION, TRAINING, AND EXTENSION

An early assumption in the Academy plan was that research, evaluation, training, and extension could be integrated in a single new type of educational institution concerned with rural development. The Pakistanis and their American advisers believed that the concepts which undergird the United States land-grant-university tradition were relevant as guides in chalking out the major features of such an institution. This hypothesis was adopted in the selection of staff and in their training at Michigan State University. Experience at Comilla has demonstrated the basic workability of the concepts in the Pakistan setting. Thus it was quite consistent that a laboratory area was chosen for experimentation; that the problems of the villagers became the agenda for experimentation and research; that the results of the experimental efforts were documented as a base for developing new instructional materials which were used for the instruction of officers and village leaders in the extension of validated practices; and, that research became a principal tool for further documentation and evaluation. The integration of these interrelated parts of the development process is well expressed by Ahkter Hameed Khan, the director of the Academy: "The pioneering role of the land grant college is indeed an approach most suitable for a Pakistani training institution. The desire for practical involvement, the belief that old knowledge must be tested and new knowledge acquired through unending research, the urgency to make scientific knowledge useful by extension —these are the basic attitudes which developed in the United States, and could start the same process for us, too."

Beyond these action-related, descriptive, fact-finding, and assessment efforts, some more theoretical research and evaluation were later undertaken by the Academy in collaboration with other Pakistan research and developmental agencies.

The Expansion of Comilla's Program to Other Areas

The secretaries of the provincial departments have found it to their advantage to join the Academy in relevant development experiments and, when the experiments proved workable, to expand them to other areas. Those facets of the Comilla effort that have proven operative have been expanded to other areas, with adaptations as needed, and at

The Setting, and Operating Assumptions 19

a rate thought feasible by those most closely associated with the administration of the various aspects of the program.

The Comilla thana council demonstrated, by a pilot public works project in 1961–1962, that village roads and drainage and irrigation canals could be constructed by local project committees. These local projects made use of unemployed villagers in the yearly slack period from January to April. This thana pilot project became the prototype of a province-wide works program in 1962–1963 and succeeding years.

The Comilla Thana Training and Development Center, too, has become a model for expansion by the Department of Agriculture and the Department of Basic Democracies and Local Government within the province, with the whole bundle of Comilla-type programs launched in three scattered thanas located in each of the other three divisions in East Pakistan in mid-1963, and in seven more thanas in 1965–1966. In almost all thanas in the whole province, more limited development centers were later set up by the Department of Basic Democracies and Local Government in collaboration with other departments.

The expansion of the Comilla programs to other areas involved the thorough conceptual and operational training of key personnel, the readying of the people of the area to be served, the uses of both private cooperatives and governmental programs for development, and the making of administrative arrangements which constructively redefined the roles of government officials to the villagers, to one another, and to the wider concerns of government itself.

The Comilla Program in the Context of Community Development

The Comilla program bears some resemblance to more conventional community development programs in a number of respects. The felt needs of people form the starting point for program planning and administration; strong emphasis is placed on social organization and motivation; decisions are based on the consent of the participants with varying amounts of persuasion, education, and communication techniques; and the social goals of human betterment are paramount.

But the Comilla program differs from many community development programs. A heavier emphasis is placed on economic and technological factors; the program is more rigorous in its demands on participants, including sanctions for deviation from agreed-upon policies and procedures; the program is more experimental, with the use of a laboratory area as a testing ground for ideas which may later be dropped or substantially modified before being advocated for adoption elsewhere; and it is more comprehensive, relating to food production, family planning, the expansion of the role of women, and the involvement of both the private and public sectors in the whole rural development process.

This summary may have given the reader some clues as to the character and meaning of the Comilla project. The rest of the book is devoted to illustrating and elaborating the history of the first ten years of the program.

2. Origins and Institutional Development

The conditions in the area to be served by the Comilla Academy militated against modernization: a high rural population density and miniature farms, lack of machinery and credit, low agricultural yields, undermotivated public servants and an ineffective extension system, widespread illiteracy and ill health, and a social system that severely limited the contribution of women to development —with all of this complicated at many a point by the vagaries of the climate. It is not hard to understand why the villagers had all but lost that elemental ingredient of action toward modernization: hope.

Some of the key leaders of the newly created Pakistan, including Director Khan, had a general understanding of the problems which had to be solved to bring the rural sector of East Pakistan into the mainstream of modern living. They knew that some major breakthroughs would have to be devised to help alleviate the plight of the villager and make him a contributor to the achievement of national goals which were in process of formulation. Some of the broad outlines of needed processes of modernization were understood, even though the sequence of actions was but dimly perceived.

The government also had the experience of older, pre-Partition efforts to deal with rural problems and the then current and very large community development program (V-AID). This program was being assisted by the United States government and the Ford Foundation. V-AID had been established along the lines of the older program of the government in India which emphasized work in development areas and the use of multiple-purpose village-level workers. The V-AID workers were being trained in especially created training institutes in both East and West Pakistan. The program, set up in 1953 as a semiautonomous agency,[1] was within a couple of years under way with high hopes for success. One deficiency emerged early, namely the need for the training of the higher-level officials responsible for the policies and general administrative supervision of the program and of others associated with it. It was at this point in the evolution of the V-AID program that the highest officials of the government of Pakistan began to formulate plans for meeting this deficiency and called for advice upon the United States advisors to the V-AID program and on the officials of the Ford Foundation. The sequence of steps which led to the

---

[1] V-AID was outside the Ministry of Agriculture and other nation-building ministries. This organizational weakness, along with other defects, contributed to the demise of V-AID in 1961. For an account of the work of the agency and of earlier attempts to improve the lot of the villagers, see speeches of Akhter Hameed Khan, *Rural Development in East Pakistan* (Spring, 1965), and *Community and Agricultural Development in Pakistan* (Spring, 1969), East Lansing, Michigan State University, Asian Studies Center, Occasional Papers Series. (Akhter Hameed Khan had served as the director of the East Pakistan V-AID program for one year (1954–1955) and then returned to his previous position as principal of Victoria College, located in Comilla.)

Origins and Institutional Development 23

establishment of the two Academies for Rural Development is now described.

The Origins of the Academies

The origins of the Academies for Rural Development[2] in Pakistan may be seen from the record of a meeting of high officials of the Pakistan government in January 1955. The working paper for this meeting stated:

For some time the Village-AID Administration has felt the necessity of establishing training academies not only for the higher level administrative staff in the Project Development areas ... but also for training and for reorienting the provincial extension staff generally and such staff of the nation-building departments as would be operating within the *tehsils*[3] in which Village-AID Project Development areas are located. The necessity of such Academies is also felt because it is hoped ultimately to provide to the Government Administration through the operation of the Village-AID Programme, a bias for Welfare (as distinct from the current law and order bias) especially in the rural areas. To implement this idea, it is necessary to train fresh batches of Civil Service of Pakistan and Provincial Service officers for at least a period of six months at these Academies and subsequently to get a selected few of them to assume charge of Project Development areas for a period of say one year and thus prepare them as Welfare Administrators.[4]

The curriculum of the Academies was to include provision of information about administration at the various

[2] The general political and administrative setting at the time of the founding of the Academy is described at the beginning of Chapter 4.

[3] *Tehsil:* a local unit of government in West Pakistan generally comparable to a thana in East Pakistan.

[4] Minutes of the meeting of January 18, 1955 (East Lansing, Michigan State University, Pakistan Project files).

levels in each of the provinces. Special attention was to be given to the effective use of the technical knowledge available at the tehsil and thana level which would include training in such subjects as cooperatives, agricultural credit, financing, budgeting, social welfare, economics—with special emphasis on rural economics—role of cottage industries, home economics, and so on.

The basic idea was therefore to reorient more effectively Government personnel to the necessity of becoming real servants of the people and to work hand in hand with them. For example, in the past, farmers were expected to come to Government Farms or demonstration plots, to see the demonstration of improved practices being carried out by trained government personnel. Such demonstrations were carried out in ideal conditions which farmers could not generally produce. Therefore, they showed very little interest in these demonstrations. Now, the methodology was to go to the people in the villages, to carry out such demonstrations on their own farms and preferably to get the farmers to demonstrate to themselves the new techniques. Our Administrative Probationers were no doubt given a vast fund of general knowledge in several fields, in addition to administrative training but were lacking in a welfare bias or social training. . . . It was not intended to produce technical experts at these Academies but sound welfare officers.[5]

These basic ideas were accepted by the prime minister in October 1955, after consultation with the representative of the Ford Foundation in Pakistan with particular reference to the possibility of external funding of some of the costs anticipated for the first few years. The government decided among other things to obtain the assistance of an

[5] Minutes of the meeting of January 18, 1955 (East Lansing, Michigan State University, Pakistan Project files).

American university to help with the further planning of the Academies and to provide continuing advisory assistance in the development of the Academies' programs. The services of Michigan State University (MSU) were enlisted for this purpose, with Ford Foundation financing.

In June 1956 a team of four faculty members, under the leadership of Professor Floyd W. Reeves, after intensive observations and consultations throughout Pakistan, prepared a draft "scheme" for submission to the government. This proposal provided for establishment of two Academies with substantially the same functions previously approved by the government. They were to be set up under a single board chaired by the prime minister and made up of ranking ministers and representatives from each of the two provinces. The board was to be responsible for policy, with administration assigned to a director for each Academy, appointed by the board. Each Academy was to have a full-time staff of ten social scientists, two of whom would be specialists in research, and as many as six part-time subject-matter specialists.

The two directors and the initial staff members were to be highly qualified as to academic backgrounds and attitude. Worldwide recruitment and relatively high salaries were suggested to attract this type of Pakistani personnel. The training of the directors and staff members would be done over a period of a year, roughly nine months in an American university, preceded by six weeks of orientation in Pakistan and followed by six weeks of observation of rural development programs in selected Asian and European countries.

The survey team proposed operational and capital budgets for the first four years (1957–1960) in the substantial amount of over Rs. 12 million.

This plan was presented to the government in August 1956. In June of the following year memoranda of agreement were reached between the government, the Ford Foundation, and MSU for technical assistance to the Academies, including funding of more than one million dollars from the Foundation for both Academies. On July 4, 1957, the government formally approved the "Scheme for Pakistan Academies for Village Development—Peshawar and Comilla." The major difference between the approved plan and the MSU proposal was that the two Academies were set up under separate boards rather than a single national board under the prime minister. Between July and December MSU appointed a campus coordinator of the project and a MSU resident representative in Pakistan; it also sent a second team of specialists, again headed by Reeves to advise and consult with the government, officials of the Ford Foundation and of the United States International Cooperation Administration, and to clarify numerous aspects of policy, organization, and administration of the Academies. The Greek firm of Doxiadis Associates was selected to design the Academy buildings. The architectural services were to be financed by the Ford Foundation and the construction, except for imported items, by the government.

On December 19, 1957, two boards were established for the "Pakistan Academies for Village Development East/West Pakistan" and their composition, powers, and related matters set forth.

SELECTION OF STAFF MEMBERS

A major recruitment effort for high-quality staff had already been launched. Applications were invited from qualified Pakistanis at home and abroad. Fifty persons applied, of whom 37 were interviewed in Karachi, Lahore, and Dacca by panels made up of Pakistani officials, a United States International Cooperation Administration representative associated with the V-AID program, and the resident MSU representative. Several other candidates were interviewed in London, Chicago, Washington, D.C., and Denver, Colorado. It took nearly a year to get the Academies staffed under these highly selective procedures, in which special consideration was given to academic training, professional experience, age, residence, language facility, and attitudes expressed regarding the projected work of the Academies. Selectees had to be endorsed by the Academy boards, and appointments were made on a probationary basis subject to successful completion of the training program. Appointees agreed to sign a bond to serve the Academies for five years.

Of the directors and 19 faculty members at the time of recruitment, four had Ph.D.'s, and the remainder had M.A.'s. The mean age was 35 years; the range, 24 years to 50. About half were or had been government officials. Sixteen had studied in universities in one or more countries outside of Pakistan.

THE TRAINING PROGRAM

While the directors and faculties of the Academies were being selected, intensive work was being done by Michigan State University faculty members on the major features of the training program as set forth in the scheme. Two university faculty members went to Pakistan in early 1958 to work out a training program with the Pakistanis and the university resident representative there.

The concept of administration which the Academy was trying to develop was described by George Gant, representative of the Ford Foundation in Pakistan, as "development administration." "The objective," said Gant "is to utilize the disciplines and techniques of public administration, sociology, economics, psychology, education and extension in the formulation of a program of learning and work experience for enrolees in the Academies which will prepare them to perform effectively [their] administrative and supervisory tasks in the development field, with particular reference to rural development. Such a program will not be successful if it only assembles teachers and offers courses in public administration, economics, sociology, etc., in the compartmentalized form traditional in both the United States and Pakistan."

The philosophy of the training plan devised at MSU was set forth as follows: "The Academies for Village Development are conceived to give direction to public administration in a rapidly changing culture. The primary function of the Academies is to teach concepts of human relationships to supervisory and administrative personnel of the Village-AID program and the nation-building departments. The efforts of these Academies will be directed toward changing the existing concepts of public administration from one of law and order to one with a developmental emphasis. . . . All phases of training are to be guided by the assumption that the major determinants of the experiences of the Academy faculty lie in Pakistan. . . . The efforts of the [faculty] trainees are to be teaching, research and the integrated approach. All of these are to be considered in their applicability to the broad concept of community development. . . . Present research findings in Pakistan are quite limited and social research is a relatively unexplored field."[6]

The training program had three major parts: (1) The

[6] Albert E. Levak, "A Generalized Training Statement for the Faculty of the Academies for Village Development" (East Lansing, Michigan State University, Pakistan Project files).

training in Pakistan, for about six weeks, included observations of administrative operations and problems at the national, provincial, regional, and village levels. The training at the national level involved conferences with representatives of government, United States International Cooperation Administration, the Ford Foundation, and other agencies as related to the expected role the Academies were to have in development matters. At the other levels of government emphasis was placed on field observations and conferences with administrators of V-AID and other government programs. Some interviews in the villages were arranged.

There were two shortcomings in this Pakistan phase of the training program: only the two directors and eight faculty members had then been selected; and the training activities were restricted to West Pakistan.

(2) The most substantial phase was the nine-month training at MSU from June 1958 to March 1959. When this training began, the group included the two directors and 17 faculty members, subsequently increased to 19.

The group was rather heterogeneous and faced many adjustment problems. Its members had to adjust to a new culture and to one another; and, upon their return to Pakistan, be prepared to relate themselves to a new venture in which each would for the first time teach his or her particular discipline to public officials within a framework of "developmental" public administration, use new teaching techniques to supplement the lecture method, and participate with their associates in an interdisciplinary approach.

To facilitate their adjustment on the campus at East Lansing, a central office was set up for them, with a separate office for each director. Secretarial services were provided, as was also a library of materials on Pakistan.

After a few weeks the training program that had been

planned at MSU was found to be less than satisfactory, especially in achieving the integrated approach to the several disciplinary backgrounds of the faculty members. The program was revised in consultation with the directors and Academy faculty members. The major elements of the revised, more flexible program were: a three-term Academy development seminar for the entire group; individual graduate courses; and group and individual field observations. In addition there were short-term seminars organized around such topics as teaching techniques and social science research, and a colloquium on Pakistan for non-Pakistani students and MSU faculty members.

The heart of the training program turned out to be the Academy "development seminar." This seminar met for two hours a day, four days a week, with all Academy faculty members present. It was the principal vehicle for securing understanding of the job ahead and appreciation for each other, and for developing a sense of purpose. The seminar's first term was concerned with the cultural forces playing on man to shape his personality, and how these forces might be modified and controlled. The focus was deliberately broad to lay the groundwork for the more specific topics which were to follow and in part to avoid controversies over specifics at this early stage in the program. In addition to the general treatment of concepts in literature and lectures by several outstanding experts in education and community development, fourteen papers were given by the Pakistani trainees dealing with conditions in Pakistan as they relate to family and kinship, beliefs and attitudes, landlord-tenant relations and village social structure, a short history of public administration in Pakistan, and other topics.

The second term of the seminar focused on "The Public

Administrator and Social Change." Members of the seminar interrelated specific information on the structure and function of the nation-building departments of Pakistan and the contributions which social science could make to the solution of problems of public administration. A bibliography of development literature was compiled, which was later used in making up the original booklist for the libraries at the Academies.

The initial two terms set the stage for the final one which was devoted to the development of a "Blueprint for the Academy." For this task the group was divided into committees covering curriculum, off-campus activities, faculty organization, student relations, and administrative organization. Each seminar member participated in two committees, with assignments made on the basis of the academic and professional backgrounds of the members. Each committee prepared a report which served as a basis for discussion and for selection of those elements which were finally incorporated into "A Tentative Operational Outline" for the work of the Academies. Some of the sessions of the final seminar were conducted by one director of the Academies or the other, with participation by members of the faculty of that Academy. This arrangement provided an opportunity to focus on the distinctive problems which would be faced by each faculty in the two provinces.

The faculty members took graduate courses for credit, or as auditors, as thought relevant. All members took some work, with a range of from two to ten courses, largely in political science, psychology, education, agricultural economics, and sociology. The earning of a degree was not encouraged, but some members completed enough formal course work to earn another Master's degree.

Field trips on an individual and group basis were taken

by the directors and faculty members to learn more about practical problems of development, including visits to the Upper Peninsula of Michigan where a coordinated effort was being undertaken for the development of this depressed area, and to the Tennessee Valley Authority. Some national and international conferences were attended. Extensive use was made of the academic resources of MSU and to some extent of other institutions.

(3) The final phase of the training involved visits to European and Asian countries. After a visit by the whole group to Jamaica, the faculty divided into two tour groups, each composed of staff members from both Academies. One group observed development activities in Japan and the Philippines; the other group observed similar work in England, Norway, and Sweden.

The faculties returned to Pakistan and reported to their respective Academies in May 1959. At each Academy they began their work in temporary quarters made ready while they were abroad; the new buildings were under construction.

The Governance of the Academies

The original scheme for the Academies anticipated the necessity for a strong board of governors to provide policy and broad managerial guidance for the creative work which was expected of the new training and research institutions. Although the plan for a single board suggested in the scheme was changed to a board for each Academy, the basic concept of a strong board at the head of the Academies was clearly retained, and the government maintained only broad policy control.

The chairman of the boards was the head of the ministry

responsible for V-AID and later for the National Development Organization (NDO). The chairmanship thus moved from Economic Affairs to Health, Labour and Social Welfare, to National Reconstruction and Information, and back to Health, Labour and Social Welfare. The secretary (career head) of each successive ministry served as vice-chairman of the boards. Members common to the two boards were the secretaries of Finance and Establishment of the central government and the chief administrator of V-AID and the National Development Organization. In addition the finance secretaries to the government of East and West Pakistan, respectively, and nominated members from each of the provinces, served on the boards.

The functions of the boards are to formulate major policies for operation of the Academies, more specifically to request and receive grants-in-aid; approve budgets and authorize expenditures; authorize, in broad terms, instructional and research programs; appoint instructors and other staff members; erect, construct, and alter buildings; and delegate powers to the directors and other officers of the boards.

The Ministry of Finance ultimately determines the magnitude of the budget, and general control is exercised under audit and other governmental procedures. But within these restrictions the boards have had wide latitude for conducting their business. Major administrative responsibility is assigned to the directors of the Academies who by an early decision of the boards should be "persons of considerable seniority and sufficient status as to be able to undertake training senior Civil Service of Pakistan Officers like Divisional Commissioners, Secretaries of Government of East Pakistan and Deputy Commissioners; therefore in principle their status should be the same as that of Divisional Commissioners."

In the latter part of 1960 the boards of the two Academies, meeting jointly, formally reviewed the direction which the Academies were taking. Charges of "deviation" by the Comilla Academy in East Pakistan from the original purposes had been make in some quarters; it was said that the Academies were performing functions which properly belonged to other parts of the government. In response to these charges, the board set up a working party to look into the matter. Particular attention was given in this review to the financial aspects of the operations (largely expenditures for the buildings), to the powers and authority of the directors, to the numbers of trainees and character of the training programs of the Academies, and to the research being undertaken. Special attention was directed to activities of the Comilla Academy such as work with cooperatives, a poultry project, dairy project, and related experimental and demonstration activities.

After extensive review of documents and discussion "the Chairman expressed his satisfaction with the work carried on by both the Academies. The board agreeing with these observations, resolved that neither of the two Academies had deviated from the original objectives and that they should be allowed to grow according to their own genius and the requests of their training clientele."[7]

This decision had the effect of legitimizing the previous decisions of the Comilla board to approve experimental and demonstration project work at the Comilla Academy and to clear the way for continued development of the training,

[7] Record of the proceedings of the joint meeting of the boards, October 30, 1960 (East Lansing, Michigan State University, Pakistan Project files).

Origins and Institutional Development 35

demonstration, and research work in response to the needs of East Pakistan.

CREATION OF TWO PROVINCIAL BOARDS

Recognizing differences in the setting for each of the Academies and in conformity with general efforts to "provincialize" and decentralize government operations, the government, by official order, created two largely provincialized boards for the Academies in October 1962. The basic changes were in the chairmanship and in the membership.

Thus, the East Pakistan board is headed by the chief secretary of the government of East Pakistan, with members representing the central Ministry of Finance and the Establishment Division, the provincial secretaries of Finance, Agriculture, Basic Democracies and Local Government, and of Education, the registrar of cooperatives, the vice-chancellor of the University of Dacca, two nonofficials appointed by the governor, and the director of the Academy as member-secretary. The membership of the board is therefore representative of the major users of the instructional and research services of the Academy.

The East Pakistan board has met on an average of three times a year with an average attendance of 12 members. Agenda and background papers for the meetings are prepared by the secretary and distributed in advance of the meetings. Careful minutes and other records of the deliberations are maintained.

FINANCIAL SUPPORT

Rupee expenditures for Comilla's new buildings, including roads and grounds, totaled approximately Rs. 5,100,000, and Ford Foundation contributions for architectural design, architectural supervision, and imported building material amounted to approximately $210,000.

Financial support for the annual recurring expenses of the Academy has increased from approximately Rs. 400,000 in fiscal year 1960 to Rs. 850,000 in 1968. The central government provided 75 per cent of these funds until the board was provincialized, and 60 per cent since then. Of special significance in these overall expenditures is the component for research, which in its various aspects has ranged from approximately Rs. 37,000 to over Rs. 250,000 a year.

Ford Foundation support for the technical assistance contract with MSU from 1956 to 1969 totals $1,935,082. This includes provision of resident foreign advisers, research and administrative services from East Lansing, library support, funds for staff development, and imported equipment items. In conformity with Ford Foundation policy on the duration of technical assistance programs, a final contract was entered into by the Ford Foundation with MSU to cover the Pakistan project for the period from 1967–1970. Ways of maintaining a continuing relationship beyond 1970 between the Academy and MSU and possibly other universities are being explored.

A summary of the funds made available for the Academy and its programs from all principal sources is given in Appendix VII. In addition to the above figures which deal with the period from 1959, when the Academy opened, there was the cost of the one-year training of the director and nine Comilla staff members then appointed. The costs for training all but two were borne by the United States International Cooperation Administration; the two were financed by the Ford Foundation.

The Academy's Philosophy of Development Administration

From its original conception, the Academy was an institution for the training of government officials having present or potential responsibilities for development programs in Pakistan, and for the conduct of research on rural development problems. It is clear that something a good deal more than a traditional academic approach to training and research was contemplated, but the precise form which this new program would take was left to the imagination and efforts of those who would execute the program. At Comilla, as will be seen in succeeding chapters, the Academy from the very beginning conceived the idea of a pilot development program, with training, research, and demonstration dynamically integrated into the life of the rural community and the structure of the Pakistan public service.

The key method for giving effect to the Academy's philosophy of development administration has been the use of a development laboratory. Three months after the Academy opened the director, Akhter Hameed Khan, received permission from the V-AID administration to start demonstrating what a development laboratory might be like in an area designated by V-AID (80 square miles) as one of its "development areas." Four months later the chief secretary of East Pakistan designated the whole of the Comilla thana (107 square miles) as a development laboratory, and delegated to the director considerable latitude to conduct programs and administrative experiments in this already established unit of government.

The ways in which the Academy used the laboratory to conduct numerous experiments in agricultural production, public works, women's work, family planning, and related fields are described in later chapters.

In 1963, when the new campus and buildings at Kotbari were completed, the Academy faculty moved there. This new campus is in the lower edges of the Lalmai-Mainamati Hills that rise some 100 feet above the surrounding deltaic plain. It is about six miles from Abhoy Ashram,[8] which until then had served as the temporary campus. Since then, the Abhoy Ashram has been used as the headquarters for the laboratory program, for the central cooperative association, and for the thana training and development center. The Kotbari campus, with its library, hostels, classrooms, and auditorium serves as the headquarters for the training of provincial and national officials, for research and evaluation, for communications and the graphic arts, and for the overall administration of the Academy. The "Academy," "laboratory area," and "pilot program" have become, over time, highly interrelated. Although formal organizational, budgetary, staffing, and other relationships and controls are maintained, in practice it has become difficult at times to be sure what is being done by the Academy, what by the central cooperative association, or what by government departments. The problems encountered in the modernization of the rural community have become the central concern of all the separate organizations, with formal structure and relationships taking a secondary place.

TRAINING AT THE ACADEMY

The nature of the training planned and carried out by the Academy may be seen in succeeding discussions of the

[8] A Gandhian retreat site, "The Retreat of the Fearless," located a mile south-east of Comilla town, was founded in 1923. It was used by the Academy from mid-1959 to April 1963.

various Comilla programs. Training is a crucial part of the entire effort, covering a wide range of subjects and a wide range of trainees, for periods of a few days to as much as six months.

Great emphasis has been placed on flexibility, with adaptation of programs to meet the specific needs of the particular group of trainees. Set courses have, accordingly, been largely avoided. From the very beginning the topics discussed and the training method have been based on the assumption that what government officers needed most was to learn how to apply their knowledge to practical local situations. This involved using the experiences of the trainees to supplement the knowledge of the Academy faculty, in a free discussion between the two. In these discussions the trainees would share their thinking about how village conditions could be improved. At the end of the course they made critical evaluations of the training they had received, and the programs for later groups were adjusted in the light of these criticisms.

Even when there were several groups of the same category of officials, as for instance the training of the circle officers for the province-wide works program in 1962–1963, the syllabus was changed as needed in response to the staff's cumulative experience and to the comments of the trainees at the end of each group's training period.

Thus the training has afforded government officials the opportunity of meeting their colleagues in an atmosphere of academic freedom. Discussion is encouraged, work is reviewed, operational opinions are exchanged, difficulties are aired. No academic diplomas are given, and no entries are made in personnel folders.

The Academy's training activities may be divided into three phases which are not mutually exclusive. During the first two years, the training was primarily focused on the results of elementary, but somewhat systematic, explorations of rural problems in Comilla thana and on some early findings of the pilot experiments. The second phase, from 1961 onward, began with the recognition by the government of the importance of the Academy's pilot projects (cooperatives, rural public works, and so on). Here were programs that were yielding results and, since they might well be expanded to other areas, large numbers of thana and district officials of various departments came to the Academy for on-the-ground training. The third phase, that of the Academy serving as consultant to the policy makers in rural development, is essentially an outgrowth of the second phase and is one which is increasing in importance as the program matures and more stable results are achieved. This development is illustrated by the Academy's active collaboration with relevant officials in holding seminars (on agricultural development, use of International Rice Research Institute [IRRI] rice varieties, family planning, and other topics) for key policy and administrative personnel and for researchers and scholars.

Exclusive of the training programs for villagers, somewhat over 6,000 persons were trained at the Academy from 1959 to 1966, of whom slightly over 3,700 were officials.[9] Circle officers, Civil Servants of Pakistan, East Pakistan civil servants, and officials associated with education, agriculture, and cooperatives constituted a large part of this number. Although comparability of statistics on training beyond 1966 (when a field check was made) is not possible, the Academy's annual reports since then indicate that in 1966–1967 a total of 1,618 government officers, foreign

---

[9] For details, see Appendix VI, Table B.

scholars, and others participated in orientation trips, seminars, course programs, and other training activities of the Academy at Kotbari; the number similarly trained in 1967–1968 was 4,780.

More than 11,000 villagers from Comilla thana (on a yearly subject-matter basis) were trained at the Thana Training and Development Center (TTDC) at Abhoy Ashram during the period 1959 to 1966. The largest category was the once-a-week trainees. The volume and range of training activities has continued to grow since 1966, as will be noted in the several chapters on programs which follow; but again comparable statistics with the earlier years are not available. A total of 2,175 villagers received training at the TTDC during 1967–1968.

The types of instruction given at Abhoy Ashram to villager trainees are discussed in the succeeding chapters. The rationale for the recurring instruction is simple enough. The villagers need brief periods of training, away from the village, that will not interfere with their farming activities, over a long period of time, cheaply, and in harmony with the culture of the area. So they come to the Academy weekly or fortnightly or monthly, or seasonally, to learn new ideas and techniques gradually and comfortably. Then they, as the chosen representatives of their village groups, go back and share what they learned with their village neighbors.

EXTENSION

As in the case with training, the extension activities of the Academy will be best seen in the discussion of individual programs in succeeding chapters. A mixture of extention methods is used, the emphasis being on practical activities, often on a group basis. Some are adaptations of

Western methods, such as field demonstrations, talks, and use of pamphlet materials. Others are new, such as the use of an "organizer" in the cooperatives and in the family planning program, and the use of the model farmer as the agricultural extension agent—a major departure from the conventional American land-grant-university extension system.

Tours are organized from time to time for villagers to see nearby areas where performance is better. Field days are sometimes held in cooperative villages for the farmers to exchange experiences. A rally may be organized to inaugurate a new facility, such as a cold-storage plant. Annual rallies, held for each of several Academy-sponsored activities, are attended by hundreds of men from the villages, some women, and many children. As experimental programs have matured to a point where operating assumptions have been reasonably well validated, manuals have been produced and used extensively in training for wider application of the program. The public works and irrigation pilot projects in Comilla thana are prime examples of the value of manuals for extension.

In broad outline, the extension work centers around these tenets: the members of each voluntary village group must select their own leaders; the training of these local leaders must be frequent and continuous, with new ideas contributed by government officials, Academy instructors, advisors, and the village leaders themselves; and each village group must assemble weekly to hear what its representatives learned at the Academy and to discuss how to apply what was learned, and to tell their representatives what questions they should bring up when next they go to the Academy.

RESEARCH

The relationship of research, demonstrations, and training was set forth by the director, Akhter Hameed Khan, to the board of governors in late 1960 in this note:

The Academy was designed to conduct both training and research programs. It was for this reason that two research specialists were placed on the staff, and instructors with high academic qualifications were selected. To emphasize merely the number of trainees in the training course and not allow time and energy for research and experimentation would destroy the original idea behind the scheme, viz: of an institution where fresh thinking would be done . . . and where knowledge provided by social science would be made applicable to rural conditions of Pakistan. . . . In order to provoke thinking and discussion it would be necessary to prepare teaching materials based on first-hand experience of rural conditions and the adaptation of economic and social theories to these conditions. . . . It would be extremely dangerous to rely on foreign textbooks exclusively and lectures alone as this would soon reduce the training course to lifeless routine and repetition. Keeping the need of first-hand observation in view, we have adopted the Comilla thana as a laboratory for social and economic research and experiment. The instructors are carrying on projects in their own fields in order to make their teaching realistic. . . . If this opportunity is denied, the Academy would lose its distinctive feature of a blend of theory and practice. . . .[10]

From the beginning, accordingly, research was made one of the essential elements in the program. A description of

[10] Proceedings of the "Sixth Meeting of the Board of Governors," October 29, 1960 (East Lansing, Michigan State University, Pakistan Project files).

the kinds of research conducted and some of the problems encountered are found in Chapter 8.

Succeeding chapters describe, and to a degree analyze and interpret, significant policies and operating experiences in several aspects of comprehensive rural development during the first ten years of the Academy's life.

3. A New Village-based Cooperative System

Although no precise formula was available to the Academy at the beginning of the program, several working hypotheses had been formulated as to just how villagers could be helped to increase their production, and thus secure a solid economic base for improvement of living standards. General village conditions and the attitudes of villagers were known to the director, Akhter Hameed Khan, but great restraint was exercised in developing a blueprint for the program from this base. Instead of relying on this knowledge and prescribing what needed to be done, systematic consultation with village groups and leaders was the first order of business for the faculty, together with making simple surveys of village conditions. The director and faculty members went out to villages for informal talks. Representative leaders and groups—farmers, religious leaders, potters, artists and others—were invited to the Academy for long discussions of problems being faced and of possible solutions. These gatherings were referred to as "camps" because some of them lasted into the second day. It did not take long to state the problems, but the way out seemed to be obscure and remote. One conviction did appear to emerge, namely, that new ideas had to be tried, and that perhaps the Academy's efforts would turn out to be more helpful than previous attempts to solve the problems. Of central importance at this stage was the reputation which the director enjoyed for being genuinely interested in the people's welfare. There wasn't much to work on except faith, but this they had, and it provided a base from which to start.

The New Village Cooperatives

Even though the director and the faculty had no prescription or formula, they were not without some hunches which the consultations with the villagers did not negate. These, briefly stated, became the working hypotheses around which activities began to revolve.

1. A viable private economic organization was needed which could serve as a basis for collaborative effort, and through which mechanization and other improved methods could be introduced. The central need, initially, was for the creation of capital through savings.

2. The village would be recognized as the basic unit, with those families whose heads decided to do so becoming members of a local voluntary group.

3. Some linkage would be needed between these voluntary groups in the villages and the Academy. Since it would be impossible to work directly with individual members of these groups, some form of representation would be needed. The method suggested was for each village group to select its representative, called the "organizer," who would serve as fiscal agent and learner-trainer. Soon thereafter one or two alert farmers and early adopters would be selected as "model farmers."

4. A training method would follow logically from the above in which the organizers and model farmers would

A New Village-based Cooperative System 47

come to the Academy for weekly training sessions, followed by village meetings where the ideas learned would constitute the "lessons" for the villagers.

5. The early technical "inputs" would be furnished largely by a team of Japanese rice-cultivator demonstrators furnished by the Colombo Plan, who would use the Academy's own farm and some land in nearby villages for demonstration plots, and who would teach at the weekly meetings and work with the model farmers.

6. Inasmuch as only the simplest techniques such as line sowing and improved fertilization could be adopted at first by individual villagers (considering the size of land holdings and other available resources) early emphasis would be given to these techniques and extended soon thereafter to joint planning, joint purchasing, credit, and joint use of machinery.

Putting the six hypotheses together it seemed best to develop the program within the framework of cooperative principles which were known to the director, faculty, and advisors. The broad principles of the cooperative movement—savings, educational meetings, joint planning and action—were adopted even though the past record of local cooperatives in the area was essentially a record of dismal failure. For in these earlier "multipurpose societies," as they were called, no regular savings were being made by the members, there were but few loans taken, and most of these were not being repaid; the membership met only in annual meetings that were indifferently attended. Although the director felt that the theoretical principles of the cooperative were sound and should be retained, it was apparent that some basic changes in the conventional practices would have to be made.

In March 1960 the Academy appointed a special officer

for cooperatives; he had had more than a score of years of experience in organizing cooperatives and was willing to make changes. Most crucial of all, it was obvious, was the matter of how to secure the interest and participation of the villagers. This involved explaining patiently and repetitively how individual and group action would be of benefit to them. The villagers wondered that the special officer for cooperatives should continue to come to their village. They were pleased when he would stay with them for the Friday meeting at the mosque. He often said little except to encourage them to talk among themselves. Often they sat silently for minutes at a time. And why? This didn't seem to bother him. When he left he would tell them when he could come back, if they wanted him to. Yes, they wanted him to come. So they would meet again, with again perhaps not much said. But each time there was more talk than the time before, until at length the truth was out—that each had looked upon his situation as unique, unbearable, and unsolvable, something to be endured by himself and his family, that no one else would be interested in anyway. But the cooperative specialist was interested, especially as the villagers began to realize they had in common this bond of misery and hopelessness. The villagers began to take interest when he and the director would meet with them to talk about the need for organization, capital formation, credit, simple improvements in their agricultural practices, and especially about setting up low-lift pumps in the dry season, or opening clogged drainage canals to lessen the damage from the monsoon flood. But for the Academy to help them, the Academy people explained, the villagers would need to do certain things thought necessary to form a viable cooperative group, called a society. They should choose a chairman from among the more elderly and respected

A New Village-based Cooperative System

members of the group; his position would be largely honorary, and would afford moral support to the organizer, a younger, active man who would be asked to take part in pioneering activities.

Soon after mid-1960 the Academy standardized the conditions a local society would need to meet to be a part of the Academy's new cooperative program. In addition to choosing a chairman, the group should (1) organize itself and later become a registered cooperative society; (2) hold weekly meetings with compulsory attendance of all members; (3) select a trusted man from the group and send him to the Academy once a week for training (he should become the organizer and teacher of the group); (4) keep proper and complete records; (5) do joint production planning; (6) use supervised production credit; (7) adopt improved agricultural practices and skills; (8) make regular cash and in-kind savings deposits; (9) join the central cooperative federation; and (10) hold regular member education discussions.[1] These ten conditions, which were alluded to in the earliest discussions and shortly thereafter were more formally articulated, are more fully described in the first annual report of the cooperatives published by the Academy in 1961 under the title of "A New Rural Cooperative System for Comilla Thana" by Henry W. Fairchild and Shamsul Haq. Subsequent annual reports, the last published in 1969, affirm the basic soundness of these principles and record the evolution and growth of the cooperatives operating under these principles.

Early in 1960 village-based cooperative societies were organized at South Rampur and Monsasan, and ten days

[1] Henry W. Fairchild and M. Zakir Hussain, *A New Rural Cooperative System for Comilla Thana* (Second Annual Report, 1962), Comilla, PARD, July 1962, pp. 14–15.

later at Tongirpar. In each instance the society was organized around a low-lift irrigation pump. No systematic plan had yet been worked out to make the pumps available to the villagers. Even so the cash savings made by the society members at their weekly village meetings were beginning to provide a basis on which later credit-worthiness could be established and loans to the local society could be made.

Ten cooperatives were organized by the end of May 1960—seven village-based agricultural societies, a vegetable growers' society, a women's cooperative, and a weavers' cooperative. The membership of the agricultural cooperatives was made up almost wholly of the smaller and middle-sized farmers. The larger farmers, usually with five to ten acres, leased out their lands and often were moneylenders and so had little or no interest in becoming members of the local cooperative society.

The first annual report of the academy summarized the progress of the first few months: "We have shifted the emphasis to training and education, and provided instructive material, technical guidance, and short courses of training; we have selected and trained extension agents from among the local people; and we have emphasized the importance of permanent organizations in the shape of village cooperatives and association of progressive farmers."[2]

THE ORGANIZER AND THE MODEL FARMER

The *organizer* of the village-based cooperative society is the key man in the new cooperative system. Chosen by his fellow members, he is the liaison between the village society and the Academy. He brings to the Academy the weekly cash savings and the problems of his society, and

[2] "First Annual Report of the Academy, 1959–1960," Comilla, PAVD, May 1960 (mimeographed), p. 4.

A New Village-based Cooperative System 51

takes back the ideas he learned at the Academy to the entire membership at the society's weekly meeting.

As the local cooperatives became better organized, the *model farmer* emerged as the second most important person in the village cooperative. The model farmer system became operative in November 1961. Five distinctive features of the model farmer as a new type of agricultural extension agent are (1) He is a resident village farmer who serves his own society rather than an outsider who serves several villages. (2) He is selected by the other members of a local voluntary cooperative group rather than by the Academy or some other agency. (3) He comes to the Academy one day each week for training, and so provides liaison between the farmers and the Academy. (4) He is one of a group of village farmers who as a unit serve as innovator (individual innovators are rare). (5) He is taught by the Academy staff and advisors (later largely by the departmental representatives).

The weekly training at the Academy of the organizers and the model farmers early became recognized as of first importance. Here was the Academy's opportunity to make a continuing contribution. But what kinds of training materials were appropriate? How were they to be formulated? How could they be presented effectively?

The outcome, after some experimentation, was the preparation of inexpensive lesson sheets in Bengali by the special development officer, the thana training officer, the special officer for cooperatives, and some of the departmental representatives in the thana. Much of the training material for the model farmers was seasonal to fit crop cycles, such as land preparation, transplantation of seedlings, weeding, harvesting, and storing. Attention was also given to the benefits of line sowing, composting, improved seeds, irrigation, and additional crops. These lesson sheets were further refined as the months passed, and later were brought out in pamphlets.

Topics taught to the organizers in the early years included: cooperative practices, improved methods of cultivation, credit (supervised, after being preplanned by the group), capital formation by savings, joint use of agricultural implements, joint storage of water, joint planning, formation of bullock groups, conduct of meetings, accounts keeping, and marketing of agricultural produce. These weekly presentations yielded in the first year alone nearly a score of training booklets for distribution to the cooperative members. Some of the titles were: "What Is a Cooperative?"; "Why a Cooperative?"; "Cooperation in Denmark"; "How to Organize a Cooperative"; "How to Conduct a Meeting"; "Needs of Cottage Industry"; and, "Islamic Opinion on Contraception."

FROM ORGANIZER TO MANAGER

As the business of the local cooperatives increased and took up more time of the organizers, the duties of the organizers and model farmers were combined into a new position, called a "manager." A system of incentive payments was worked out, as follows, making him an almost full-time employee of the local society:

50 paisa[3] (10¢) per month per member regularly attending the weekly village meeting and depositing a saving;
50 paisa per acre per crop brought under improved cultivation by the society;
1 per cent of the loan repayments; and

---

[3] 100 paisa equals 1 rupee.

A New Village-based Cooperative System 53

15 rs. per month for organizing the use of a low-lift pump or a tube well for irrigation.

When the jobs of the organizers and the model farmers were combined, some societies said they wanted the model farmer system continued. After a few months, most of the societies arranged to send a model farmer to the Academy fortnightly or monthly for training. Alternate training sessions were set up in selected villages; the Academy extension committee provided assistance for this work.

The regular visits to the Academy of these organizers and model farmers were a factor in the decision to office all of the department representatives at the Academy, and to add the function of teaching to their regular duties.[4]

National and Provincial[5] Government Interest in Cooperatives

In early 1961 the possibilities for compulsory cooperatives as instruments for the introduction of farm machinery

---

[4] See Chapter 4.

[5] Since April 1963 the East Pakistan Cooperative College has been located on the Academy Kotbari campus. The College uses a battery of classrooms alongside those used by the Academy. It houses its trainees in one of the four hostels on the campus. The auditorium, the recreation room, and the shops on campus are facilities in common for both institutions.

Established in 1960 by the provincial government, the Cooperative College operated in or near Dacca until it was transferred to the Kotbari campus. The staff is made up of a principal and six instructors.

There is a close working relationship between the faculties of the Academy and the College, but except for the one-week orientation course for directors and members of cooperative societies each year, the major part of the training in each institution is performed by its own staff. One or more representatives of the College usually were being discussed at the national level. On February 6, President Ayub Khan had called for a "system of *compulsory* cooperative farming in which the owner of a holding becomes a co-sharer to the extent of the price of his holding."

A working party was established to implement the presidential directive, whose terms of reference were (1) to report on the manner and the scope of the introduction of compulsory cooperative farming, which should be as comprehensive as possible, and on the Law needed to introduce it; (2) to examine the relationship between the proposed setup and the Agricultural Development Corporation which may come into existence as a result of the Food and Agriculture Commission's Report; and (3) to review the scheme of the consolidation of holdings in view of the proposed setting up of compulsory cooperatives.

The report[6] included an Appendix written by the director of the Comilla Academy, Akhter Hameed Khan. It is a detailed plan for an experimental pilot project in agricultural production and related economic and social activities based on the early experience at Comilla; excerpts from this Appendix are:

---

participate in the regular weekly Academy faculty meeting, and some of the instructional materials used in the College are based on the experiences of Comilla cooperatives.

Two other campuses of provincial education institutions are located in the edge of the Lalmai-Mainamati Hills adjacent to that of the Academy. They are a Teachers' College and a Polytechnic School; each was built in the early 1960's. In these same hills are the sites of some fifty ruins of royal fortresses, Buddhist monasteries, and Hindu shrines which archeologists have dated between the sixth and the thirteenth centuries.

[6] *Report on Mechanization in Cultivation through Cooperatives and Block Farming*, Rawalpindi, Ministry of Food and Agriculture, **Government of Pakistan Press, 1961.**

A New Village-based Cooperative System

The problem of increasing agricultural production is a problem of better organization and the introduction of improved farm practices.

The Agricultural Commission has suggested that these ends may be achieved by declaring selected areas as agricultural blocks and developing farming cooperatives. There has been to date little research work in this field in our country. We are handicapped by the absence of experience and data. During the last one year the East Pakistan Academy for Village Development has done some experimental work in the organization of village cooperatives. There are now 25 cooperatives working in Comilla thana. The experience thus gained has shown that the villagers are eager to use modern agricultural machines and other implements; that they are willing to overcome the handicaps of small land holdings through joint planning and adoption of improved methods of agriculture and irrigation. . . .

The experiment has suffered many handicaps. In order to develop it into a pilot project, initial investment in the form of tractors and equipment is required. . . .

It is considered necessary to choose the village as the unit because in East Pakistan it has a social entity which all members recognize and are loyal to. Each of the village cooperatives will have the advantages of a large farm while individual possession will be retained. . . .

In East Pakistan the thana seems to be the most feasible unit for organizing federations of single-purpose cooperatives.

Director Khan's statement continued with the aims of the proposed cooperative project in its first year to: increase the number of village-based cooperative societies to 60; develop institutions at the thana level to service them; introduce joint planning and joint management and retain the individual ownership of farms; make use of tractors and irrigation pumps; introduce new crops and improve farm practices; encourage savings and provide credit, joint marketing, and subsidiary occupations; experiment with special programs for women; develop vocational education; develop village leadership; and provide for continuous critical appraisal and analysis of data on various aspects as the project takes shape.

The director's statement concluded with an outline estimate of staff requirements, financial implications, the expected returns from the proposed pilot project, and comments on administrative supervision, banking, machines and tractor station, supplies and stores, advisory services in farm planning and irrigation, and a farmers' school.

The statement did not go into the question of compulsory versus voluntary cooperatives. However, the subcommittee of the working party, established soon thereafter, of which Director Khan was a member, did examine this question. The subcommittee's report read: "Consolidation of holdings is likely to create strong discontent among the people. The farmers hold their small parcels of land as dear to them as their lives, and they are likely to resist any attempt of consolidation of their holdings on a compulsory basis. . . . After thorough discussion, the committee held the view that the experiments that are now being carried on in Comilla should be intensified with the active participation of the cooperative and agriculture departments."

A Yugoslav team of experts, invited to advise on cooperatives, after visiting Comilla supported this view, and suggested to the government of Pakistan that the Comilla experiment be further developed.

Support for the Comilla approach also came from a leading cooperative official of West Pakistan in his "Note on Cooperative Farming (Compulsory or Voluntary?)." He commented on the difference between the concept of a cooperative, which is internationally accepted as a volun-

A New Village-based Cooperative System 57

tary group, and that of "A Joint Agricultural Enterprise," the name he would give to any group formed by compulsion to carry on mechanized production. He recommended this term . . . to preserve the sacredness of the term cooperative society." He went on to state that the big landowners can use machines on their present holdings; that the small farmers can make effective use of them if they are willing to organize themselves voluntarily into cooperative societies; and that if all the available machines are not so used, only then should "A Joint Agricultural Enterprise" be formed.

This view ultimately prevailed, and the idea of compulsory cooperatives was abandoned.

The Central Cooperative Association

In the early summer of 1961, the secretary of the central Ministry of Agriculture came to Comilla to study the cooperatives in order to prepare a plan for their expansion into other areas of the country.

In the course of his report he recommended that the Comilla-type cooperatives be further developed in the thana by an appropriate program:

> The scheme will continue to operate as an integral part of the research, training and demonstration programme at the Academy . . . under the direction of Mr. Akhter Hameed Khan.
>
> The main objective of this scheme is an experiment in methods to increase agriculture production by intensive farming through modern farming techniques and use of machinery. The approach is expected to demonstrate the importance of cooperatives in solving problems of small holdings and in providing supplies and services to those cultivators whose lands are not sufficiently extensive to justify the individual purchase

of power units. . . . The scheme also aims at providing a model demonstration area for other cooperators and to arrange for their training and a laboratory area for research and collection of data on cooperation and mechanization.

It is proposed to organize and develop 240 primary farming societies at the village level with a central association at the thana level. . . .

A one-year proposal was developed for 1961–1962, but before it could be made operative, plans were being worked out, based in part on the one-year proposal, for a five-year project.

In January 1962 a five-year mechanization project for Comilla thana was approved by the central government, after extensive discussions within the Planning Commission, Ministry of Agriculture, and the Academy. In the same month the *Kotwali*[7] Thana Central Cooperative Association (KTCCA) was registered. This new thana central cooperative association would give support to the activities of the local cooperative societies, render services that could not be provided by the societies severally and manage the projected mechanization project. It would "promote the continuation and expansion of savings of members in cash and in kind; make provisions for crop-production loans and medium-term credit to the local cooperative societies (not to individual members) for productive purposes (not for costs of funerals, weddings, parties, festivals, and the like); provide training for the members and staff of the cooperatives; carry on bulk marketing and purchasing activities; procure, maintain, and hire out useful farm machines to the primary societies; establish a research and demonstration laboratory activity to yield practical operational informa-

---

[7] See Glossary.

tion on cooperatives, farm machinery, and needed adjustments in the civil administration of the project area; and, develop by-laws and hire a staff to achieve the above goals."

The total cost of the five-year thana mechanization project was estimated at Rs. 48.69 lakh.[8] The central secretary for Agriculture requested 38.53 lakh from the Ford Foundation (especially for the foreign exchange costs) and the balance, 10.16 lakh, was to be contributed by the central government. Roughly, of the total, 9 lakh was to be a grant for organizational, educational, and training activities, and 39 lakh a loan. Of the latter amount, 8 lakh was for working capital repayable in eight annual installments from the sixth year, and 31 lakh for machinery and equipment, largely tractors and irrigation pumps, to be repaid in 20 annual installments from the fourth year. All repayments were to be made to a revolving fund to further cooperatives and the mechanization program. The assumption was that by the use of machines, credit, and improved methods the members could increase their production enough within the loan period to repay the loan and so become self-supporting. The Ford Foundation made the requested grant to the government of East Pakistan for the use of the KTCCA for the revolving fund after the central government had made its contribution.[9]

Director Khan became the chairman of the KTCCA's managing committee. Six of the other eight members, ap-

[8] Equivalent to U.S. $1,022,490. One lakh is 100,000, written 1,00,000. One lakh rupees is about $20,000.

[9] For a comprehensive report to the Ford Foundation on the five-year Comilla thana mechanization program, see Nicolaas G. M. Luykx, II, "Terminal Report on Introduction of Mechanized Farming in Comilla on a Cooperative Basis 1961–1966," Comilla, PARD, June 1967. Mimeographed.

pointed by the director and affirmed by the provincial registrar of cooperatives, were faculty members, and two were organizers of local cooperatives. The membership of the managing committee remained thus until October 1963 when it was increased to eighteen, twelve of whom were elected from among the villagers.

The first manager (called project director) of the KTCCA, an experienced civil servant, had come to the Academy in August 1959. The special cooperative officer, mentioned above, became deputy project director.

The operations of the KTCCA and the local cooperative societies were greatly facilitated by a coordinating meeting held each Saturday morning. These meetings were attended by the chairman, Director Khan, the project and deputy project directors, the training officer, interested members of the Academy faculty, advisors, and the heads of each of the sections of the KTCCA. Also present were any field inspectors and supervisors with problems that required policy answers. These meetings provided an opportunity for differences to be discussed and resolved, for continuous training of the staff, for refining operational procedures, and for program planning.

The line of administration from the KTCCA's project director and his deputy is through the inspector (a trained person, often with a V-AID background), to an assistant inspector (usually a villager who had been highly successful as an organizer), to the organizer of the local society, and to the members of the local society. The inspector and assistant inspector are paid by the central association, the organizer partly by the central association and partly by the society itself. An inspector usually serves about 15 local societies and has three assistant inspectors working under him, each of whom attends to his own society and four others.

A New Village-based Cooperative System 61

The central association has worked out a system of records for itself and for the member cooperatives. Villagers with some schooling were trained to serve as accountants, one for five or so local societies. The manager of the society keeps simple records of receipts and expenditures. Each week one of the accountants visits the society and brings its books up to date. Services of the accountant are ultimately paid for by the village society through the five per cent service charge added to each loan. The cooperative department of the province maintains auditors with the association to check the central association's books and make reviews of the accounts of the primary societies.

Once the central association had been registered, it was ready to develop programs for the member societies in marketing of farm products, bulk purchasing of supplies, provision of machinery, and in providing production credit.

With these activities underway, there were soon many other evidences of progress. In December 1962 the 100th cooperative society was organized. In February 1963 the property at Abhoy Ashram, 16 acres including grounds, farm, and two tanks, was purchased by the central association. In March the staff of the central association was expanded by five new assistants—in marketing, machinery movement and maintenance, water, dairy, and agricultural processing. In November the managing committee of the central association decided to have elections of all directors each year. This would provide wider opportunities for affiliate primary societies to participate in the management of the central organization. By December of 1964 the central association had declared a dividend of ten per cent, to be distributed to the members of the cooperative societies.

The central association has had a steady growth rate in

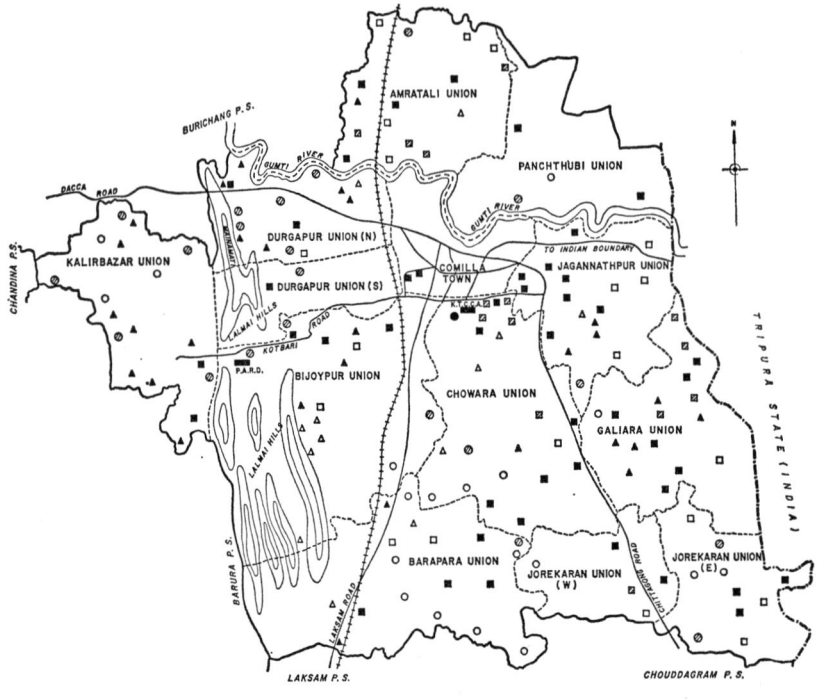

Map 2. Comilla Kotwali thana, the agricultural cooperative societies, by years, 1959–1966. Developed from information provided by the Agricultural Cooperatives Federation of the Comilla Kotwali Thana Central Cooperative Association, December 1966. Drawn by M. A. Quddus, PARD, December 1966.

cash savings, share purchases, and in loans from year to year.

SEPARATE FEDERATIONS FOR AGRICULTURAL AND NONAGRICULTURAL SOCIETIES

A little more than halfway through the five-year modernization project for the thana, there were 122 agricultural societies and 45 nonagricultural societies. At that time, July 1964, it was decided to set up for the nonagricultural societies a separate federation, subordinate to the KTCCA, under the name of Special Cooperative Societies Federation while retaining the organization of agricultural societies under the Agricultural Cooperatives Federation.

The first nonagricultural society, the Balarampur-Deeder Rickshaw Pullers Society was made up largely of very small farmers who supplemented their incomes by rickshaw pulling. Numerous other rickshaw pullers lived in the villages immediately around Comilla town. By mid-1965 there were 55 nonagricultural societies. Twenty of these were made up predominantly of rickshaw pullers. The members of most of the other 35 nonagricultural societies, even if resident in the town, had come in from the villages and still had family contacts there. Why then set up a separate association? Because the members of these nonagricultural societies were handling money throughout the year, rather than primarily at harvest periods as in the case of the farmers. Hence, they could amass savings more quickly and could therefore make use of more loans. On the other hand, the nonagricultural societies were less cohesive and less stable than the agricultural ones, with their recognized village elders. The nonagricultural societies needed closer supervision and more continuous guidance from the specialists in cooperative operations at the Academy.

As of June 30, 1966, there were 163 societies in the Agricultural Cooperatives Federation with 6,126 members, and 58 societies in the Special Cooperative Societies Federation with 2,860 members. The 58 nonagricultural societies

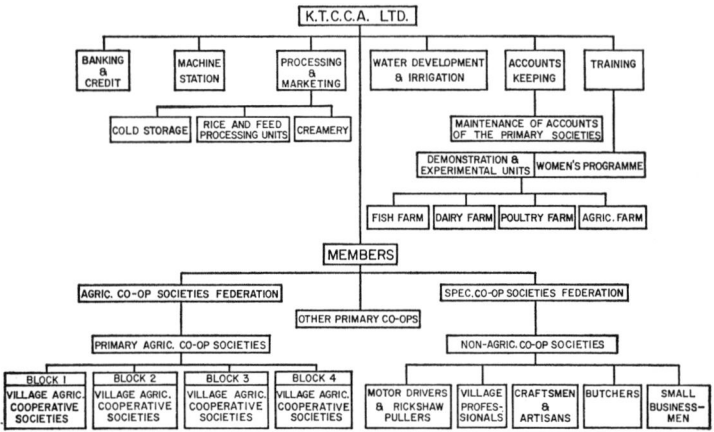

Chart 1. Structural and functional dimensions of Comilla cooperative system, 1968.* Taken from "Eighth Annual Report . . . A New Rural Cooperative System for Comilla Thana," Comilla, PARD, 1969, p. 3.

represented a score of different occupational groups: 23 rickshaw pullers, 13 small traders, 3 merchants, 2 masons, and one each of blacksmiths, bookbinders, butchers, weavers, potters, carpenters, tailors, press workers, motor drivers, motor mechanics, food grain dealers, trunk makers, fishermen, sweepers, village doctors, women, and factory workers. By mid-1968 there were 261 agricultural societies

* The two cold-storage plants and the creamery at Comilla in January 1969 (subsequent to the drawing of this chart) were transferred to the new province-wide Industrial Cooperative Society. The members of the new Society are the KTCCA and the thana cooperative association in each of the ten other thanas where Comilla-type programs are in operation.

with 11,518 members and 78 societies in the Special Cooperative Societies Federation with 3,936 members.

In mid-1966 the KTCCA operated 25 tube wells and 4 low-lift pumps for irrigation. In mid-1968 the number had increased to 91 and 37, respectively. Acres irrigated by tube wells increased from 1,127 in mid-1966 to 3,891 in mid-1968, and by the other pumps from 178 acres to 1,292.

In 1966, the KTCCA had twenty 35-hp tractors for rent to the societies, and under certain conditions to nonmembers. The number of tractors had increased to 35 in 1967 and dropped back to 28 by mid-1968. The number of acres plowed or disked increased from 1,583 in 1966 to 4,840 in 1968. The tractors were also used for hauling and other operations.

Trained tractor drivers, pump drivers, mechanics, drillers, and others related to the expanded program of mechanization increased from 261 in mid-1966 to 1,068 in mid-1968. These drivers and mechanics, largely from the cooperative villages, are keeping the tractors and pumps in operation. Many of them are finding employment elsewhere in East Pakistan.

The KTCCA rents out its machines on a first-come first-served basis. Information about the equipment for rent is avilable to all societies. A control board, first displayed at Abhoy Ashram and later at the machine shop, is kept up to date. It shows where each machine is, how long it will be there, and where it is next scheduled to go.

Savings, Credit, and Loans

Within the new cooperative setup at Comilla, savings came first, credit-worthiness next, and then loans. The systematic accumulation of membership savings and share purchases was a primary goal from the beginning of the effort.

These membership savings helped to achieve credit-worthiness for the local society at the same time the local society was providing the villagers with an ongoing organization to which to belong.

One of the first societies to establish a regular savings program was the vegetable growers' society, organized in November 1959, which adopted the policy of requiring savings in the amount of one-sixteenth of each sale. Within the next six months, each member of the seven agricultural societies, organized in as many villages, began to make a cash deposit, however small, at each weekly meeting.

Director Khan and the special officer for cooperatives were looked upon as a bit queer by the villagers for insisting upon cash savings. The villagers would say among themselves: "What does the man mean—telling us to save?" And, "When we tell him we are too poor to save, he says that is why we must save." The essence of this situation was stated by the Michigan State University coordinator of the Pakistan Project:

> Director Khan and his staff offered the villagers the almost impossible suggestion that only *they* could help themselves in the last analysis—through their individual and joint efforts. Although often starving, they would have to save; although illiterate, they would have to learn new methods; although torn with factions and animosities in the village, they would have to learn to cooperate and pool their efforts. Yes, the government would have to change; but *they* were the key elements in even the reform of government, as impossible an idea as that seemed to be.[10]

---

[10] Richard O. Niehoff, *Technical Assistance in the In-Service Training of Pakistan Civil Servants since 1958*, Michigan State University, Asian Studies Center, Occasional Paper No. 3, Spring 1966, p. 19.

The savings in the early days appear tiny indeed. During April 1960, savings of the first seven agricultural societies ranged from Rs. 12.00 to Rs. 65.00. The per-member monthly savings ranged from Rs. 0.60 (12 cents) to Rs. 2.65.

The first 25 agriculture societies as of June 1961 had cumulative cash savings of Rs. 23,041. In addition, 21 of these societies had in-kind savings of 2,680 *maunds* of *paddy*,[11] at not less than Rs. 10.00 per maund, or Rs. 26,800, giving a total of about Rs. 50,000. By 1967–1968 the total savings and shares of the agricultural and nonagricultural societies totaled Rs. 1,452,378.

The cash saving is regularly entered in the member's passbook, week after week. It is also entered in the record book of the local society for that week. These transactions take place in the weekly meeting and, in addition to saving money, give further incentive for learning to read. "Was the right amount entered?" an illiterate man may wonder. Here is a good reason for him to learn to add and subtract.

The first cash savings were made largely on faith in the integrity of the Academy's administration, and more particularly in Director Khan and the special cooperative officer. For, as mentioned, there was no effective banking for the local societies until the KTCCA was organized. In the meantime, however, membership savings were being made and have continued to be made, as indicated by the figures cited above.

PURCHASES OF SHARES

The by-laws of the KTCCA also encouraged the accumulation of capital through the purchase of shares by mem-

[11] See Glossary.

bers. A share capital issuance of Rs. 500,000 in 50,000 shares at Rs. 10 each was authorized. This overall amount could be changed at any meeting called for the purpose, and by amending the by-laws accordingly.

The purchase of shares by the societies has been rather slow, but even so there has been a steady rate of increase. The cumulative shares, purchased by the agricultural and nonagricultural societies combined, increased from roundly 1,140 in 1962 to 4,660 in 1963; to 8,680 in 1964; to 21,110 in 1965; to 40,830 in 1966; 49,470 in 1967 and 85,870 in 1968 (roughly Rs. 860,000). In this last year the average share holding of the members of the agricultural societies was Rs. 47.67 and of the nonagricultural societies Rs. 78.65.

Some shares have been purchased by the membership from increased earnings; but most of them have been purchased under conditions laid down in the by-laws of the KTCCA: that each local society upon joining the central association purchase Rs. 50 of capital stock as an admission fee into the association; that a society retain its membership in the association by purchasing Rs. 50 of capital stock annually thereafter; that dividends earned on capital stock be paid to a member society in the form of additional capital stock; that an amount equal to five per cent of any loan be purchased in capital stock before the loan can be given; and that upon the payment of a loan a capital stock purchase service charge of five per cent of the amount be made.

The rules for the cooperatives provide for a further hedge against risks, namely that each loan be protected by a reserve fund in the member society equal to 25 per cent of the loan being taken. If the reserve fund is less than that, five per cent of the principal of the loan must be deposited

A New Village-based Cooperative System 69

in the central association. A similar procedure must be followed until the reserve fund has reached the stipulated level.

Monies thus secured increase the capital of the central association, and make it more able to procure and maintain farm machinery, promote the sinking of irrigation tube wells, get agricultural processing enterprises into operation, and so on. The village societies, too, are helped directly, for these fees paid to the central association are credited to them, and so raise their loan limits.

Even though the by-laws of the KTCCA were designed to increase its capital as fast as possible through the sale of capital shares, nearly 70 per cent of the total cumulative savings from the local societies up to mid-1963 had come from the weekly cash deposits of the members. But by mid-1968, about 60 per cent of all cumulative cash savings were from share purchases and 40 per cent from weekly cash deposits.

LOANS

Despite the difficulty of getting a production loan prior to the organization of the KTCCA, 17 village societies had by 1961 secured 25 loans totaling Rs. 108,000. The largest amount borrowed by any village society was Rs. 15,000 and the smallest Rs. 2,500. These loans were arranged through either the Comilla Cooperative Bank or the Agricultural Bank at Comilla, by all of the credit-worthy members of a society joining together in the pooling of their several collaterals (separate pieces of fragmented unencumbered lands). When a loan was granted, an Academy representative of the cooperative deposited it to the village cooperative's account in the Comilla Cooperative Bank. It could be withdrawn only by action of the general meeting of the village society, and for the purposes for which it was secured.

Such loans were put to relatively good uses. A great deal of joint planning took place in the village cooperatives in the preparation of the loan applications. The smaller farmers of the society were served through the collateral provided by the larger farmers of the group, and often had some collateral of their own that could be included. The borrowing society was encouraged by the Academy representatives to be very careful about the purpose of the loan, to keep it small enough to be repaid on time, for only so could a society get larger loans later.

These early arrangements were theoretically good enough, but there was no effective way to provide the continuous supervision needed. Furthermore, these banks had little resources of their own, and so served primarily as agents for the State Bank of Pakistan. The result was that loans could not always be had, and those that could be had often came late. This situation was made yet more intolerable by the villagers' tendency to be late in their applications for loans.

The operations of the KTCCA were designed to correct the basic problems described. It would have resources of its own, make loans promptly and in the amounts needed, further refine the joint planning already started, and provide continuous and constructive guidance for the use of the loans through training and field supervision.

The lending activities of the KTCCA have regularly increased. The annual loans to agricultural societies, for example, rose from Rs. 235,664 in 1961–1962, to Rs. 725,276 in 1964–1965, and to Rs. 4,224,477 in 1967–1968. Annual loans to nonagricultural societies also rose consistently from Rs. 3,000 in 1961–1962 to Rs. 1,029,633 in 1967–1968.[12]

LOAN APPLICATIONS

To safeguard the repayment of loans, there is a relatively elaborate system of application, approval, and supervision. First a maximum loan limit is fixed for each society by the managing committee of the central association. This limit is arrived at on the basis of shares purchased, status of reserve funds, weekly cash savings, in-kind savings, production capacity, previous loan repayment record, the level of the "cooperative spirit" of the society, and the ability of its members to work together as a unit. Second, a joint production plan must accompany the society's loan application.

The joint plan will usually be keyed back to an overall annual plan worked out for the society as a whole. The totals of such a plan are made up of all the items of all the members. Here is laborious business—the compilation of details by small farmers, many of whom are illiterate, and none of whom are accustomed to joint planning. A loan application shows for each member: the number of adults and minors in the family; total land possessed; exact uses of the land down to as little as 1/100 of an acre (called a "decimal") for chili, for instance; and the uses each member plans to make of his part of the loan, with the exact amount entered, as relevant, for commerical fertilizers by types, wages for farm labor, type and amount of seed by crops, rent of a tractor or irrigation pump, and money needed to purchase insecticides or implements or bullocks. The plan is reviewed by the area inspector and the assistant

[12] *A New Rural Cooperative System for Comilla Thana* (Eighth Annual Report, 1968), Comilla, PARD, April 1969.

inspector. They then assist the organizer in drawing up a composite loan application for the interested members of the society, to be submitted to the central association. The loan application is studied by association officials. If it is acceptable, a check is made out, usually within a couple of days. The check is drawn to the organizer of the society and is deposited in the central association to the credit of the society. Withdrawals are made on the joint signatures of the organizer and the project director of the central association for the purchase at wholesale prices of the production items or for payment for services as set forth in the loan application.

TYPES OF LOANS

The most common types of loans (short-, medium-, and long-term) made by the central association are crop production loans; in-kind loans to tide a family over a period of food shortage, to be repaid in kind; milk-cow loans, to be repaid by milk regularly supplied to the dairy processing unit operated by the central association; loans for the release of mortgaged lands, that is, lands whose titles had been given to moneylenders for loans (so great was this need that after considerable hesitation the central association decided to permit up to one-half of the loan ceiling to be used by the members of a society for this purpose); loans to societies for the hire and purchase of machinery, including repair services; and loans against a pledged crop to pay land revenue tax; interest to moneylenders; and wages for laborers at harvest time. In the last few years loans have also been made for land improvement, electricity, irrigation, and for other similar production purposes.

Annual production loans are made by the central association to the village agricultural societies at 15 per cent interest per annum, repayable in cash, which is allocated as follows: 7 per cent for use of the money, 5 per cent for overall cooperative services, that is, training, accounting, and so on. The remaining 3 per cent is refunded to the village society for its expenses or distributed as dividends. Other types of loans are made on a similar rate structure.

To escape the necessity of selling paddy at the depressed harvest-time price, a member of a cooperative society may take a loan of 60 per cent of the market price of such produce as he deposits with the society or the central cooperative association. The repayment of the loan is made when the produce is sold, which is when the price goes up. After the payment of interest on the loan, the village borrower gets the entire benefit. This arrangement, a very attractive one, has led to an increase in the membership of the local societies. The program was of benefit to noncooperative farmers, too, for it reduced the amount of paddy sold on the harvest-time market.

When the size of loans made is considered in relation to membership, it is apparent that the loans taken by the member groups of the Special Cooperative Societies Federation are larger than those for the Agricultural Cooperatives Federation societies. Some of the larger Special Cooperative Societies Federation loans through the KTCCA have been for trucks. Five trucks have been purchased by rickshaw-pullers' societies and one each by three other societies: the merchants, butchers, and motor engineers. Four buses have been purchased at around Rs. 47,000 each. Other purchases through KTCCA loans include a blacksmith shop (Rs. 37,000), a printing press (Rs. 45,000), trunk shop (Rs. 11,000), an aluminum-shaping shop, a doctors' cooperative shop, and six auto rickshaws. Managerial and technical problems have been encountered with the press, blacksmith, and aluminum shops, and their loan repayments have been slow. The Special Cooperative Societies Federation is trying to help solve these operational problems through the training of managers, and in some instances by replacing them with more qualified people. Repayments on most of the purchases for motorized equipment are ahead of schedule, as is also the case with the doctors' cooperative shop, trunk shop, and a small contract operation of the masons' society.

LOAN REPAYMENT

The repayment record of the cooperative loans at Comilla has been one of its outstanding differences from most of the other cooperative endeavors in the province.

On a cumulative basis, from 1961–1962 to 1966–1967, the percentage of overdue loans to agricultural societies was 1.2 per cent and for nonagricultural societies 1.6 per cent. There have been some extensions of loans on justifiable grounds, such as crop damage from floods, breaches in the Gumti levees, storms, and sometimes illness or death. No effort is spared by the KTCCA to assure the collection of every loan made. Each society is kept advised of its fiscal responsibility. It is warned that any irregularities will be dealt with promptly, and that recourse to the courts will be made if needed.

Failure to repay loans is hardly tolerable within the Comilla cooperative system. Societies in arrears, or otherwise not living up to the ten-point set of rules noted earlier, may be put on probation until they meet their outstanding obligations. Or, if they persist in their delinquency, or lose interest in meeting the conditions of membership, they are dissolved by the central association.

A score of agricultural societies, some of them earlier

A visit from President Ayub Khan and East Pakistan's Governor Momen Khan, March 1963 (PARD)

Sign promoting IUD device before the shop of one of the 500 agents selling nonmedical family planning supplies (Fred Ward, Ford Foundation)

Installing pipe for a deep-bore tube well for irrigation (PARD)

Samples contrasting three panicles of mature IR-8 rice and three panicles of an unimproved variety (Fred Ward, Ford Foundation)

Another money-making project of the women's section of the Academy: weaving cloth on handlooms—but first the yarn must be prepared as the woman is doing here (Fred Ward, Ford Foundation)

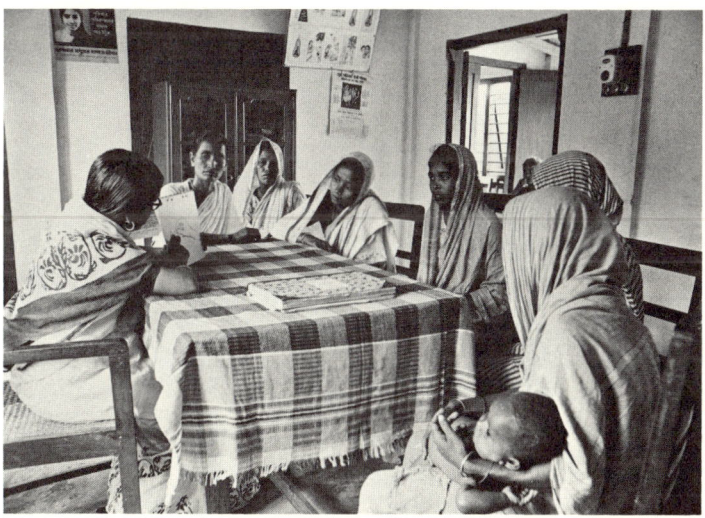

A group of village midwives being given birth control information by health visitor (Fred Ward, Ford Foundation)

Villagers operating a foot-pedaled rice thresher (Fred Ward, Ford Foundation)

A village "feeder school" in session (Fred Ward, Ford Foundation)

The Sonaichuri intake through the levee of the Gumti River nearing completion (PARD)

Villagers making jamma (rock-like fragments of hard-burned brick used for practically all cement work and road paving), for the public works program (Fred Ward, Ford Foundation)

Money-making activities sponsored by the women's section of the Academy: (top) making clothes for the family and for sale; (bottom) silkscreen printing of cotton cloth for saris (Fred Ward, Ford Foundation)

The old way and the new of readying a field for rice seedlings (PARD)

A weekly meeting of a group of organizers (managers) of village-based agricultural societies (Fred Ward, Ford Foundation)

A village representative at the machine shop, making arrangements to rent a tractor (Fred Ward, Ford Foundation)

A low-lift irrigation pump, one of the early experimental installations of the village-based cooperatives (Fred Ward, Ford Foundation)

A New Village-based Cooperative System 75

highly successful, were put on probation in November 1965 for failure to repay loans when due and to make deposits. Each one of them requested that their resources be retained by the central association. Seven months later all but four had repaid their back loans and otherwise requalified for membership in good standing. The four others remained on probation. These censures naturally raise the question as to whether other societies, too, may in time exhibit similarly poor performance.

Thirty-six societies have been discontinued. Eighteen of these were agricultural societies, with 983 members, and 18 nonagricultural, with 658 members. Some few of these societies were asked by the central association to withdraw; but most of them lost interest, and performed so poorly that they dropped out on their own initiative. Several of those that were discontinued have been reinstated, however. The lack of a good organizer (manager) among the membership is a most common cause of failure.

The good record of loan repayment at Comilla is the result of systematic training and planning. Loans are made to be used, and loans that are used constructively can and will be repaid, thus creating an enlarging revolving fund. It is in the creation of a revolving fund that thrift plays so basic a part. For borrowers will make the most constructive use of credit when they are borrowing against their own credit-worthiness and that of their neighbors, in short when they are borrowing from themselves.

The financing of the cooperatives and other activities at Comilla has generally been adequate, what with the support of the government, the grant from the Ford Foundation to the five-year modernization program, and the PL-480 counterpart funds made avilable for the thana's intensive public works program.

The basically sound financial position of the KTCCA is indicated by its ability to negotiate loans for its needs. In 1966–1967, applications were made for an operating loan of Rs. 3,000,000 from the State Bank of Pakistan, and a foreign exchange loan of Rs. 6,000,000 for mechanization from the funds loaned to Pakistan by the World Bank. Both loans were granted.

There was no lending agency capable of offering reasonably priced credit to the average village farmer until the KTCCA was established. The regular banks were in the larger towns, and for all practical purposes loans were not available to the farmers whose operations were small and whose collateral was slight. Furthermore, most villagers were in debt to the local moneylenders. The KTCCA became the banker to the local society, which was in turn the banker to the individual members.

THE FIRST RURAL BRANCH OF A COMMERCIAL BANK

The strict conditions under which the KTCCA made loans and the good record of loan repayments led to the opening of a branch of a commercial bank, United Bank, Ltd., at Abhoy Ashram in October 1962. This branch bank served as the banker for the central association and so further strengthened the financial position of the cooperatives. The bank made the accumulated accounts of the societies more secure; removed the necessity of tying up government money by substituting loans from the bank against security provided by the central association; invested the surplus funds of the association; provided remittance facilities to the local societies (through the association) and so encouraged the use of cash; and opened a line of credit for the societies for production, marketing, trade, and other purposes.

A New Village-based Cooperative System 77

This branch bank, the first in East Pakistan to serve a predominantly rural clientele, is highly profitable as a banking venture. In addition to the business of the central association, by mid-1964 it had attracted individual deposits of more than Rs. 500,000 ($105,000) from the farmers and townspeople. While cooperative members concur in the strict production uses of their loans from the association, they also want some ready cash of their own for weddings, funerals, and festivals. These are the traditional ways of proving to your neighbors and to yourself that you can "celebrate." And this, too, is new for most of the farmers —namely celebrating with cash saved instead of with a loan from a moneylender.

The all-round success of this first rural banking venture may be further seen from the fact that a branch was set up in each of the three thanas where Comilla-type programs were begun in 1963, and in each of the seven thanas in Comilla district in which Comilla-type programs were started in 1965–1966.

Activities of the Central Cooperative Association (KTCCA)

From the outset there was a close relationship between the organization of cooperatives and the use of farm machines. When the first two tractors at the Academy, provided by the Department of Agriculture, were taken to the villages in March 1960 the farmers were curious about them and came out in great numbers to watch the demonstration. But they showed little interest the first day in having tractors used on their own farms. They saw that the tractors did the work well, but assumed apparently that the equipment was suited only to the farms of the government and the large landowners. Even so, the few villagers who were having the tractors used on a demonstration basis in their fields liked the work they did. By the end of the third day of the demonstrations, as the word began to get around, many farmers were wanting the use of the tractors and stood in a long queue at the Academy with the rent money in their hands. With so much demand, some rules had to be developed before the tractors could be further used. The villagers agreed that it was not sensible to try to use them in different villages on the same day, for then they would be on the road too much of the time. The Academy decided that a tractor would be sent to a village only when five or more farmers, with a total of eight or more cultivatable acres in a contiguous area, made a joint request for a tractor and deposited the rent money with the Academy.

At first the farmers thought these conditions would be difficult, if not impossible, to meet, because of factionalism in the villages and because of the varied interests of the farmers. Furthermore they feared, on the basis of past experiences, that any advanced rent money would be lost or stolen. Meanwhile the tractors were not in use. After a few days, however, the farmers in one village paid the rent and requested a tractor. One was sent there. Shortly after this two nearby villages qualified, and then others, many others.

Two problems had yet to be solved: the smallness of the fields, and the unwillingness of the tractor drivers provided by the Department of Agriculture to work all day in the fields. The tractors could operate in the small fields, but it was very costly because of so much turning and such heavy use of the brakes and hydraulic lifts. Also it was much harder work for the tractor drivers, who were already dissatisfied with this rural assignment.

The small-field problem was put squarely to the villag-

A New Village-based Cooperative System

ers. What suggestions did they have about how to proceed? After much discussion, they decided that they could drive stakes to mark the location of the miniature embankments between their small fields, and then let the tractor plow or disc across them. This was done. No disputes arose the first year, or later, as to the correct place for the reestablishment of the embankments. The explanation is that the farmers had formed a group for the use of the tractor and had driven the stakes themselves.

VILLAGERS TRAINED AS TRACTOR DRIVERS

Two tractor drivers came with the first two tractors, and two more with the next two tractors a year later. These drivers, with schooling up to about tenth-year level, had been taught at a workshop near Dacca. It was soon found that they were reluctant to work in the noonday sun, in the rain, or on weekends. The village farmers, though underemployed a considerable part of the year, were accustomed to working long days throughout the busy planting season. It was in the premonsoon preparation of the fields for the aus rice crop that the use of the tractor was most wanted.

The village farmers were highly displeased with the performance of the tractor drivers. There were rumors that a driver would sometimes disconnect wires or remove some small part from the tractor so it would not operate, and he could go into town. These young men had been chosen to drive the tractor because they could read and write, make reports, and remember the parts of the tractor. There soon arose a question: was not whatever superior information these drivers had being more than offset by their negative attitude toward work in the villages?

The Academy decided to train young men from the villages to operate the tractors. The villagers liked this idea.

To the young men in the villages tractor driving was prestigious work. The first group of 40 villagers began their tractor training in early September 1961. Each young man was a member of a cooperative society, or his father was. He had to be physically fit, accustomed to manual farm work, educated enough to read instructions, and interested in machines. And he had to have been selected by the members of the cooperative society. The training was done at the Academy by three skilled mechanics over a period of six weeks. Thirty-six of the young men finished the course; the other four dropped out because they were unable to learn about the machine or were unwilling to do the work.

A week after this first group finished their training a second group entered upon a five-week training period. They were chosen in much the same way as the first group, except that less emphasis was placed on education and more on work experience. In the meantime 13 local villagers, chosen by their cooperatives, had been trained to operate the irrigation pumps. Here again operators were needed who lived in the villages.

Thus were established the principles by which the new cooperative system began its mechanization program, and by which the tractors and pumps were used in the villages. That these rules were generally to the liking of the villagers can be surmised from the rapid increase of local cooperatives that occurred over the months ahead and from the increased use of machinery.

MACHINE SHOP AND TRACTOR STATION

A cooperative machine shop and tractor station was set up in late 1961 to service the few machines then in use and to prepare for the upkeep of those to be brought in later by the five-year modernization project. The shop is located

A New Village-based Cooperative System 81

two miles from Abhoy Ashram, within the Comilla municipality, in space rented from the Comilla Mohajir Karkhana Cooperative, Ltd.

The machines in Comilla thana and those requiring major repairs from other pilot thanas are serviced at this machine shop. The establishment also trains the mechanics and drivers employed at Comilla and in the expanded program in the other thanas. At first the machine shop and tractor station had two sections, maintenance and movement, each headed by a Peace Corps Volunteer. A third section, water development and irrigation, was added in 1964.

The maintenance section handles the major repairs of all cooperatively owned machines and in 1965 began in addition to provide repair service for motor cars, jeeps, trucks, and motorcycles not belonging to the cooperatives. This section also trains those who repair the machines. The movement section prepares rosters for and operates all machines, takes them to the villages, and performs minor repairs in the field. It trains tractor and pump drivers, and services tube-well pumps. The water development and irrigation section, headed by an experienced well driller from West Pakistan, by mid-1966 operated ten drilling rigs and was equipped to install large-bore wells to a depth of 600 feet or more. Well-drilling crews are trained as needed for Comilla thana and the other thanas with Comilla-type programs. Some indication of the volume of the operations of the machine shop and tractor station is indicated by the following statistics for 1967–1968: twenty-eight tractors were used in cultivating 4,840 acres of land in Comilla thana and also did a total of 1,146 days (8 hours each) hauling and other operations. In addition training was given to 241 tractor drivers, 417 pump drivers, 70 mechanics, 60 drillers, 30 assistant drillers, and to 7 high-level mechanics. The use of the shop for installing pumps and tube wells is described in Chapter 5.

The shop operated at a deficit for the first four years (1961-1965), but made a profit in 1966, primarily because of increased use of tractors. The ninth annual report of the Academy (1967-1968) still reported a deficit for the tractor station of more than Rs. 100,000 for a gross operation of Rs. 534,692.

MARKETING: SALES AND BULK PURCHASING

Marketing of farm produce has been another basic activity of the KTCCA. For what incentive does the village farmer have to produce more if there is no market for the surplus? Bulk purchasing has also been important.

The marketing section of the central association collects information about prices and makes it available to the local societies; assists in arranging sales for members' produce in the best possible market; purchases consumer goods in bulk and makes them available to the members of the societies at wholesale cost (still in the experimental stage); and links marketing with credit. With so many small farmers, mass marketing and bulk purchasing can become operative only after the villagers themselves are well organized. It has become apparent at Comilla that it is more difficult to achieve consumer cooperation than to carry on cooperative sales activites.

Director Khan estimates that the farmer normally gets about one-fourth too little for what he sells, and pays around one-fourth too much for what he buys. The causes of this double penalty are that he traditionally disposes of his surplus in small lots at harvest time, and that he makes his purchases as an individual, item by item.

A New Village-based Cooperative System 83

The central cooperative is trying to develop an agricultural marketing system that will use a standard unit of weight (see below), insure full prices for farm products sold, and make available good supplies at reasonable costs. These ends are being achieved in two ways: by the storage of farm produce at harvest time in the local village or in larger warehouses, and by arranging for bulk transport of produce to large distant markets.

MARKETING AND STORING OF PADDY,
POTATOES, AND VEGETABLES

The central cooperative arranges as needed for sales of paddy at a river-port market (Hajiganj) some thirty miles from Comilla. Whenever the price at Comilla falls more than one rupee below that of its river-port outlet, the tractor-trailers of the central cooperative haul it there. At the Hajiganj market the light maund is used rather than the heavy one used at Comilla. This difference (approximately 80.5 and 82.5 lbs.) offsets most of the transportation cost to the river-port market. As a result, the traders at Comilla are no longer able to depress the price when the cooperatives' pooled stock starts to move into the market. This tends to stabilize the price at Comilla, and so is of value to all farmers in the area.

Now, practically all of the stored paddy of the village cooperatives is sold at Comilla, by the local cooperatives themselves. The very existence of the central association's marketing-transportation arrangement makes its use unnecessary. The farmers now are convinced that they can sell more paddy at a good price, and so they more readily adopt improved methods.

Potatoes and vegetables, too, are being marketed cooperatively. The contribution of the cooperative enters the picture early, for these crops are grown in the dry winter season, and irrigation must be provided, as must also fertilizers, good seed, and insecticides.

Much care is needed in marketing potatoes, for they are perishable. So the cooperative farmers at Comilla decided to construct and operate their own cold-storage plant—a 30,000 maund capacity unit on a five-acre tract of land close to the railroad station at Comilla. It was put into operation in the 1965–1966 season. The initial project proposal had estimated that the cold-storage plant would earn an annual income of Rs. 250,000 from potatoes alone; this projection was essentially realized in 1966–1967. The next year, the net profit was Rs. 169,246. A second cold-storage plant has now been added. Potatoes stored at harvest time are sold later. The whole crop no longer need be put on the local market at once, or be hauled off to Chittagong or Dacca. Sales may still be in distant markets, but arrangements can now be made ahead of time as to the price to be paid. This is in sharp contrast to rolling into the market with a truckload of unsold potatoes, with the buyers hoping yet other truckloads will soon arrive. At best it was a buyer's market. If only the buyer has cold-storage facilities, it is he rather than the farmer who profits from the crop.

The marketing of other vegetables presented much the same problems as potatoes, except that most vegetables mature over a longer period of time and are even more perishable. In an attempt to escape dependence on the Comilla market, the central association trucked vegetables to the Narayanganj and Dacca wholesale markets, 40 and 50 miles away, Sales were made, but the cost of ferrying across the rivers consumed most of the profit. Vegetables are also trucked to Chittagong, a distance of 100 miles. This proved to be more satisfactory. When the road to Naray-

A New Village-based Cooperative System 85

anganj and Dacca is further bridged, these population centers will probably be the best outlets for vegetables from the Comilla area.

AGRICULTURAL PROCESSING ENTERPRISES

Besides the two cold-storage plants the KTCCA operates a dairy unit in the same area and a rice mill at Abhoy Ashram. Several smaller enterprises too have been started, including printing, the selling of fish, and a butchers' cooperative for crushing of bones, sale of hides, and drying of blood for feed.

Procuring a dependable flow of raw milk from the villagers and processing it have been major problems for the dairy project, but these were being partially solved by early 1965. The village producers had formed a cooperative of their own, with 228 members. It had taken loans of Rs. 65,000 from the central cooperative association, and was delivering milk to the creamery from 250 cows. By mid-March the cooperative had 241 members; more milk was needed, and more loans were taken to purchase cows. A total of 175 villagers including a dozen village women took loans for cows.

A new creamery located at the site of the cold-storage plant provides more than 500 square feet of floor space and relevant equipment, including a cool room, pasteurization facilities, and so on, for producing quality dairy products in commercial quantities. In cool weather, it has been able to ship cheese daily to Chittagong, and to sell milk locally. But the problems of marketing in hot weather have not been completely solved.

Despite numerous difficulties in supply, marketing, and finance the dairy project continues because the farmers have seen that it is possible to increase their incomes in this way. There are some hopeful considerations: the village roads have recently been improved, more winter farming may mean the opportunity for better forage for cows, the cold-storage plant now has ice for sale to cool the insulated vehicles that transport the raw milk to the creamery, and road transportation to Dacca and Chittagong is being further improved. As of mid-1966, the dairy cooperative had 302 members, scattered over the thana. Loans had been taken for the purchase of 259 cows, of which more than 30 per cent had already been repaid. A Danish dairy expert had been posted at the creamery. The ninth annual report of the Academy (1967–1968); with a gross operating budget of Rs. 579,665, still shows the unit operating at a small net loss.

The production, processing, and marketing of poultry products have been greatly aided since 1967 by an expert supplied by the Danish government. A modern slaughterhouse and freezing unit have been provided. Dressed birds and eggs are now supplied to major hotels and restaurants in Dacca and Chittagong. For this commodity, it appears that long-standing problems of production and marketing are being overcome.

The rice mill on the Abhoy Ashram campus started operations in May 1964, occupying modest new buildings erected for the purpose. The use of the mill should enable the cooperative association to sell at a greater advantage the rice that comes to it from the primary societies through repayment of loans in kind. The report for 1966–1967 showed a small excess of income over expenditures, whereas the next year the operations of the mill, with a total operation of Rs. 544,806, showed a small net loss.

In addition to the above-noted central services, the KTCCA operates a central store which operated at a small

A New Village-based Cooperative System 87

loss in 1967-1968, and a seed section which had a substantial excess of income over expenditures.

MISCELLANEOUS MARKETING ACTIVITIES

The importance of transport, vehicles, roads, and communication facilities has been highlighted in the marketing experiments of the cooperatives. The villages near the main roads have long had an advantage. In recent years the situation in numerous other villages has been improved by the local roads that have been constructed through public works programs. In some areas local societies propose that selected villages be made assembly points at which trucks could pick up vegetables for transport to distant markets.

Most of the hauling for the central association is done by its tractors with trailers. This has provided needed work for the tractors. But as the roads improve, trucks are being used more because of their greater flexibility and speed. Some trucks are used by the central association and some by the primary societies.

To help the villagers understand the marketing process and know that the association is selling their produce at the best possible price, one or more villagers selected by the societies accompany the trucks to the markets. This same practice is followed when bulk purchasing is being done for the cooperatives and for the union councils.

Some effective marketing of children's clothing and of saris and other women's wear has been done from time to time by the women's section at Abhoy Ashram; poultry products too have been marketed. There are still many unsolved market problems for practically all of these items. With further experimentation it is thought that reasonably adequate answers can in time be worked out.

A project of the central association to supply consumer

goods for retail sale by village cooperatives looked promising for a time, but it was discontinued when confronted with credit problems. A subsequent effort to achieve the same purposes through established shopkeepers also failed.

In late 1962–1963 an unsuccessful experiment was undertaken in the cooperative marketing of sugar cane, and in 1964 in selling fertilizer to the societies.

Several special-purpose cooperatives started in the early days at Comilla did not succeed. A vegetable growers' cooperative organized in November 1959 expired in March 1962, mainly because of marketing and credit difficulties. A women's cooperative which bought and sold products needed in the household was formed in March 1960; it disbanded after about two years, partly because of resistance by the men to women being engaged in this kind of business activity. Later on, other women's cooperatives, however, have succeeded. A cooperative community at Kotbari for the staff of the Academy and their families was tried out, but this never really got off the ground.

An Evaluation Study[13]

A sample study in 1966 of 45 out of 156 agricultural societies was undertaken by a four-man evaluation team, under the direction of the vice chairman of the KTCCA. A third of those chosen were considered "good," a third "bad," and the other third in between. A case study was made of each of the societies, with emphasis on management, capital formation, credit operations, accounting procedures, production practices, marketing, and social and psychological factors affecting operations. In summary, the

[13] M. Zakir Hussain, "A Field Investigation into the Management of Village Cooperatives in Comilla Experimental Area," Comilla, PARD, 1967. Mimeographed.

A New Village-based Cooperative System 89

committee's findings indicated that the good societies are characterized by able and honest leadership and the bad ones (many of them earlier good ones) by dishonest and self-seeking leadership. The members of the former have confidence in their societies, the members of the latter do not. This report also indicates that the per capita cash deposits made weekly by the cooperative members tend to reach a peak in the second or third year, then decline, and following that begin to build up again, slowly.[14]

The reasons the fifteen societies went "bad" include: misappropriation of funds or suspicion about the misappropriation of funds; factions in the societies; the autocratic way in which the chairman (not manager) of the society controlled it; lack of interest of members; promotion of a successful manager without a proper substitute; and rule by a clique. The "good" societies were characterized as having high morale, high attendance at meetings, regular savings, prompt repayment of loans, high rate of adoptions, growth in membership, and other positive responses.

Back of these immediate causes is the failure of the central cooperative association to continue to provide the needed supervision, progressive training, and close contact with the societies. The villagers perform best when the director or other ranking staff people in the Academy or the central association can personally work with them. But this became increasingly difficult as more and more societies were formed, and as program operations became more complex. "The Academy is learning the lesson," said the resident Michigan State University adviser, "that there is

---

[14] This pattern of a fast start, then a slow-down, followed by a solid if slow growth rate, was observed in many other aspects of the Comilla program, such as the use of tractors, number of acres irrigated, number of women in training classes, etc.

nothing that can be considered 'self-sustaining' in the program. Continual effective interaction is vital. . . ."[15]

It is well to remember that some of the bad societies had earlier been good ones. They had then made their weekly cash deposits, bought shares, met regularly, and had taken loans and repaid them. Most of these practices had been reversed by the time they were blacklisted in late 1965. What can be done to keep the rate of deposits from slumping after the second or third year? What can be done to keep good societies from going bad? The committee's study helped a great deal to highlight the need for the most careful and continuous scrutiny of all of the operations of the cooperatives.

The 1966 evaluation study made more apparent, too, the need for management assistance. The rapid growth of the cooperatives and the increased volume and complexity of fiscal and managerial problems which have accompanied such growth have been a persistent problem for the extremely limited number of capable managers who could be developed through experience, supervision, and training. In order to provide some guidance and assistance in keeping the development of some managerial skills somewhat apace with the growth, a Michigan State University adviser experienced in cooperative management[16] spent a substantial part of a two-year period analyzing problems and conducting seminars and other training activities. He was followed somewhat later by a short term consultant from the university who performed similar functions and produced training-management manuals which are used to continue the

[15] Nicolaas G. M. Luykx, II, at Comilla from February 1966 to May 1968.
[16] Robert D. Havener, at Comilla from November 1964 to July 1966.

A New Village-based Cooperative System 91

effort. More recently a Danish expert in marketing and management has come to Comilla to further this advisory assistance. A constant effort is made to identify managers and supervisors from the ranks of organizers, accountants, and others who have demonstrated supervisory capabilities. Promotions for these persons have been very rapid in the KTCCA.

Recent Developments

Within the framework of policies and practices described above, and reflecting in part the growth in the volume and complexity of the KTCCA and its affiliated organizations, a few of the relatively more recent developments are worthy of special comment. These developments in the areas of organization and support, extension, technical inputs, and research are briefly described below.

ORGANIZATION AND SUPPORT

1. The administration of the cooperatives, started in mid-1965 in seven additional thanas of Comilla district, has been transferred from the Department of Agriculture to the East Pakistan Agricultural Development Corporation. As a first step in the transfer, the project directors of the seven thanas, who had been appointed from the East Pakistan civil service system on deputation to the KTCCA, have been replaced by East Pakistan Agricultural Development Corporation officers. These newly recruited officers were trained at the Academy for six months before being assigned to the new positions in March 1968.

2. The Danish government has created a trust fund under which grants are made to KTCCA for advisors, machinery and equipment. Three Danish advisors are now assisting the KTCCA in the fields of dairy, poultry, mar-

keting, and management. Equipment has been provided for poultry raising and processing.

3. The major groupings of cooperative societies under the KTCCA in January 1969 included the Agricultural Cooperatives Federation, the Special Cooperative Societies Federation, and miscellaneous primary societies. As of this date, the two cold-storage plants and creamery at Comilla were transferred from the KTCCA to the new province-wide Industrial Cooperative Society.[17]

EXTENSION

Whereas the earlier concerns in extension were largely focused on getting the principles of the cooperatives firmly established, the more recent developments have become much more complex. In the financial field, investments of considerably larger magnitude and sophistication are now being made with a concurrent need for educational extension programs for the cooperative membership. In the field of agricultural modernization much greater attention is paid to improved rice varieties from the International Rice Research Institute and other sources, and much more attention is paid to substantially greater investments in fertilizers, insecticides, and other production inputs. Mechanization has received tremendous stimulation from the successful demonstration of the feasibility and profitability of irrigated crops, a development which promises to revolutionize agriculture in East Pakistan.

TECHNICAL INPUTS

The increased volume and complexity of the new developments has resulted in identifying areas where highly specialized advisory assistance is needed. Some of these new

[17] See organizational charts of KTCCA on pages 64 and 129.

A New Village-based Cooperative System 93

technical advisory inputs are provided by drawing more widely on governmental resources, but others are provided from outside organizations. Michigan State University, for example, has provided, in addition to general advisory assistance and staff development, short-term consultants on potential new crops under irrigation and more specifically on potatoes; the International Rice Research Institute has provided advisory assistance on rice crops; and the Danes have given helpful advice in the fields of poultry, butter, and cheese production and marketing and management. As the program grows, additional advisory inputs will be needed to help achieve the new potentials built upon the base of viable village cooperatives whose members have acquired a new vision, drive, and discipline for development.

RESEARCH

Although research has been built into the Academy's operations from the beginning, as will be more fully described in Chapter 8, and although increased production has been a major objective from the start, definitive findings on production and costs were possible only after the basic new social and economic organization for development had begun to produce results. Furthermore the newest of the technical inputs—improved seeds and an irrigation system—have only recently been introduced, tested, and extended.

These developments have now been made a major concern of research. Varietal trials conducted by a faculty member trained at the International Rice Research Institute are going forward on the Academy farm lands on a scientific basis. For example, fourteen varieties—nine IRRI selections, one Malaysia, two Thai, and two agricultural department varieties—were tested for the 1967 amon season. Consideration of factors such as land preparation, use of pesticides, agronomic characteristics, incidence of disease, and other factors were put under observation.[18] Similar tests were made for the boro season. A special study was also made of insecticides for rice.[19]

A number of crop-cutting surveys have been made. For example, a systematic survey of yields obtained from eleven varieties under variable sowing processes, use of insecticides, and soil types were made of scientifically selected plots in 67 villages for the 1964, 1965, and 1966 aus crops. This survey showed that cooperative villages produced an average of 21.84 maunds per acre in contrast to 14.16 maunds produced from noncooperative villages.[20]

Overall yield studies on the Abhoy Ashram farm for 1966–1967 contrasted with 1961–1962 show the following average yield of rice in maunds and *seers:*

Crop	1961–1962	1966–1967
Aus	28.34.0	34.1.0
Amon	34.20.0	38.20.0
Boro	25.35.0	47.15.0[21]

Other studies have been made of crops under mechanized irrigation (tube wells and pumps) and acreage under traditional irrigation (manual and natural). The study of 8,628 acres shows a clear trend of planting new rice vari-

[18] A. M. Akhanda, "Tests of IRRI Selections" (Amon, 1967), Comilla, PARD, May 1968. Also by the same author, for Boro, PARD, Sept. 1968. Mimeographed.

[19] A. M. Akhanda, "Study of Insecticides for Rice," Comilla, PARD, May 1968. Mimeographed.

[20] M. Safiullah, "Aus Crop Survey in Comilla Kotwali Thana, 1967," Comilla, PARD, May 1968. Mimeographed.

[21] *A New Rural Cooperative System for Comilla Thana* (Eighth Annual Report, 1968), Comilla, PARD, April 1969.

A New Village-based Cooperative System 95

eties under mechanized irrigation, while local varieties of rice and vegetables are still irrigated under traditional arrangements.[22]

Efforts to arrive at more definitive answers to questions of costs and returns of irrigated crops have been systematically undertaken in two studies. Information was recorded for several rice crops and potatoes on purchased inputs (hired labor, seeds, fertilizers, insecticides, tractor hire, tube well, and loan costs) and on family inputs and on production results.[23]

The findings of these studies were, as in the case of all other studies, made a part of the weekly training sessions. A special three-day training session for model farmers, managers, and union agricultural assistants on the cultivation of IR-8 seed and irrigation was held for different groups. The training sessions were conducted by the Department of Basic Democracies and Local Government, the Department of Agriculture, and the Academy to focus on experiences with these new resources. Lectures, film showings, field trips, and open discussions on the questions raised by the participants made up the program.[24]

Some Overall Views

Much has been done by the Academy's cooperative program; there is much more to do. In June 1965 at the

[22] M. Safiullah, "Winter Crop Survey in Comilla Kotwali Thana, 1968," Comilla, PARD, Sept. 1968. Mimeographed.

[23] Mahmoodur Rahman, *Cost and Return: A Study of Irrigated Crops in Comilla Villages*, Comilla, PARD, Oct. 1965; and *Costs and Returns: Economics of Winter-irrigated Crops in Comilla, 1965–1966*, Comilla, PARD, March 1967.

[24] "Cultivation of IR-8 and Irrigation Prospects and Problems: A Report on the Farmers' Seminar," Comilla, PARD, August 1968. Mimeographed.

inauguration of the Comilla district program, Director Khan estimated that about 30 per cent of the farmers of the thana were members of the local societies. He thought that in time the proportion would likely increase to around 60 per cent, and that then the "annual rate of savings and deposits will exceed Rs. 800,000." This projection had not quite been reached by 1967–1968, the percentage membership then being 50 per cent, and annual rate of savings close to Rs. 640,000.

Director Khan went on to say that in 1964–1965 "our transactions in [Comilla] Kotwali thana alone exceeded Rs. 9,100,000 by the end of May. Thus you can understand that rural development is not a small affair. If it is properly planned, and if the resources are there, it is a big affair and sound business."[25] By 1967–1968 transactions were three times the 1964–1965 figure—somewhat over Rs. 27 million ($5,670,000). The assets of the KTCCA at this time were slightly over Rs. 23 million.

A second speaker at this same inaugural occasion, the additional chief secretary of the government of East Pakistan, said:

Dr. Akhter Hameed Khan started the Kotwali Project, I think, in 1959. In 1958, our neighbours across the borders, China, started a new system of agricultural development and development of the rural communities. It is called the Commune System. I have had the privilege of visiting this great country for a few days and studying the tremendous experiment in human mobilisation which is taking place there. The experiment is a great success. A commune consists of an area which may be equal to a union council and has a membership of up to 22,000 people. The members have built irrigation ditches,

---

[25] *Inauguration of the Comilla District Integrated Rural Development Program, June 27, 1965*, Comilla, PARD, pp. 6–7.

A New Village-based Cooperative System

[installed] diesel pumps and can produce 3 to 4 vegetable crops a year. It is a great and sensational experiment but with one difference. We are organised in a different way. What we are doing is a voluntary effort on the part of the people. We are not forcing anyone to participate in our project. As you may know . . . we expect that not more than 60% will come into the cooperatives in the next 5 years or so. So these two experiments—the one in China and the one in East Pakistan, will have to be compared both by their results and by the human freedom that people are allowed to enjoy."[26]

The relatively few years of intensive work with the new cooperatives at Comilla have demonstrated a number of important early generalizations: villagers can cooperate, learn, create capital, adopt more progressive practices and have the will to do so; latent leadership can be discovered and put to work; and the modernization process can create confidence in moving in new directions. The next chapter sets forth the second major dimension of the Academy's work, namely to make governmental resources more readily available to the villagers.

[26] *Ibid.*, pp. 18–19.

4. Changing Concepts of Local Government

At the time when the Comilla program was getting underway, Pakistan was still struggling to find ways of creating a viable nation. The early years of this struggle had often been chaotic, plagued by the untimely death of the founder of Pakistan, Mohammad Ali Jinnah, and by political splintering and other divisive forces. Out of this background of instability, General (later Field Marshal) Mohammad Ayub Khan emerged in October 1958 as the strong man of the government of Pakistan. As president of the republic, he began a series of administrative, economic, and social reforms. Ayub and his advisors judged that the political element of the system of government inherited from the British was inappropriate; but they did not feel this way generally about the civil service system. In fact, they decided to keep it pretty much the way it was, that is, a public service led and dominated by an elite organization of men selected through comprehensive examinations of the British type and carefully trained for their future responsibilities as leaders. This leadership had proved to be generally competent and honest. But Ayub also recognized the necessity of strengthening local government, and an important feature of the reforms which he introduced was to be the rebuilding of local government through a system of "Basic Democracies" which would bring an admixture of local political leadership and higher-level technical expertise and administrative personnel, with representation from both the central and provincial governments.[1]

It was a fortunate circumstance that this arrival on the scene of strong central leadership with a plan, however imperfectly defined at first, to strengthen local government coincided with the beginnings of the Comilla Academy for Rural Development. The Academy provided an exceptional resource for trying out and developing plans for effective grass-roots democracy, and the ideas which were germinating at the Academy could never have prospered without the strong and sympathetic support of the government. In May 1959 when the Basic Democracies proposal was being developed, the chief secretary of East Pakistan had secured from the director of the Academy, Akhter Hameed Khan, statements on how the reorganized bodies might be constituted and how they might function. The V-AID program was administered along with the new Basic Democracies program under the National Development Organization until 1961, when the V-AID and the National Development Organization were abolished. From then on the Department of Basic Democracies and Local

[1] Back of "Basic Democracies" is a long history of efforts in the subcontinent concerned with the government and the people, more than 80 per cent of whom are villagers. Landmark statutes include: Permanent Land Settlement Act of the late 1700's; Village Chaukidari Act of 1870; Local Self-Government Act of 1885, and several others, up to the act establishing the Village Agricultural and Industrial Development program launched in 1953 (V-AID). For a systematic study of the antecedent effort to establish effective local government, see Elliott Tepper, *Changing Patterns of Administration in Rural East Pakistan*, East Lansing, Michigan State University, Asian Studies Center, Occasional Paper No. 5, August 1966.

Government was given responsibility for the Basic Democracies program and for collaboration with the Academy in experimental work in the thana council.[2]

It will be seen in this chapter how the Comilla laboratory area came to be extremely important in the evolution of the government's development programs, most strikingly in connection with the public works program, for in the Comilla thana the idea of vitalization of local government was early put to the test of application. Here it was shown that local political leaders and government administrators could work together if the conditions were right. Under the old system a villager had to come to the government offices in the city and sit in the outer office and wait. Officials, always disinclined to go to the villages, found it convenient to stay in their offices complaining that there were too many villages, none of them was convenient, and there was no place to meet. So the Academy at Abhoy Ashram became the headquarters of the government body, the thana council. It was rural enough, just a few simple buildings around a large rectangular tank (pond), and it was convenient enough for the village people and the government people. Also, it had some technical and informational resources to add to those that the government men brought with them. This thana council, later functioning within the Thana Training and Development Center

[2] See A. K. M. Mohsen, *The Comilla Rural Administration Experiment: History and Annual Report 1962–1963*, Comilla, PARD, Oct. 1963, for a systematic account of the efforts by the Academy, and others, previously, to develop effective rural government. See Appendices C1 and C2 of Mohsen's report for the text of Director Khan's recommendations to the chief secretary; a major effect of these recommendations was to forge closer linkage between developmental programs and civil administration. Mohsen's materials are relied upon heavily in the early part of this chapter.

Changing Concepts of Local Government 101

(TTDC), went to work and became the pattern for organizing rural development work for the province as a whole. When the government men did finally leave their city offices and move to the Academy's campus, they left some of their deeply rooted traditions also. In the experimental and educational atmosphere of the Academy, with small farmers coming and going freely as equals, they discovered two-way communication for the first time, and soon found themselves, like their academic associates, educators instead of merely judges of issues and issuers of directives.

Basic Democracies: Comilla Thana Council

The Basic Democracies order of October 1959 established a five-tiered system of councils,[3] at the union, thana, district, division, and provincial levels (later changed to four when the provincial council was supplanted by the provincial legislature). Operational integration is partially

[3] The councils are made up of elected, appointed, and ex-officio members. The lowest unit is the union council, representing several villages, with all of its members elected. The next unit is the thana council, made up of the chairmen of the union councils plus an equal number of government officials and appointed citizens. The higher tiers are at the district, division, and provincial levels. The number of councils for each tier in East Pakistan, with chief officer:

Province (The provincial council was superceded by the East Pakistan Assembly in 1962.)	1	Governor
Division	4	Commissioner
District	17	Deputy commissioner
Thana council	411	Circle officer
Union council	4,053	Chairman

There are also these units in East Pakistan, which are not included in the five-tier Basic Democracies system:

Subdivisions	54	Subdivisional officer
Villages	64,000	(no legal head)

achieved by having the chairman of each union council serve as a member of the thana council next above it. Union council chairmen are also represented on higher tiers of the system. Thus the village is represented, though in diminishing proportions, in each of the higher tiers of councils. The union councilors are elected, one from each ward with a population of around 1,250. Each union councilor is an elector in the general elections. The councilors of a union select one of their number to be chairman of that union council. The union councils were assigned certain specified taxing and other powers and development responsibilities, and the thana council had major responsibility for coordinating development programs.

The thana council is the lowest level of local government which has trained civil service officials in agriculture and other fields to carry out governmental efforts in rural development programs.[4]

The Comilla thana council in mid-1961 had 24 members of whom 12 were chairmen of the union councils, seven were government officials, and five were appointed nonofficials. The seven official members were the subdivisional officer, the executive officer of the thana called the circle officer, the V-AID development officer, and four of the departmental representatives posted in the thana. The thana council met monthly at Abhoy Ashram primarily because the Academy had already begun intensive pilot rural development projects in the thana. The subdivisional officer was chairman, and the circle officer was vice-chairman.

[4] See Richard O. Niehoff, *Basic Democracies and Rural Development*, Michigan State University, Asian Studies Center, Reprint Series No. 1, Fall 1966. See also Niehoff and George M. Platt, *Local Government in East Pakistan*, Dacca, Government of East Pakistan, January 1964.

Changing Concepts of Local Government 103

Even though the Basic Democracies order required thana officials to report on departmental programs to the thana council and to develop activities with union councils, this kind of relationship was alien to official habits, and attendance at thana council meetings was irregular. Accordingly, it is not surprising that at the council meetings those official members present had done most of the talking. This was in accordance with customary behavior between officials and villagers. But gradually specific needs in the villages were beginning to be discussed by the union council representatives.

The new working relationships prescribed in the Basic Democracies order between elected members of the council and the public servants related to the council emerged slowly and carefully. An early step (December 1960) was an exploratory visit to three union councils in Comilla thana by the additional subdivisional officer who was posted at the Academy and given overall charge of the development area, to discuss developmental needs and possibilities of the unions. He later met with all of the thana departmental officials to tell them what he had learned. He reminded the departmental officials that the Basic Democracies system required that each of them make a report to the monthly meeting of the thana council. He knew the union council chairmen wanted many things done, and he knew the officials were not accustomed to being confronted by ideas from village leaders. But how was the new Comilla thana council to function unless the union council chairmen brought their problems and development plans to it? And how were the thana departmental officials to be effective unless they addressed themselves to these problems and plans?

The first confrontation was a lively one. The village

leaders said the farmers could not get the short-term loans they needed, that their growing crops were not being sprayed, that their cattle should be inoculated, that more efforts should be made to control cholera and smallpox, and that many of the tube wells for drinking water were inoperative.

The thana departmental officials answered that their main trouble in getting things done in the village was the lack of local cooperation. They made special reference to the union councilors, some of whom to be popular would lay unfounded blame on the officials for lack of action. They pointed out that no more loans could be made until those already made had been repaid. The people and cattle, they said, could be inoculated only if they were assembled at agreed-upon central points.

Times without number the village leaders had sent reports of their problems to one official or another, and had stated what they needed done. But never before had they as a group representing all the unions met with the thana departmental officials as a group. Here was an action-oriented forum in which the village leader could say what he wanted to say, and in turn hear what he himself as a leader would need to do before his requests could be effectively met. The official, accustomed to reporting only to superiors in his department, would in the presence of his fellow officials and the village leaders report on what his office had done in the past month and what it expected to do in the next, and a record of the proceedings would be distributed to each member as a monthly reminder of the extent to which performances were up to expectations. Thus were roughed out the basic elements of a vitalized thana council at Comilla.

These beginnings were built upon through trial and error

over the months that followed. The departmental officials, each housed in a separate office in the town, tended to keep aloof from one another and from the people. There was more that needed to be done than they could possibly do, especially since much of their time was spent in preparing reports to their departments.

From January 1961 the thana council began meeting on a fixed date. Copies of the agenda were sent to each council member well ahead of the meeting. The officials came with prepared reports, decisions were made, and the full proceedings of the meeting were distributed. At this first regularly scheduled meeting, reports of cholera and smallpox cases resulted in 12 inoculators being sent out the next day, one to each union. They were to stay until all the villagers had been served. When it appeared that further inoculation of cattle was necessary the union council chairmen agreed to assemble the cattle as needed for the district animal husbandry officer. Upon request, the agricultural officer agreed to put on cow-dung-pit demonstrations in each union, arrange for loans, supply fertilizer, and make sure the union agricultural assistants (the local employees of the Department of Agriculture) worked closely with the union councils.

To get better acquainted with local conditions, the additional subdivisional officer, circle officer, and development officer accepted invitations to visit each of the union councils during the next two months, and the additional subdivisional officer began to spend several hours each week with the departmental officials, often in company with their field staffs or the union councilors.

The union council members began to assume their new roles as communicators, organizers, and planners for their unions instead of the old roles of advocates and petitioners;

a good working model of the thana council as a development forum and action body began to develop.

Significant steps were taken when the circle officer moved his office to the Abhoy Ashram campus to be closer to the staff of the Academy and its training and planning activities, and when an orientation course was given to all of the union councilors, in successive groups. These short courses covered variously the functions of the union councils and the duties of members; planning for development, with steps and contents of the plan; improved methods—including the kinds of departmental help, supplies, and services available and suggestions for seasonal preventive work, such as pest control, vaccination, inoculation, and so on; and the organization of cooperatives. Shortly thereafter, training in these same subjects was given at the Academy for the union agricultural assistants.

The departmental officials, union chairmen, and agricultural assistants were beginning to work together as a team. It became clear, for example, that when village leaders mobilized the people to assist in giving inoculations to cattle, the departmental officials could get vast amounts of work done in short periods of time. These and other accomplishments growing out of the coordinated approach were duly included in the reports of the officials to their departmental superiors.

When the V-AID program was terminated in June 1961, Director Khan arranged with the chief secretary of East Pakistan for the continuation of the work of the Comilla thana council as a special training model to be financed by the provincial government. This plan, it was intended, would provide a working model for the training of officials and would serve as a basis for research on possible further improvement of rural administration. Academy faculty members served in advisory capacities to the development efforts, attended meetings of the council, and began to document the proceedings and methods for later use in instructional programs, the principal one of which was a province-wide training program for officials and others involved in the public works program described below.[5]

The Comilla Thana Pilot Public Works Program

As the thana council became more effective, the villagers felt freer to bring their needs to its attention. How could production be increased except through the use of credit? But how could new production loans plus the old crippling debts to the moneylenders, be repaid unless the damage from floods could be reduced? And what sense did it make to increase the inputs of labor, tractor hire, fertilizer, and insecticides if the crops were going to be drowned out? How could the villagers get a good price for the paddy and other farm produce unless a truck could get to the village to haul it away?

Such were the kinds of problems faced by the farmers, and especially those in the low-lying 25-square-mile Dakatia-Kodalia river area south of Comilla town. Here for five years in succession prior to 1961 the spring aus crop had been severely damaged, and the amon had often been transplanted two or three times before the seedlings could keep ahead of the rising flood water.

Attempts to solve the problems of this area illustrate the developing roles of the thana and union councils. In the

---

[5] While the public works program became the major concern of the union councils of Comilla thana and of the Comilla thana council itself, attention was concurrently given to taxation policies and collections, refugee problems, problems of dealing with border smuggling and other matters of considerable importance.

areas where the flood damage had been greatest, the union councils near the end of the rainy season built cross dams in the channels to impound irrigation water for some dry-season farming. This did not prove very satisfactory, for the water gave out toward the end of the dry season. But it did make it possible to produce some winter crops. Also, in the building of these cross dams, the union councils found that they were as competent in organizing earth-moving projects as they had earlier been in organizing the inoculation campaigns for the departmental officials.

With continued pressure from the unions most affected by flood damage, the thana council had little choice but to give added attention to it. Hardly any agenda item could be discussed without the matter coming up in one way or another. If it was made an agenda item, it consumed most of the time of the meeting. If it was not on the agenda, it would be discussed as an unscheduled item.

There were many causes for the flooding. Foremost of all, the area was flat and low-lying, and drainage channels in and around it were crooked and clogged. The clogging was from the increased siltation out of the Indian hills to the east as more land was being cleared for cultivation, from encroachment on the channel beds by land-grabbers, from uncleared bushes growing on the banks, from the profuse growth of water hyacinths, and from fish traps that had been strung across the channels by permission of the district board. Furthermore, the flooding in the area had recently been worsened by the efforts of the East Pakistan Water and Power Development Authority (EPWAPDA) to improve it. Some of the channels that had been opened up to drain the area brought in more water than they discharged.

This was the situation in early 1961 when the Comilla

thana council was becoming a functioning organization. The leaders of the affected unions were determined to do something to correct the problem before the coming of the summer rains. But to do anything that could make any real difference involved interthana cooperation in addition to interunion cooperation, for much of the water had come in from Chowddagram thana, to the south.

After much discussion among representatives of EP-WAPDA, the thana councils of Comilla, Chowddagram, and Laksam, the deputy commissioner of Comilla district, and Director Khan of the Academy, it was agreed that an embankment might be built on the Dakatia River near Hemjora village to keep the excess water out of the low area in Comilla thana. The representatives of Chowddagram thana objected, saying the construction would result in the flooding of their fields. At length it was decided, under a tripartite agreement between EPWAPDA and the Comilla and Chowddagram thana councils, that an embankment could be constructed, with the provision that the EPWAPDA would cut it if it flooded the Chowddagram areas heretofore unaffected.

The embankment was built in April and May, 1961, with nearly half of the funds coming from the Department of Agriculture's minor irrigation schemes. The remainder was from the union councils and local people. The execution of the plan was a joint venture of the local union councils under the guidance of the Comilla thana council.

A few weeks later heavy rains came, and the Chowddagram area flooded. The people there gathered and tried to cut the embankment, but they were prevented from doing so by the builders who had built it, who gathered en masse to strengthen it further as the waters rose.

For a week the opposing groups faced one another.

Officers patrolled the site to maintain the peace while the authorities tried to decide what to do. A proposal that a diversion canal be cut to drain off the flood waters was verbally agreed to, and work was begun on it. But before it was completed a flash flood one night breached the levee of the Gumti River near Comilla town several miles to the north, and all officers were called there. The Chowddagram people then quit work on the diversion canal and cut the embankment. The low-lying area in Comilla thana was soon severely flooded, and more damage than usual was done in yet wider areas.

All knew that these efforts had not brought the desired relief, in fact had made bad matters worse. On the other hand, all had seen that the union councils could organize a massive earth-work project, could mobilize local labor, and could construct with dispatch, and at low cost, an embankment that could withstand some floods. So, despite the greater-than-usual damage, the people of the flooded areas had gained a new faith in their ability to contribute to the solution of their problem. But how were they to get the needed guidance for their efforts to be successful? Only an overall plan would suffice. Such a plan required more organization, more trained personnel, and more fiscal resources than were available.

EMERGENCE OF PUBLIC WORKS PROGRAM

In Comilla thana alone there were 110 miles of drainage channels that needed to be cleared, and additional ones needed to be dug. Only one per cent of the land was irrigated in the dry season. Improvement or construction of some 350 miles of village roads was necessary. Unemployment was chronic in the rural areas. These problems presented a challenge to the leadership of the Academy and the new Comilla thana council, a challenge to be met through a pilot public works program, which had the twofold purpose of creating an infrastructure of drainage, irrigation, and village roads, and providing needed employment during the slack-work season.

Creation of the public works program received a major assist from the head of the Harvard Advisory Group to the national Planning Commission, Richard V. Gilbert, who conceived the idea of using United States counterpart funds and surplus wheat to help finance such a program.

After considerable discussion with the director and faculty of the Academy, the thana council in October 1961 approved the proposal for a thana-wide pilot public works project. It was agreed that the next monthly meeting of the council would review projects sent in by the union councils. In the meantime, the following lists of questions and related assumptions were compiled by the Academy staff for guidance of the effort.[6]

Questions	*Related Assumptions*
What kinds of public works can be started easily in rural areas?	Public works to develop a comprehensive system of drainage, irrigation, and communications can usefully be carried on for several years in Kotwali thana. Such works can be started quickly and easily.
To best execute such rural public works, what should	The most effective and least expensive organiza-

[6] From *Report on A Rural Public Works Programme in Comilla Kotwali Thana*, Comilla, PARD, June 1962.

be the organizational and administrative agency?	tional-administrative agency would be the thana council and its constituent members, the union councils. The circle officer, as representative of the civil administration, and as the secretary of the thana council, should serve as the chief administrative officer of the program.
What should be the role of union councils?	The role of the union councils is central and vital. The councils should prepare the schemes in consultation with the villagers themselves; organize the work (employ labor, disburse wages, keep accounts, ensure correct specifications, etc.); and undertake subsequent maintenance.
Is the requisite technical competence available?	The union councils and village leaders can supervise earth-work competently. Farmers are very knowledgeable about local drainage. Small schemes prepared by them are generally sound. Engineering assistance, however, is needed in the case of large projects.

Changing Concepts of Local Government 113

Is it possible to mobilize village laborers extensively and sufficiently in large numbers to carry out such works?	Large numbers of laborers can be employed from approximately November to May under the supervision of union councils on extensively scattered projects.
Will they accept wheat or other food-stuff as wages?	The laborers will accept wheat in part payment of their wages.
How much will local farmers contribute voluntarily in labor, land, or money to the support of such works?	Local contributions in land, labor, and money would be forthcoming for projects designed and implemented by the local people for their own benefit.
What would be the economic benefits of such a works program and to whom?	Rural public works would relieve distress caused by unemployment; increase agricultural production; build the much-needed development infrastructures of drainage, irrigation, and communication; create managerial and technical skills; and strengthen local governmental bodies and enable them to raise more taxes.

In preparation for the anticipated launching of the rural works projects, the thana council enlarged its staff several weeks before the work was to begin. It trained the new members, and twice called the union councilors to the

Academy, in groups, for training. For the first course, 182 came; for the second, 132.

The November 1961 meeting of the thana council to consider programs submitted by the union councils approved 21 projects, estimated to cost a total of Rs. 322,000. Numerous projects, many of them ill defined, had been sketched out initially by the villagers in the local wards. These had been screened and consolidated by the union councils, and then drastically revised and integrated by the thana council, with the help of the Academy staff. This consolidated plan was then reviewed and accepted by the EPWAPDA engineers in Comilla with some modifications and approved by the deputy comissioner of Comilla district and the provincial government, which sanctioned it on December 24, 1961.

The sum of Rs. 260,000 was provided by the Department of Agriculture from its minor irrigation schemes appropriation. This amount, half of which was to be in rupees and half in wheat (provided under PL-480 program) plus the voluntary contributions expected from the union councils and the local people, would provide the necessary funds.

A substantial measure of local responsibility was achieved through the use of project committees whose members were trained in methods of measurement, preparation of "muster rolls" (employment lists), fiscal controls, and related procedures.

Each project was carried out and maintained by a local project committee, headed by the union council member resident in the area. This committee made a bond for the proper use of all funds. The thana-wide program was under the direction of a thana council committee made up of the Academy's chief training officer, the instructor of public administration, one Michigan State University advisor, a Peace Corps Volunteer engineer, the subdivisional officer, and the circle officer.

Funds were drawn from the government by the deputy commissioner, and from his office in turn by the circle officer, who advanced them on a weekly basis upon the joint signatures of the chairman of the union council and the union councilor who was chairman of the project committee. After the first advance, funds were replenishable weekly to these local project committees on the basis of the record of the daily wages paid to the laborers during the previous week.

The records of the local project committee's measurements of earth moved, wages paid to the laborers, and engineering matters were checked by representatives from the thana council. The circle officer certified the correctness of all records.

Any disputes that arose between the project committees and the laborers, or with landowners affected by the operations, were settled by the union councils. The union councils were especially enjoined to make certain a few dissident landowners should not be permitted to obstruct the progress of a project and thus deprive the majority of landowners of its benefits.

Since half of the wages of the laborers were paid in wheat, a mid-day meal of *khichuri* (a dish of whole wheat, rice, pulse, and spices) was served on the job at low cost.

IMPLEMENTATION OF PUBLIC WORKS PROGRAM

Work got underway with the establishment of 44 project committees. Several of the larger projects were divided into two or more smaller ones, each operating under a separate committee. The thana council arranged for the training at the Academy of the members of the project committees. The chairmen and secretaries were given special instructions to acquaint them with the major elements of their tasks: the measurement of earthwork, the keeping of muster rolls of workers, and the recording of wheat distribution. Weekly instructions were given to the chairmen and secretaries at the circle officer's office when they came to submit the records of work done the past week, and to receive the advances of cash and wheat for the next week. These project committees received no pay; rickshaw fares were paid from program funds.

Problems arose early in the program. Some project committee chairmen tried to get weekly advances without rendering full accounts. Such requests were refused. Though this slowed up the work some at first, it served a good purpose, causing the thana council to assign a person to each committee to make certain all accounts were reported correctly and promptly.

Clashes between individuals, between villages, and with the union councilors were usually resolved, but not always. One dispute, even after being taken to the subdivisional officer for resolution resulted in the project being abandoned. In another instance involving two union councils, their differences could not be resolved; the project was dropped. So, too, with an irrigation project involving Comilla thana and Burichang thana. The latter was not willing for water to pass through it to irrigate land in the other. An international dispute too arose. It occurred along Comilla thana's eastern boundary with India, where a watercourse ran over into India for a short distance. When the Indian police objected to the cleaning out of this section of the old channel, a new channel to complete the project was dug on the Pakistan side.

Then there were many instances where encroachments upon the channel beds had narrowed them, sometimes to one-third or one-fourth of their width. These had to be widened. The encroachers were usually the larger farmers, often union councilors, who over the years had become accustomed to having their way. However, once a project had been started, and the width to which the canal would be cleared had been agreed upon by the project committee, most landowners permitted the filled-in earth to be removed.

The wheat payment was far from popular at the outset. One reason was that the value assigned to wheat was higher than had been expected, but, most bothersome of all, the wives were unaccustomed to cooking it. Some workers preferred to work for a smaller cash wage, and some sold the wheat at reduced prices and bought rice. The mid-day meal of khichuri on the job was not popular, either, for most rural laborers were accustomed to eating with the family, and, moreover, since food was scarce, they wished to share what they had with their families. The children began to come to the work place for a mid-day meal, and the atmosphere became one of holiday and feasting, at some cost to project efficiency.

In subsequent years only cash was paid, it being assumed that wheat, which was then priced lower, would be bought if the laborers had money with which to buy it. The assumption proved correct, for the overall consumption of wheat was at about the same rate as if half wages had been paid in it. The difference, an important one, was that those who wanted to purchase the cheaper wheat could, and that those who did not, could buy rice—and at a cheaper rate than if their neighbors had not begun to eat substantial amounts of wheat.

The public contribution in cash was not forthcoming from the union councils, as had been hoped, and traditional ways of raising it were resorted to: higher wages were shown than were actually paid to the laborers and more earthwork was reported than was actually moved. Since the thana council workers assigned to the project committees refused to certify these deceptions, the work on almost all the projects came to a standstill. The director of the Academy at this point warned the project committee members that the situation would be reported to the government and that criminal cases would be instituted against each of them for corrupt practices. He also threatened to go to every village and tell the people about these malpractices of their so-called leaders. In the end the director declared that if the public contribution could be paid only at cost to the laborers or by other deception, it should be dispensed with entirely. Public contribution was discontinued, and the work was resumed.

ACCOMPLISHMENTS OF THE THANA PILOT PROGRAM

Of the original 21 projects for drainage and irrigation, six were abandoned, three new ones added, and near the end of the dry season eight sand dam projects were organized. Accomplishments included clearing of 34 miles of drainage canals, construction of 14 miles of embankments, half of which also served as roads, and building of 26 two-foot culverts-cum-floodgates and six sand-erosion control dams.

In all, 8,000,000 cubic feet of earth were moved, by 46,000 man-days of labor, at a cost of Rs. 202,000.

Shortly after the pilot thana works program was completed a full report was prepared.[7] Director Khan summa-

[7] A. K. M. Mohsen, *Report on a Rural Public Works Programme in Comilla Kotwali Thana*, Comilla, PARD, June 1962.

rized his views thus: "A comprehensive programme of public works was designed and carried out within the short period of six months; the thana council and the union councils proved themselves remarkably efficient in planning and executing this project; the union councils mobilized and supervised the labourers much better and more cheaply than private contractors would ordinarily do; the village leaders' own skills in earth work and their ability to follow the engineer's instructions were fully demonstrated; . . . foundations were beginning to be laid for a good drainage system. To a certain extent, flood risk in the area was reduced. Managerial skill was created and the position of the union councils was greatly strengthened."[8]

Two months later a manual was produced telling just how the program had been carried out in Comilla thana, and how a similar program could be launched in all other thanas in the province.[9] More specifically, the manual covered such important subjects as: need for public works planning, organization, training, finance and account keeping, engineering plans, supervision, and evaluation. This report and the manual were basic documents for the training of personnel in the expansion the next year of the works program.

LARGER THANA WORKS PROGRAMS FOR 1962–1963

The Comilla thana council planned for larger projects in 1962–1963, as the first part of a three-year plan. To prepare for this, the union chairmen were given additional training

---

[8] *Ibid.*, pp. 6–7; also quoted in *An Evaluation of the Rural Public Works Programme, East Pakistan, 1962–1963*, Comilla, PARD, October 1963, pp. 7–8.

[9] *A Manual for Rural Public Works*, Comilla, PARD, August 1962.

in May, and in June all twelve of them submitted projects totaling nearly Rs. 2,000,000 for the three-year period, subsequently scaled down to Rs. 335,000 for the year 1962–1963.

This program attempted to move rather quickly into masonry work on bridges, regulators, and culverts. There were many technical difficulties, for work could not begin until the designs had been drawn, and furthermore the procurement of cement and iron rods took time. And even after the designs had been finished and orders for needed materials given, there was often a shortage of cement. Masons worked more slowly when paid by the day instead of by the job. The project engineer, a Peace Corps Volunteer, became involved in the tube well program for irrigation and was unable to give as much supervision as was needed while masonry projects were underway. The result was that some of the construction work did not hold up.

There were some organizational difficulties, too, growing out of too little publicity about rates, and ineffective reporting by some project committees and union council chairmen. Field supervision was not always well scheduled, and not enough training was provided for the masons or for the project committee chairmen and secretaries. Several instances again arose of cheating and of disputes about the donation of land needed for roads or canals. As in the year before, cheating was dealt with firmly, and projects were closed down when needed land was not donated.

To correct some of these inadequacies, the thana council increased its supervisory staff from six to nine workers, and a list of "advisable precautions" pointing up the need for correct operating procedures and continuous checks against possible irregularities was worked out by the training officer of the Academy.

In an effort to take care of the shortage of bricks, especially in the areas of the thana remote from the main roads, and to reduce the price generally, the union councils launched a brick-burning project early in 1963. The project was financed by a loan from the United Bank, Ltd., upon the security of the KTCCA, which also procured the coal. Some 3,200,000 bricks were burned, of which about 1,000,000 were used in the public works projects. Many of the remaining bricks were of an inferior quality, sales were slow, and repayment of the loans was poor. In overall, this brick-burning program of the union councils was not a success in itself. But it did make brick available on time that year in remote places at reasonable prices.

Though there were technical and organizational difficulties, the 1962–1963 thana rural works program, like the one the year before, was highly productive: 42 miles of village roads built to specifications, 12 bridges, 55 culverts, 11 drainage canals, and three regulators. The lessons learned were put to good use by the Academy in its training of officials for the expanded province-wide works program for the following year, and in the later intensified works efforts in the thana.

At the end of each year, the situation in Comilla thana was reviewed, and another year's plan was worked out, again as the first unit of a new three-year plan. This kept in focus what had been done, what was being done, and what still needed to be done.

In 1963–1964, Rs. 800,000 were used for the regular works program in Comilla thana. The thana council allocated less than half of it for earth work, and the remainder for bridges, culverts, flapgates, regulators, brick surfacing of roads, and the maintenance of previous works.[10] In all,

[10] In addition, as set forth in Chapter 5, Rs. 600,000 was spent on irrigation and another Rs. 600,000 on rural electrification that year. See Appendix VI, Table E.

116 project committees were formed, and training began for them in November and December. The training program took account of the experience gained in the two previous years.

The result of these successive works programs was that by mid-1964, all of the 31 local markets in the thana had been connected with a road. Most of the villages could be reached by some sort of vehicle. This is no mean achievement in a flood plain where every road must be elevated from five to ten feet to avoid flooding. The village roads and the drainage system had been made possible by the movement of more than 40 million cubic feet of earth, the construction of scores of bridges and regulators, and the installation of hundreds of culverts, many of them with flap gates.

It is the oxcart and the bicycle that can get to the village first, and then the pedal rickshaw. At the end of the third year of the thana's works program, many villages had reached only the pedal rickshaw stage. But having reached it, most were looking forward to roads that would accommodate a jeep, and then a truck. Many of the new roads zigzag around the fields. This fact, of itself, is an evidence of local planning.

The thana works program for 1964–1965 was smaller than the year before and less effectively carried out. The reason, apparently, was that this was the presidential election year. The election came on January 2, early in the dry season just when the public works projects would normally be started. Some work was begun in February, but soon closed down, for no program funds were released by the government until a month later. Despite an expected allocation of Rs. 400,000, only half that amount was made available, and not all of this could be used before work had to be stopped because of the arrival of the monsoon. A total of Rs. 178,662 was used in the regular works program. The largest single item was for the construction of village roads, followed by construction of bridges, excavation of canals, and so on.

The funds for 1965–1966 were a little more than Rs. 316,000. The largest expenditure, nearly a third of the total, was for grants to the union councils. The second largest was for road maintenance, followed by expenditures on canals and on culverts.

Taking the period of 1961–1966 as a whole, the total expenditure for regular rural public works was Rs. 1,830,490. The seven largest expenditures (each more than Rs. 100,000) in rank order were: road construction, bridges, culverts, canals, grants to union councils, embankments, and road maintenance. The high priority on roads is clear, with the control of water next most important. Union council allocations were usually spent for a school building, a community hall, or a small office building for the council's use.

Subsequent allocations for public works for Comilla thana (Rs. 198,000 in 1966–1967 and 328,000 in 1967–1968) were focused on irrigation projects and maintenance of channels and roads. The developments in irrigation are discussed in the next chapter.

TRAINING FOR THE PROVINCE-WIDE
PUBLIC WORKS PROGRAM

The Comilla model for the public works program was found most useful for a province-wide program administered by the Department of Basic Democracies and Local Government. Rupees ten *crore* (approximately $20 million) were authorized for the 1962–1963 program and twenty crore for the year following. The Academy, working very closely with the secretary of the department, carried on a massive training program each year for circle officers and other officials. The training materials included the report and manual for public works mentioned earlier. Villagers who had worked on local project committees participated in the training as resource persons. For the 1963–1964 program, for example, 343 circle officers were trained at the Academy for seven days in eight groups, plus assistant directors, directors, divisional commissioners, and other officials of the Department of Basic Democracies and Local Government for shorter periods. The secretary participated in these training sessions.

A small part of the allocated funds was used for two comprehensive evaluation reports, for the 1962–1963 and the 1963–1964 province-wide programs. The evaluation reports were authorized by the secretary and conducted by faculty members of the Academy.[11] Based on a representative sample of the total program, the studies examined the objectives and assumptions, planning and training phases of the effort, and actual execution of the program. The reports dealt candidly with any deficiencies in the administration of the program and illustrated successes and failures in case studies of well-administered and poorly administered projects. The effect of the program, on balance, was clearly on the positive side. One of the appendices presented in the first evaluation report was a paper prepared by Akhter Hameed Khan for governmental policy makers (members of the Economic Council and the Planning Commission)

[11] A. T. R. Rahman, et al. *An Evaluation of the Rural Public Works Programme, East Pakistan,* 1962–1963, and *ibid.,* 1963–1964, Comilla, PARD, 1963 and 1965, respectively.

on "The Public Works Program and a Development Proposal for East Pakistan, April 1963." Accomplishments to date were summarized, and projections for the necessary funding of rural public works were set forth. The evaluation reports and the discussions and reflections which they precipitated provided guidance for later programs in East Pakistan, and for the launching of the program in West Pakistan.[12]

Further Development of the Thana Council

The above account of the development of rural public works has momentarily obscured our mentioning the other functions of the thana council. The regular work of the council has included monthly meetings, in which a wide range of subjects has been discussed and numerous actions taken. The representatives of the nation-building departments posted in the thana have carried on their services: Agriculture has sold fertilizers and improved seed, and promoted the spraying of crops; Animal Husbandry has vaccinated and treated cattle and poultry; Fisheries has distributed fingerlings and encouraged tank fish production; Supply has brought in coal, cement, and wheat; and the union multipurpose cooperatives have made loans and sold farm supplies. Outbreaks of smallpox, cholera, and other endemic diseases have been kept in check by the health officer in collaboration with the union councilors and other village leaders. These service activities have been improving

---

[12] Richard V. Gilbert, "The Works Program in East Pakistan," *International Labor Review*, Vol. LXXXIX, No. 3, March 1964. Gilbert as head of the Harvard Advisory Group to the Planning Commission, was a chief author and advocate of the public works program.

gradually as the Academy's programs have expanded and as the thana council has become a more effective channel of communication between the officials and the villagers.

The attendance of the thana agriculture and other officers at these meetings was appreciably improved by a reminder from the district office that attendance and reporting were parts of their official duty. Other officers who were not obligated to attend found the thana council an effective body and also came. Included in this category were representatives of the Agriculture Development Bank and others. The interest of the union council chairmen remained high, and the length of the meetings was extended to afford them more time for participation.

A total of 742 man-days of training was given in 1962–1963 to union councilors and secretaries of local project committees. The council's training dealt with the functioning of the Basic Democracies system, and with the implementation of the rural public works program. Bengali leaflets and pamphlets on these and other subjects were prepared and used effectively.

For the year ending in mid-1964 the regular work of the council continued to center on the reports of the departmental representatives and actions thereon.

The pilot work of the thana council was continued in 1964–1965, although special grants from the Department of Basic Democracies and Local Government were terminated the year before. This was done to demonstrate that councils in other thanas, too, could with their resources carry on training programs for union councilors, coordinate departmental activities, and plan and execute special works programs.

The thana council's work for 1966 centered around planning for the thana public works program and training

128 newly elected union councilors. The council also assisted in the training of the thana fisheries officers from throughout the province. A manual for this purpose was developed cooperatively by the Academy and the Departments of Fisheries and of Basic Democracies and Local Government.

SHIFT OF DEPARTMENTAL REPRESENTATIVES
TO THE THANA HEADQUARTERS

In January 1963 the headquarters for five department officials, previously located at different places in Comilla town, had moved to the council's headquarters on the Abhoy Ashram campus. They were the officials for agriculture, animal husbandry, fisheries, education, and plant protection. The move was made so they could work together more effectively as a thana team, and be more available to the farmers. The circle officer, as already mentioned, had moved his office there nearly two years earlier. Two other officials, the sanitary inspector and the supervisor of the union-wide multipurpose cooperatives, while still officed in town, came to the council headquarters for the monthly meetings and to take part in interim conferences as relevant. The 24 union agricultural assistants were brought to the Abhoy Ashram campus and trained for work with the departmental representatives, or otherwise as determined.

The shifting of the departmental officials to the thana headquarters and the reassignment of the agricultural assistants were in response to the administrative reorganization in the thana as the Academy's experimental programs continued to expand. To provide training for the increasing number of villagers who were coming each week to the Academy, the thana departmental representatives took on the added function of teaching. Making the departmental representatives into "teachers" proved somewhat difficult, since this was an entirely new role. Although the departmental representatives were at first skeptical, they soon found that as teachers they were able to increase their influence, working on a sustained basis with hundreds of villagers chosen by the local cooperatives or union councils. When they went to the villages, they began to be received as teachers and friends. Being in touch with the people, they were often called to the villages to advise on some specific need that had arisen, whereas before that they had spent most of their time talking with people who dropped into their offices in the town, and in preparing reports. In connection with adding the role of teacher to the duties of the thana officials, the Academy staff made a study of the number and nature of the various monthly reports required by the Department of Agriculture. The number was then reduced from more than a score to less than a half dozen, thus affording the thana official much more time to carry on activities that were worth reporting.

In overall, conviction was growing among officials and local leaders that effective training procedures were being worked out, that development work could be achieved, and that a system of collaborative decision making was maturing. Together these efforts were creating an administrative infrastructure that would support the Academy's modernization programs.

Thana Training and Development Center

Through deliberate experimentation the Comilla program had produced a working model for rural development, the Thana Training and Development Center (TTDC), established in February 1963. A main function

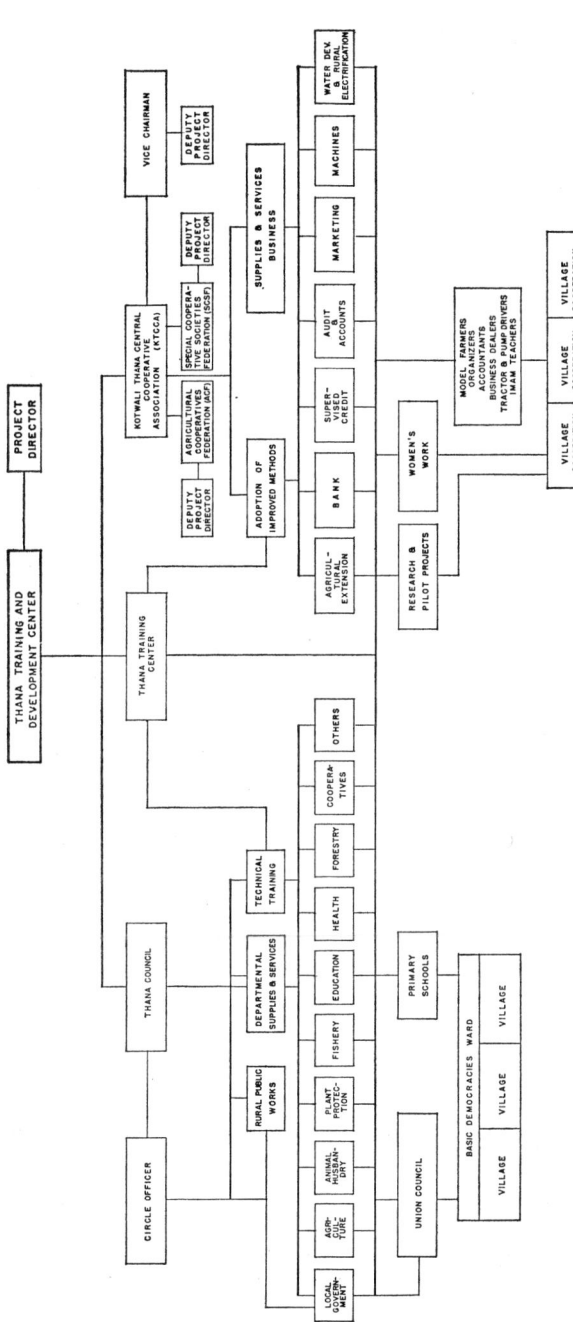

Chart 2. An organizational chart for a thana training and development center. Adopted from A. K. M. Mohsen, "The Comilla Rural Administration Experiment, History and Annual Report, 1962–1963," Comilla, PARD, October 1963, Appendix A, p. 82. This chart represents relationships as they were in mid-1966.

of the center was to coordinate the various public and private development activities in the thana, and especially the work of the thana council and the central cooperative association. The center became a prototype for organizing and administering governmental and private rural development programs in the thanas throughout the province. These principal ingredients came to focus in the TTDC, in addition to the central cooperative association:

1. *The union councils* and wards are the statutory bodies which represent all the people. They provide the grassroots base for identifying basic problems and for elementary planning, and administering the mass efforts of villagers who participate in the development process. In addition, union councils collect taxes, adjudicate local disputes, and perform other functions. The participation of the chairmen of union councils in the work of the thana council provides linkage for broader policy planning and administration.

2. *The thana council* furnishes leadership for coordinating development efforts at the thana level. Thana departmental officers provide trained personnel (in agriculture, animal husbandry, fisheries, and other fields) and government resources such as allocations of funds for public works and supplies and supervision for the governmental inputs. The TTDC is a convenient organization through which other officials of government not normally located at the thana level, such as engineers from EPWAPDA, can make contact.

3. *Village representatives* and leaders—union council members, committeemen for public works projects, cooperative organizers, model farmers, accountants, supervisors, plus *Imams* (prayer leaders at local mosques), women leaders, teachers, and other participants in the rural develop-

ment programs—become the clientele for the instruction programs, often on a once-a-week basis.

4. *The educational processes* are facilitated by the physical location of government offices, with Academy personnel and advisors at one place, plus the gradual acceptance by the officials of a redefined role as teachers instead of desk-sitting issuers of directives and reports. Committees for training, extension, and other functions, made up of civil officials, Academy instructors, KTCCA supervisors and advisors, establish procedures and assignments of responsibility that make possible a reasonably high degree of order out of what might otherwise be a chaotic mass of well-meaning but undirected effort. As time passed, the educational materials supporting the process were refined to include simple extension lesson plans, graphic material, booklets in English and Bengali, field observations, manuals, and other devices. Periodic rallies and annual meetings have been highly useful in dramatizing achievement and increasing morale.

An important distillate of these educational processes has been the creation of new approaches to "extension" which deviate from conventional approaches. The emergence of village leaders in the process is a key finding which influences planning of all development programs fostered by the Academy.

5. *The physical facilities* of the Academy (including the KTCCA) have contributed significantly to the organization and program resources of the TTDC. These facilities include classrooms, the offices for the thana officials, demonstration farm, tank (for fisheries work), soil-testing laboratory, dairy, cold-storage plants, dairy-processing plant, rice mill, a health and family-planning clinic, and others.

6. *The built-in research component*, staffed with Acad-

emy instructors and researchers, provides a documentation and analytical service which contributes guidance for the TTDC and for formulation of province-wide policy by the Academy's board of governors made up of provincial officials responsible for rural development. The numerous reports (monthly, annual, and special) and the research studies, in turn, provide instructional material for officials who come to the Academy for brief orientation or longer periods and to numerous officials (including the president of Pakistan) and foreign visitors who are interested in finding out how the Comilla experiment works.

The basic evolving model described above was essentially accepted by the government of East Pakistan in mid-1962. A young civil service officer was assigned on special duty to examine the organization and methods for the purpose of replicating the model set up in one thana in each of the other three divisions of East Pakistan. After six months of study, he spent an additional six months training key personnel for the selected thanas. Comilla-type centers were established in Natore, Gaibandha, and Gouripur thanas. Physical facilities (old V-AID training centers), were available comparable to the Abhoy Ashram campus and the normal complement of officers were on duty in the thanas. Later the Comilla model was established in seven other thanas of Comilla district and still later less elaborate TTDC's were provided for in four-fifths of the other thanas of the province. These and other expansions are described in Chapter 9.

In summary, Director Khan, in commenting on the nature and purpose of the TTDC, explained that its

... composition varies from Imams with flowering beards, champions of orthodoxy, to diffident village women coming out into a strange world. It includes union council members (the most influential segment of village society), organizers of village cooperatives (the emerging leaders of small farmers), model farmers (innovators and adopters of new methods), accountants (educated persons marooned in the village), teachers, enumerators, doctors, midwives, drivers, bricklayers, and the youth.

When we designed this educational center as a forum for village leaders, we were aiming to reproduce in our area the beneficial influence of the early Danish folk-school movements. We hoped to overcome despair and defeatism by bringing together the active, the energetic and the purposeful, taking them out of the stagnant village repeatedly and putting them in contact with each other and with experts, thus making them receptive to new ideas and aspirations.

From scattered and helpless individuals, these villagers coming weekly to the center were to be transformed into workers for uplifting their neighbours by exemplifying confident action in the midst of cynical despair. Perhaps in two years the borrowed branch has imperceptibly grafted itself on to more local roots, viz., the weekly congregation of Muslims. The training conference has become for organizers or model farmers, Imam teachers or women leaders, a way of life, a moral and intellectual necessity, a source of inner sustenance, like the Friday assembly. Only thus can be explained the unfailing attendance. When the appointed day comes, it seems, all work is abandoned; in heat or cold or rain, they wend their way to Abhoy Ashram, then go back satisfied and encouraged. The intermingling, the long discussions, the analysis of their problems, the demonstration of new methods followed by attempts to diffuse what they have learned, then they return to revise and learn more—this elaborate and unceasing education process re-shapes their habits of thought and action.

Undoubtedly the most wholesome influence is that of the new relationship between officers and villagers, a friendly partnership, like that of teacher and students. There is guidance and supervision without undue subordination. There is trust arising from mutual knowledge. Village leaders still retain their traditional politeness; but gone are the silent docility and the sycophantic respect, born out of false fear and false hope. They have now a realistic view of government and its agencies at the thana, not as mysterious and dreadful forces like Almighty God, who give or take as they please, but as human agencies with limited resources, established for their benefit, and solicitous of their loyalty. This small psychological shift produces big results—the seed is becoming a tree.[13]

To further institutionalize the TTDC at Comilla, the thana council in 1964 purchased a five-acre tract of land near the Abhoy Ashram campus upon which to construct a dozen dwellings for the staff. Dwellings were provided for the circle officer, eight departmental representatives, and three other officials. By early 1967 these staff quarters were occupied.

In broad outline, the experimental administrative adjustments made at Comilla have been useful to the government and to the villagers: the vitalization of the thana council by making it a planning body for development activities, the thana pilot public works program which tested the ability of the union and thana councils to carry out rural development work, and the emergence of the TTDC to coordinate public and private development efforts. These achievements were utilized in the further steps that were taken to launch a pilot program in irrigation, so essential to the modernization of agriculture in East Pakistan.

---

[13] Akhter Hameed Khan and M. Zakir Hussain, *A New Rural Cooperative System for Comilla Thana* (Third Annual Report), Comilla, PARD, July 1963, pp. 15–16.

5. Irrigation and Rural Electrification

Recognition that finding a solution to the problems of flood control and water for irrigation would require the combined efforts of villagers and various government units, together with the confidence acquired through its successful experience in managing the public works program, led the Academy to establish a thana-wide pilot program in irrigation and rural electrification. This program was developed in cooperation with the East Pakistan Water and Power Development Authority (EPWAPDA) and with other units of the East Pakistan government. In keeping with the Comilla philosophy, emphasis was placed on having the villagers themselves responsibly involved in all aspects of local planning. The need for an administrative system acceptable to the villagers to carry out the operations and collect the necessary charges for service was recognized; flexibility in planning was stressed to assure minimum disruption of crop production as a result of large-scale construction programs; in short it was considered reasonable to sacrifice some engineering efficiency in order to gain a greater measure of social efficiency.

"This pilot project in irrigation and rural electrification," said Director Khan, "grew out of the need for a practical demonstration of a comprehensive developmental plan for a single thana." He continued:

> Only when this has been done can a definitive report be written setting forth how such a project is being carried out, the problems encountered and how they were overcome, the costs involved, the expected benefits, the types and amounts of training required, and the organized efforts needed from administrators, technicians, and villagers to launch and operate such a project. Once enough experience is gained to write such a report, we expect to follow it with a manual setting forth in detail how, with adaptations needed for differing local conditions, a generally similar activity can be launched in other thanas. We know these are large goals. We dare undertake them only because of the crucial need for field information on them."[1]

Such information was needed in national and local planning. With information from a practical demonstration which was designed to determine the amount of capital that could be constructively used (or "absorbed") in the development programs in one thana, it was thought possible to plan development programs for the entire province on a much more realistic basis than had up to then been possible, taking into account the costs and the capacity of government and people to plan and to carry out projects.

The immediate background of the "absorption test" then was the effective use of Rs. 200,000 in the Comilla pilot works program of 1961–1962 and the expansion of this program to the other 410 thanas of the province in 1962–1963 through an expenditure of Rs. 100,000,000. Director Khan thought that this amount could profitably

---

[1] *The Comilla Pilot Project in Irrigation and Rural Electrification*, Comilla, PARD, November 1963, Preface, p. i.

Irrigation and Rural Electrification

be increased eight times, but many government leaders thought that neither the officials nor the local people could mount so large an undertaking.

The final outcome was that the sum of Rs. 200,000,000 was made available for the third year of the works program in East Pakistan (1963–1964), of which amount Rs. 2,000,000 was set aside for Comilla's absorption test. West Pakistan was allocated one-half the amount allotted to East Pakistan.

The sum allocated for the thana absorption test for roads, bridges, *khals*, and embankments was Rs. 800,000; for the Sonaichuri irrigation project, Rs. 600,000; and big tube wells and electrification, Rs. 600,000. The thana council would prepare the plans for the regular local works projects, in consultation with the union councils as in the two previous years. The other two project items would be drawn up jointly by EPWAPDA, the KTCCA, and the thana council.

In addition to the assistance from EPWAPDA and its consultants, the United States Agency for International Development (AID) officials, especially the agricultural advisors in Karachi and Dacca, took a keen interest in the project, gave counsel on it, and provided two technical experts who made quick on-the-ground estimates of the adequacy of the early planning.

Members of the Harvard Advisory Group to the Planning Commission studied the proposals as they related to overall planning needs, and assisted in the preparation of the detailed analysis as to costs and expected benefits.

Early Irrigation Projects

The Academy's experiences in its laboratory area had early focused on water problems—too much water in the monsoon months, and too little most of the remainder of the year. But not much was being done. The Department of Agriculture was operating a few small low-lift diesel irrigation pumps in the villages around Comilla. These pumps often proved disappointing, for the supply of water in the canals and tanks[2] would be exhausted before the end of the dry season, thus defeating the hopes for a winter rice crop. In June 1961 a flash flood had breached the Gumti levees, damaged the aus rice crop in extensive areas, and prevented the planting of the amon crop, making it urgent for those villagers whose crops were ruined to produce a rice crop the following winter. Thus they were willing to use pumps as suggested by the Academy. Maybe there would be more water in the canals and in the tanks than the year before, and maybe the premonsoon showers would come early. When certain hunger is the alternative, risks are more readily taken.

Thirteen village youths were selected by as many cooperative societies for training as pump operators at the Academy. Additional pumps were ordered. The EPWAPDA became interested the following year, 1962, and proposed that Comilla thana be made a pilot project area for their activities, especially irrigation. This meant that electrical power could be made available for experimentation with larger-scale pumping operations, and especially tube wells to tap the underground water. Such wells had already been tried out by EPWAPDA on a small scale in other areas.

---

[2] An excavation that serves as a reservoir during the dry season. The tank is usually rectangular in shape, from 10 to 20 feet deep, and may be of any size from less than a quarter of an acre up to more than 20 acres. The dirt piled up from the digging raises the land above the flood level, and so provides high ground for dwellings and other buildings, market places, etc.

A test boring of a four-inch well had been begun at the village of South Rampur, under the guidance of EP-WAPDA engineers, to be powered from the substation of the Karnafuly power line near Comilla town.

A Peace Corps Volunteer trained in engineering was put in charge of planning for the thana project. Assistance was sought from the government of West Pakistan, which agreed to sell a boring rig and casing pipe to the KTCCA, and to provide the services of a mechanic. Technical assistance was also provided by a superintending engineer from the government of West Pakistan. Agreement was reached that by using available village labor under the supervision of the mechanic a contractor's services would not be needed, and so the costs of sinking the well could be much reduced.

The first use of the six-inch boring rig from West Pakistan would be at the village of South Rampur, for it had been decided that the four-inch well already sunk there should be pulled and the larger one installed. The four-inch well, which had become operative during the monsoon, had shown there was subsoil water that could be pumped up for irrigation. Farmers from villages all around came to see it. There were many requests for well sites in other villages, usually adjacent to the largest tank. It was also thought that many or all of these proposed wells might later be powered by electric pumps.

The six-inch well at South Rampur[3] was finished in November 1962. When a diesel pump was temporarily installed, there was a steady full-pipe flow for all to see.

---

[3] See Mahmoodur Rahman, *Irrigation in Two Comilla Villages*, Comilla, PARD, June 1964, for a discussion of problems and the results of introducing tube well irrigation in the villages of South Rampur and South Kalikapur.

Water at this rate would irrigate scores of acres. But would it continue to flow throughout the dry season? There were those who doubted. Some said the water was coming from the tank beside which it was sunk. This idea faded out completely when in the next dry season the tank was pumped full, time and time again, to irrigate the fields by gravity flow.

The villagers had other doubts. Did the land need to lie fallow, to rest, a part of each year? Many farmers thought a third crop would "hurt" the land. But the Academy reported that three crops could be grown successfully on the same land. Had not just that been done for the past two years on the Academy's demonstration farm at Abhoy Ashram by the Japanese experts and the Pakistanis working with them? Yet, although it could clearly be done for a few years, there was as yet no certain proof that it could be done on a continuing basis. To the villagers a third crop was a new practice, except for the very small patches around their dwellings for winter vegetables. To cultivate whole fields in the dry season was looked upon by many as an unnatural thing to do. Quite aside from whether there is any scientific basis for the farmers' notion that the land needs to rest, how much of a handicap would this type of thinking be to the optimum use of irrigation by the villagers?

In January 1963 an electric pump was put on the well at South Rampur. Its confident hum was the herald of a new day, as some months before had been the chug-chug-chug of the diesel engine on the low-lift pump. Just push the switch and the electric motor goes to work, and it keeps on working until the switch is pulled.

By the end of February 1963 two more six-inch wells were in operation, one at the village of South Kalikapur and

Irrigation and Rural Electrification 141

the other at Monogram. On the Gumti River there were then five sets of pumps on rafts; electric pumps were used at three of these and diesels at the others. A total of more than 900 acres was being irrigated by tube wells and pumps on rafts.

A Thana-wide Irrigation Plan

In mid-1964 it was expected that within the next four years a total of some 18,960 acres would be irrigated by the three methods: 6,000 from the Sonaichuri gravity-flow project, being the farm lands within a mile of the main canal from the Gumti River and in the lower areas of the old river basin; 960 acres from the river-raft pumps; and 12,000 from 200 deep large-bore tube wells. These estimates, however, proved to be too optimistic, as a summary of the total acreage irrigated between 1962–1968 will later show.

The composite irrigation plan envisioned a continuous supply of water for every village in the thana. A ready supply of water would provide for highly dependable winter crops, whether boro rice, potatoes, or vegetables; it might also make poultry keeping, dairying, and other livestock operations more attractive, particularly since it is these winter crops and livestock products that are most readily amenable to agricultural processing, including storage for potatoes. Furthermore, since there are dry spells nearly every year during the monsoon, adequate irrigation then would increase the rice, jute, and sugarcane crops appreciably. Many years the aus or amon paddy yields have been lowered 20 per cent or more from dry spells during the monsoon.

The Sonaichuri project, according to the engineers, could eventually command a maximum of about 14,770 acres and the river rafts about 960 acres on a continuing basis. Since there is a total of about 38,000 acres of farm lands in the thana, the tube wells—the most expensive and as yet unproven source of water—would need eventually to provide for some 22,000 acres.

The installation and use of tube well irrigation is often a complex matter—complex because each local society must assume responsibility for the charges, and each local society is made up of individuals who, until the organization of the cooperative society, had had little or no experience in formally organized group action. There were several things the villagers wanted to know before they were ready to agree to pay the charges to the KTCCA and start winter farming. Could they afford the cost of the water? Would the flow of the water be dependable? Could they market profitably what they grew?

As set forth below, many a serious question too arose among the villagers with regard to the Sonaichuri project. There was less uncertainty among the villagers about the river-raft irrigation. These pumps were put in place by the KTCCA upon agreement with the local cooperative societies, or on contract with a group of local farmers. The water from the river was lifted over the levee, stored in a reservoir nearby, or taken directly to the fields.

The three types of irrigation, as originally planned, are being worked out on a complementary and integrated basis as to areas covered and charges made for water. The tube well provides a discrete unit to determine the cost of water per cubic foot per second. The fact that this cost is considerably greater than that for the Sonaichuri gravity-flow and for the river-raft pumps will, when the same rate is charged to all, make a profit from the latter. Such profit can be used, as determined, by the thana council or the

Irrigation and Rural Electrification 143

KTCCA for further irrigation and drainage projects. The per acre cost of the Sonaichuri project is low because it will serve only the areas nearest the project which are most cheaply reached. This reduces costs for structures, pumps, and the additional land for canals that would be required to take the water to the higher and more distant areas.

Once the overall plans for the three irrigation projects had been agreed to, they then had to be broken down to each individual farmer. And again a host of questions arose. How is the water to be distributed? How will it reach a particular field? How can essential production credit and supplies be had on time?

The villagers soon learned that they themselves would need to work out the answers to the water-flow problems in their own cooperative society. They learned, too, that allegations of unfair treatment would have to be resolved among themselves. Then there were questions about the availability of the tractors when needed for land preparation and hauling, whether good seed potatoes could be obtained, and whether the use of the cold storage would be a paying proposition. Again, the answers lay largely with the local society's advance planning and the necessity for it to file requests for supplies well ahead of desired deliveries. And, about the storage, "It's new, too; try it and see," they were told.

Then too, an old fear arose in connection with the Sonaichuri project. The farmers wondered how water could be taken from the Gumti without running the risk of flooding the countryside. This fear of flood waters from the Gumti has been an active one among the farmers. Flash floods have long been breaching the levees practically every year. Among the possible relief measures there had been discussions about diversion outlets. Was this Sonaichuri project, the villagers wondered, a disguise for a diversion outlet? The representatives of the Academy and EPWAPDA assured the villagers that the levee could be cut, the intake sluice gates installed, and the levee replaced in a single dry season; and that with the sluice gates installed the levee would be as strong as before, or stronger. This was hard for the villagers to believe.

So in late 1963 when the Peace Corps Volunteer engineer and his helper from the Academy went into the area to survey the four-mile canal that would carry the water from the intake on the Gumti to the Sonaichuri basin, they were ordered out by the local people. No answers they could give would placate the farmers. To the area then went representatives from the Academy administration, the thana council, and the KTCCA. They called the people of the area together to talk about the proposed project. They had with them maps, designs of the sluice gates, estimates of costs and of the values of increased yields from an irrigated third crop. They also took with them village leaders from areas with irrigation tube wells and low-lift pumps on the river. At the end of the first day the Academy representatives estimated that it would take about twenty meetings to convince the many villagers affected of the desirability of the project.

Subsequent meetings were held all over the area. After some weeks, and some adjustments in the proposal, the needed local approval of the plan was secured. In the end it was agreed that all of the land required for the main canal, regulators, sluice gates, and so on, should be paid for. The price of the land was worked out by the villagers involved. And even though the price was high, it was thought to be cheaper in money and in time than it would have been to go into the courts. And furthermore, this procedure met

THE SONAICHURI PROJECT

The excavation at the site of the Sonaichuri intake sluice gate was started through a local project committee of the works program in February 1964. After a brief religious ceremony, several scores of laborers with their short-handled hoe-shovels and head baskets began the work of cutting the Gumti levee for the installation of the four 100-foot conduits, three feet in diameter. The beginning of the work had been delayed, as noted, by the objections of the villagers through whose lands the main canal leading to the Sonaichuri basin was to pass.

Other difficulties soon arose. In mid-March there was an outbreak of cholera among the workers. For more than a week labor recruitment was difficult. Also, the final settlement for the land on which the excavated earth needed to be placed was held up. Then by late March water had begun to seep into the river end of the excavation, making it impossible to start the concrete work there for the conduits.

The result was that only three-fourths of the excavation work had been done by mid-April, when heavy premonsoon rains disrupted the operations. With the project as a whole already five weeks behind schedule, it was determined on April 18 to stop the work on the river end of the excavation, and to construct a temporary half-circle levee-embankment around it to prevent a breach from a major flood. More cubic feet of earth went into the half-moon temporary structure than had been taken out of the cut in the levee. Within a little more than a month the new embankment was complete, tamped down as it was being built, and sodded over to help it withstand the monsoon flash floods. And well it was that all this was done, for a flash flood did come in July. The levee did breach at another point, four miles downstream, opposite Comilla town.

The work on the landward end of the excavation was completed in late April, and concrete casting work was soon begun for the conduit pipes at that end. In late June all work had to be discontinued because of the frequency of heavy rains. By then the landward end of the masonry head had been finished, and 40 per cent of the conduit pipes had been put in place.

The fabrication of the three-foot reinforced concrete pipes, 4.5 feet long, for the conduits had been done at the Abhoy Ashram campus. A total of 88 pipes and 36 joining collars were made in 65 days, beginning in late December of 1963.

Since there is no rock or gravel in the deltaic area, only the barest essential minimum of these expensive outside materials was used in the concrete work. This meant that a lot of *jamma* (fragments of broken brick) had to be made for the pipes at Abhoy Ashram and for the concrete work at the site of the intake sluice gates. Piles of jamma, tons and tons of it, were made with hand hammers. Only very hard over-burned brick can be used. And a hard brick can be cracked only by placing it on a larger harder object, usually a 15- or 20-pound rock, and giving it a sharp blow with a hammer. And when it is cracked, yet other blows are needed, again and again, until no piece is larger than a walnut. A score or more of men worked, stroke after stroke, all day long, with every stroke landing on the piece of hard brick between the fingers!

Each jamma maker sits atop his own little pile of fragments. Each pile is neat, the better to measure the amount that has been made. All those who make jamma in the Comilla area are men and boys—the women are traditionally housebound by purdah. Except for a portable concrete mixer, operated by a small gasoline engine, all the work in making the pipes and installing the sluice gates is done by hand.

The work on the Sonaichuri project was reactivated in November 1964, early in the dry season. The temporary half-moon levee was removed, but the completion of the sluice-gate installation was delayed by the late delivery of heavy sheet-metal piling (66 tons). In March 85 per cent of the total casting intake had been finished, and 80 per cent of the earth had been removed from the four-mile main canal, and four bridges across the new canal had been started.

In 1965–1966, the final work was done on the intake structure—the canal was dressed and turfed, and preparations were under way for the construction of regulators and pipe outlets.

To help popularize the project, the Academy published 200 copies of a booklet in Bengali entitled the "Sonaichuri Irrigation Project." The booklet was designed primarily to inform the union councilors and leaders of the cooperative societies of the procedures the farmers needed to follow to secure irrigation water for the next dry season beginning in late 1966.

By October 1965 eleven cooperatives had worked out plans to irrigate five blocks of land, with a total area of 228 acres. The acreage actually irrigated was 211. It was expected that about 400 acres would be irrigated by this project in the 1966–1967 dry season, in nine blocks of around 45 acres each. Though no firm target projections were made for the years ahead, it was believed that the acreage would about double for the next two or three years, but just when the whole of the command area of 14,770 acres might be irrigated could not be foreseen. As of mid-1968 the Sonaichuri project provided water for the irrigation of 974 acres.

LOW-LIFT PUMPS ON RIVER RAFTS

Low-lift pumps on five rafts on the Gumti River were in operation in 1964, three being installations powered by electricity, the other two by diesel fuel. The farmers arranged among themselves to distribute the water. Some 500 acres were irrigated for winter crops that year; the water charge to the farmers was a flat Rs. 40 per acre per season. In 1965, the river-raft program was operated by the government; it was organized late in the season. Many of the farmers who used water did not make their rental payments in full or on time, which led to the belief that irrigation water could be had from the government at little or no cost. As a result very little use was made of pumps on river rafts in 1966 and in 1967. By 1968, however, more than 300 acres were irrigated by low-lift pumps.

DEEP TUBE WELL IRRIGATION

The tube well irrigation program is carried on by the water development section of the KTCCA. It handles the drilling of wells and the training of needed skilled workers in Comilla thana and in the other thanas where Comilla-type programs have been started.

The tube well program has suffered from many difficulties, one of which was that tube well water has been found to be relatively expensive: Rs. 71 per acre per year, compared to Rs. 21 for the Sonaichuri water, and Rs. 31 for

Irrigation and Rural Electrification

water from river rafts. Moreover the water supply was found inadequate some years in some of the six-inch wells at the levels to which they had been sunk and with the type of pump used. Also some of the cooperatives were encountering financial difficulties, and (as mentioned earlier) ten were blacklisted by the KTCCA in 1965. As a result, fewer wells were in operation in 1966 than in the preceding year. However, this was looked upon by the KTCCA as more than offset by the overall increase, though slight, of acres irrigated, and especially by the marked increase of acreage per tube well in operation when the charge was shifted from a per acre basis to Rs. 1,000 (plus fuel) per well. By 1967 the number of tube wells increased to 46, and by early 1968 to 91. As of June 1968 the number increased to 118, most of which were of the six-inch size.

The development in the Comilla thana of irrigation by surface pumps and deep tube wells from 1962–1963 to 1967–1968 is indicated in the following composite table:[4]

	Number of surface pumps	Acres irrigated	Number of tube wells	Acres irrigated
1962–1963			2	36
1963–1964			12	423.70
1964–1965	3	129	34	1006.08
1965–1966	4	178	25	1127.25
1966–1967	17	726	46	2350.42
1967–1968	37	1292	91	3891.54

[4] *Ninth Annual Report of the Academy, 1967–1968*, Comilla, PARD, September 1968.

In addition, in the ten other thanas with programs patterned after the Comilla model, a total of 15,591 acres was irrigated by pumps and tube wells.

The progress cited above was accompanied by an enlarged training program for engineers, assistant engineers, drillers, and assistant drillers, aided first by Peace Corps Volunteers and later by British Volunteers. Concurrently, land preparation by tractors greatly increased, and mechanical weeders, threshers, and seed drills were introduced.

The cost of sinking tube wells varied from Rs. 16,000 to Rs. 35,000, depending on depth of drilling needed and other factors.

Rental income from tube wells and surface pumps for 1967–1968 aggregated Rs. 124,114 as against Rs. 48,350 for maintenance costs. Average costs per acre for irrigation varied considerably by crops, from approximately Rs. 40 for potatoes to as much as Rs. 50–60 for rice varieties and watermelons.[5] Other costs and returns are reported in "Costs and Returns: A Survey of Irrigated Winter Crops in Comilla" (PARD, 1968).

The expanded program of irrigation was accompanied by four highly related developments: the use of improved seeds; some diversification of crops; greatly increased use of commercial fertilizers and insecticides; and the use of tractors in land preparation. Fertilizer use increased from approximately 22,000 maunds in 1962–1963 to over 48,000 maunds in 1967–1968. Similarly, use of insecticides increased from almost 8,000 pounds in 1962–1963 to more than 57,000 pounds in 1967–1968. Likewise the number of acres cultivated by tractors increased from approximately 1,500 acres in 1962–1963 to over 4,800 acres in 1967–1968.

[5] *A New Rural Cooperative System for Comilla Thana* (Eighth Annual Report, 1968), Comilla, PARD, April 1969.

Irrigation and Rural Electrification 151

The KTCCA also gave leadership and supervision to the production of improved rice and seed potatoes on its own lands and on selected seed multiplication farms managed by village cooperatives. All of the factors mentioned above taken together moved agricultural production a relatively long way toward modern methods.

Expanded Province-wide Irrigation Program

Based largely on the experience with irrigation in the Comilla thana and in ten other thanas organized on the same principles, the government of East Pakistan launched in November 1967 a province-wide program to stimulate the cultivation of IR-8 seed and other new rice varieties, and to promote, over a period of four years, the organization of 40,000 groups of farmers to use irrigation pumps. The program was preceded by a massive training and research effort organized by the Academy in collaboration with the planning departments of the other three major partners in the program—the Department of Agriculture and the Department of Basic Democracies and Local Government, and the Agricultural Development Corporation. Under this partnership, the Department of Basic Democracies and Local Government has responsibility, through the circle officers, for mobilizing villagers and organizing irrigation groups; the Department of Agriculture for training model farmers in methods of improved cultivation of the new varieties; the Agricultural Development Corporation for supplying pumps, insecticides, fuel, and seeds; and the Academy for training and evaluation.

Detailed training materials were prepared by the Academy, including maps, manuals on the cultivation of IR-8 seed and other new rice varieties, visual aids, and so on. A total of 1,098 trainees came to the Academy for three-day intensive training in nine groups. The trainees came from 16 districts and the Chittagong Hill Tracts, and included 385 circle officers (for development), 377 thana agricultural officers, 30 inspectors, 28 supervisors, and others. The whole training effort was infused with the urgent necessity of growing more food to increase supplies, to save Rs. 40 crore which were being spent on the import of food grains, and to mobilize and modernize the villages of East Pakistan. The successful organization and management of the public works program was used as precedent for undertaking this huge modernizing effort.

The instructional methods included lectures by the director and faculty members of the Academy and officials from the participating agencies, supplemented by the visual aids mentioned above. Field trips were taken to six irrigation villages in Comilla thana that used surface water, pumps, and tube wells for irrigation. The training report[6] cites 63 key questions and answers that covered such substantive matters as methods of compensating landowners for irrigation sluices, methods of establishing priorities for water, and related questions, and such managerial questions as compensation for model farmers who participated in training sessions, and needed clerical assistance. The training program was adjudged to be highly successful in launching the program. The status of this province-wide irrigation program in 1968–1969 will be seen in Chapter 9.

Rural Electrification

The provincial government had a special interest in learning from the pilot project what uses the villagers would make of electricity, especially since existing generat-

[6] M. Azizul Huq, *Training Report on Organization of Irrigation Groups and Cultivation of IR-8*, Comilla, PARD, November 1967.

Irrigation and Rural Electrification

ing capacity was far from being fully used. A system of main radial lines was planned for Comilla thana to serve the scores of widely scattered irrigation tube wells envisioned. This would put electricity within reasonable reach of all the villages. Many a line would surely not pay for itself at first. How many of the lines would later become productive investments? Under what conditions? In what period of time? Would any lines remain unproductive? If so, why? "Against the array of unknowns," said an Academy report, "we welcome the interest and cooperation of the Government in our efforts, as we proceed experimentally. If, for example, the village farmers do not take up the use of power for irrigation as presented in our estimates, this is knowledge which is well worth the price of securing, for it will keep the Province from going into much larger projects without this knowledge. If on the other hand, the use of electricity grows in the rural areas as we believe it will, the detailed costs and benefits will be available for use in planning much larger programmes in the Third and Fourth Five-Year Plans. These details would provide a basis upon which to secure more capital assistance than would be warranted by a purely theoretical feasibility survey."[7]

The first five-mile rural line was built in 1962 to the tube well at South Rampur. After several months, lines were run to three river-raft pump installations on the Gumti. The construction of these lines yielded information about costs per mile, electricity used by the pumps, and attitudes of the farmers about the line crossing their land.

It was on the basis of these small experiments that the Academy invited the EPWAPDA to develop a plan to cover the entire thana. In preparation for the development

[7] *The Comilla Pilot Project in Irrigation and Rural Electrification* (revised edition), Comilla, PARD, August 1964, pp. i–iii.

of a plan, EPWAPDA posted an assistant electrical engineer at Comilla in April 1963. The power wing of EPWAPDA agreed to take the responsibility for the installation of facilities in collaboration with the KTCCA. The plan as developed featured six radial feeder lines, from six to nine miles in length, extending out in all directions from the substation near the center of the thana.

In June 1964 a five-mile segment of one of the six main radials was started to pass near four new six-inch irrigation tube wells, and one large local market site. There was no lack of labor willing to be taught how to perform this new task of electric-line building, but farmers sometimes refused the workmen the right to string up lines across their fields. They complained that the linemen tramped the crops, and besides an electric line was a new and unknown thing. After some discussions and a few changes in the plan, the work got under way again. It was then decided that no line would be started until the entire right of way has been secured; and no connections with a deep tube well pump, or a pump on a river raft, would be made until it was certain that the farmers to be served were well enough organized to make effective use of the water.

These precautions emphasize a basic truth learned at Comilla, namely that under the conditions in East Pakistan the establishment of responsible local group organizations with voluntary membership is a prerequisite to effective use of modern technological services. Conversely, it has been found that the prospect of having these modern services can be used as a catalytic agent to speed up group organization.

The ownership of the thana-wide electric distribution system is shared by EPWAPDA and the KTCCA. The former supplies the substation equipment and accessories,

Irrigation and Rural Electrification

and erects and maintains the main radial lines, including transformers, lightning arrestors, and so on. The latter erects the distribution lines. The electrical current provided by EPWAPDA is billed to the KTCCA. The association in turn collects from the consumers the price of the current along with the association's own expenses, including amortization and maintenance.

It was assumed in the proposal that the system would operate at a deficit for some years. The size of the deficit would depend upon the rate at which the wells became operative, and whether current was used for local enterprises and village households. To have a record of the use of electrical current by the tube wells, and for other purposes, the KTCCA was prepared to do detailed metering. But as of mid-1967 the use of current from the KTCCA was limited to the twelve 1.5 cubic foot per second tube well pumps and the one 2.0 cubic foot per second pump on a river raft, and to the few electric lights in or near the ten pump houses. Two rural markets had electric lights, but for each the current is provided from EPWAPDA's main line. No village household or rural business had yet taken current from the feeder lines of the KTCCA. By mid-1968, however, 54 pumps had been electrified.

As of mid-1966 EPWAPDA had constructed four radial lines totaling 44 miles; two lines (16 miles) remained to be done. In 1965, Rs. 400,000 of public funds were used on rural electrification in Comilla thana, and the year before that Rs. 600,000. No public works funds were available for this project in 1966, and no radial lines were built. Such expenses as did occur were met by EPWAPDA and the KTCCA.

Because of lower operating and maintenance costs, it is clearly to the advantage of a cooperative society to use electric energy rather than diesel fuel to power the pumps. For example, a comparative study made in 1963 of average costs per acre irrigated by diesel-powered pumps was Rs. 22 as compared with Rs. 7.3 for electrified pumps.

As time passes and the EPWAPDA radial lines are completed and the number of wells increases, there is reason to expect that the use of electric current for pumping will be greater. The use of electrical power for pumping is, however, only one important use of this type of energy. Of possibly equal importance is the growing use of electric power for operating the cold-storage plant, rice mill, dairy, and other central services provided by KTCCA. It may take some time before the villages are illuminated electrically, but there is no doubt about the use of electricity for important income-producing rural development industry and services.

In retrospect, the great amount of planning involved in getting the irrigation and rural electrification projects launched seems to be warranted by results, not so much because of what has already been achieved, as by the delineation of the complexity of the problems involved, which again follows upon Comilla's main forte, namely to learn the answers from experimentation in the local situation.

The Comilla experiments in irrigation and rural electrification, along with flood control and village road construction, indicate vastly larger opportunities for development investment than had been previously anticipated by development planners.

6. The Women's and Family Planning Programs

Akhter Hameed Khan said in 1963 in speaking on the role of women in Pakistan:

One cause of our misery and poverty is that we keep our women-folk at home, guarded over constantly. We keep them indoors. We have almost imprisoned them. We do not educate them, and because they are confined they cannot educate themselves; so they are nearly all illiterate, they are timid. And so long as the women are uneducated, development can hardly be expected in our country.

If the mother is illiterate, if she has no courage, how can one expect courage in her children? The mother is the teacher. . . .

I think our country can never progress until we can emancipate the women.[1]

It was a major accomplishment to involve the women in the development programs. This will be understood better if first the woman's place in the village is portrayed. In brief, indispensable as she is, she is the overlooked one. From the time she was born, a boy would have been pre-

[1] Akhter Hameed Khan, *The Role of Women in a Country's Development* (translation of a talk in Bengali, March 5, 1963), Comilla, PARD, July 1963, pp. 2–3.

ferred. She grows up illiterate, is betrothed at eleven or twelve, married at twelve to fourteen. The first child is soon born, then another and another; around one-sixth of them die before they reach their first birthday. Tired and worn from drudgery and child-bearing, the mother is an old woman at thirty-five, already a grandmother—for her surviving girl children have in the meantime grown up the way she did.

She stays at home, seldom leaves the compound of her husband's immediate extended family. It is her job to take care of the children, winnow, store, and husk the paddy, grind the spices, do the cooking and washing and sun the bedding, serve the *pan* leaf and betel nut, tend the chickens and the cow stall, and perhaps cultivate a kitchen garden.

The contacts the Bengali village mother has with the outside are extraordinarily limited. She may visit her kinspeople once or twice a year if they do not live too far away. Though the mosque is a weekly meeting place for the men and boys, as is also the local market, the village women do not go to either.

The village wife and mother is busiest on family occasions—festivals, births, circumcisions, betrothals, marriages, and deaths. Kinswomen help in the feeding of scores, or hundreds, of men and boys, usually gathered under a gaily-colored canopy in the compound yard. The kitchen and house are full of women and girls, overflowing to the area of the cook pots to the side or back of the house. No man or boy stares at the women and girls. They are kept nearly out of sight. If a man should glance appreciatively toward them now and again, the glances would be accepted as if not seen. A strange man in the village seldom if ever meets a woman, although he knows the women are there. For as he walks along the village paths he gets a glimpse of a *sari* now and then, or from an opening in a nearby wall he sees a pair of eyes fixed on him.

Her husband may be involved in a litigation in the court in the town about the land, or in taking a loan from a moneylender, or he may be arranging for their son to go to school, or for the marriage of their daughter—all of which are *his* responsibilities. If he needs any advice, he usually gets it from men in the village or at the market or in the town. Generally, the father in the Bengali village looks askance at anything that may affect the status quo of relations between men and women.

If her husband is landless and dies, and she is without a son and does not remarry, a woman may become dependent on the village. In such a case, she may be assigned to this task or that by the village headman. Her status is the lowest. It is the destitute widows in the villages who become midwives, untrained and often unpaid.

The wife and mother in the village adjusts herself to life as it comes. She is told by her father, or a matchmaker chosen by him, whom she will marry and when. If her first child is a boy, praises be! If a girl, maybe the next, or the next, will be a boy. If there is no son, she may be divorced and will have difficulty in remarrying. For a divorced woman to remarry and forthwith have a son is like another life for her.

The mother reaches the peak of her intrafamily influence when her son marries. For it is she who directs the household activities of the daughter-in-law, and so greatly influences the rearing of the grandchildren. The mother and daughter-in-law relationship may be a happy one, or it may be otherwise.

A New Approach for Women's Work

The demise of V-AID in 1961, though a loss in some ways, served as an incentive to the Academy to develop a more realistic program for village women. Soon after the women V-AID workers had withdrawn from the villages, the activities they had started died out, primarily because the workers were outsiders, and had spent most of their attention upon the women of the more prosperous rural families who were least interested in change. No local women had been trained as trainers of other village women.

Through arrangements with the provincial government, the Academy retained three of the V-AID women workers along with the other National Development Organization personnel then working in the Comilla area. The three women workers became members of the women's staff at the Academy, whose first task was to develop ways to get village women interested in cooperative activity. Added to this group were one woman member of the newly arrived (October 1961) group of Peace Corps Volunteers, a lady instructor (who arrived on campus in early 1962), and the Academy's sociologist.

After much discussion it was decided that the emerging women's program would be through the family, and that lasting progress would come to a village only when all members of a family were involved in and influenced by new ideas and methods. To bring about this development, a program of intensive education and emancipation for the wives with the support of their husbands would be necessary. Emancipation was defined as involving a process of teaching women how to be more effective as contributing members of their families.

The Women's and Family Planning Programs

Starting in December 1961, the sociologist began systematic discussions with the organizers and supervisors of the village cooperatives upon their weekly visits to the Academy, and with the membership of the societies in the weekly meetings in the villages. His aim was to acquaint the men with the proposed program for women, and to win their support for it. He found that the men were well aware of the sorry state of their women. "What was new," says the first report on women's work, "was the idea that something could or ought to be done about it."[2]

The men in nine cooperative villages agreed that a women's program might be started. The cooperative organizers were then asked to arrange a meeting of the village women with the staff of the women's program, assisted at times by the sociologist's wife and the eldest daughter of Director Khan. "In the initial stages, the women were mainly curious as to why strange people had come, and especially why they wanted to talk with them. What was said was less important than the mere fact that strangers were interested in them. For most of the women, it was their first experience of a group meeting. They discovered that they had many problems in common."[3]

The purposes of these village meetings of women were to let them discuss their problems, to tell them about the Academy, and to learn if they would be interested in coming to the Academy to take part in the program that was being formulated for them there. It was learned that even

---

[2] Florence E. McCarthy, *Women's Education and Home Improvement Program* (First Annual Report, January 1962 through March 1963), Comilla, PARD, April 1963, p. 10.

[3] Florence E. McCarthy and Martha J. Raper, "The Women's Programme at Comilla," Comilla, *Journal*, PARD, Vol. IV, No. 1, July 1963, p. 29.

though a cooperative society might have been in the village for as long as 18 months, very few women knew what a cooperative was or how it functioned, and that in many cases the women had hardly heard of the Academy or of its work. Women were often as reluctant to leave the village to go to the Academy as their husbands were to send them, or to let them go. However, some ventured that if their husbands would give them permission they would go.

ORIENTATION AND TRAINING AT THE ACADEMY

In burqas and sandals (often borrowed), the first group of village women, many with children, came to the Academy for orientation on the morning of January 1, 1962. These first women "were frightened and shy, and not at all sure why they had come. It took tremendous courage for them to come, for they were moving against the traditions of their society. The Director, watching the women pass by on their inspection of the campus, commented: 'I could tell people that this is happening, but they wouldn't believe me. So we will wait, and in time they will come and see for themselves.'"[4]

Once the first group had come, others followed.[5] It had early been agreed that the women who came would tell other women of their visit and encourage them to come. By the end of January, 96 women had been thus oriented. On the other days of the week the staff went to the villages and visited the women who had come to the Academy.

The first women orientees were told that a training program would be developed for them at the Academy. If

[4] *Ibid.*, p. 29.
[5] A total of 1,350 women were involved in one-day orientation through the fall of 1964. The orientation program was discontinued for two years but was resumed in 1966.

interested, they were asked what training courses they thought the Academy should set up for them. By the end of February a "Programme of Women's Education and Family Planning in Selected Comilla Villages" had been developed, which was to be a part of the larger cooperative program. The first two training courses for women were in fact set up within the framework of the "organizer system" which afforded a regular weekly training experience at the Academy for the "teacher," and, through the teacher, for the village group. Before the training of the teachers had been completed, three of the nine villages withdrew from the program. Two could not accept so great a departure from the traditional ways, and a third was disrupted by factionalism.

The first two weekly training classes for village women were started at the Academy in March. One dealt with child care, the other with maternity diseases and family planning. Since this whole idea was unprecedented, it was decided that each of the six participating village cooperatives would send to the first courses only a few women chosen from among those who had visited the Academy, who had been endorsed by the local cooperative society to take the training, and who had agreed when trained to set up classes in the villages. Twenty-three village women took these first two courses, meeting one day a week for nearly eight weeks. Attendance was good, arrivals on time, or early, usually by cycle rickshaws, with fares paid by the Academy. The teaching was done by the instructor of women's work and her staff, with a lady doctor brought in for sessions as needed.

During the following years courses were given in literacy, sewing, spinning, poultry raising, gardening, sanitation, first aid, silkscreen printing, and so on. The trainees liked best those classes that afforded opportunities for discussion, and that contained materials whose value they could assess through their own experience. Being largely illiterate, they appreciated simple visual aids such as flannel boards, flash cards, and line drawings.

The number of women trained at the Academy (in addition to one-day orientation programs which served to introduce women to training opportunities at the Academy) increased from 112 up to March 1963, 277 from then until June 1964, dropped back to 214 during the next year, and then down to 70, but was back to 232 in 1966–1967. Later reports of the Academy indicate a continuation of this upward trend with an expanded program of training offerings. Greater emphasis is now being placed upon the more intensive training of selected women leaders.

MIDWIFE TRAINING

A midwife (*dai*) training program of three days was begun about the same time as the basic orientation program; a total of 299 midwives came to the Academy for it. But since midwives needed a good deal more instruction, arrangements were made for four at a time to spend a month at the Maternity and Child Health Centre at Comilla town. As of 1966 a total of 111 midwives had had the one-month course of training. Upon completion of the course, each trainee received a midwife kit from CARE, making a deposit of Rs. 10 to the Academy for replenishing the contents. These midwives then came back to the Academy one day each week for refresher training with a Peace Corps Volunteer nurse or a local doctor. Even this was minimal training; but it was a beginning.

More extensive midwife training of one full year was instituted in 1965 for about ten each year of the most

The Women's and Family Planning Programs

promising women who had finished the month's course. This training is done at the Comilla Health Centre and the local district hospital through scholarships provided by the Department of Health of East Pakistan and UNICEF. Current (1968) reports of the Academy indicate that the midwife training program is continuing and becoming more rigorous and professional in character.

NUMBER OF WOMEN TRAINED IN THE VILLAGES

The classes in the villages[6] conducted by the Academy-trained women were held on a fixed day and hour each week, at first attended by one or more of the Academy staff members.

It was mostly the poorer women who were willing to admit they needed to learn, would listen to new ideas and try new methods. Class members were at first from the teacher's immediate family or neighborhood. Some women later came from more distant portions of the villages, but it was generally the teachers who would venture into another neighborhood to gather together a class and teach.

Whereas at first many staff visits had been required to interest women in coming to the Academy for orientation and then for training, increasingly the penetration of the village came through the women who had been to the Academy, and especially through those who had taken courses and were teaching classes, and through the female family planning organizers.

The benefits of the women's learning are clear in the villages, in courtyards, gardens, and households. But even more important is the fact that the women now leave their homes regularly and for a new purpose, that they meet with other

[6] Through mid-1966, 412 courses had been held in the villages with a total attendance (on a year subject-matter basis) of nearly 10,000.

women regularly in the villages, that they rarely, if ever, miss class, even during inclement weather. Where previously there was no place for women in the development process, the opportunity is now being created. That the women are so eager and responsive is tremendously noteworthy and exciting.

At each stage of the program it has been necessary to win and keep the support of the village men. Some unpleasant repercussions occurred before the staff learned to sense when it was necessary to prepare the men further for next steps in the development of their women. Outlines of new courses to be taught to the women will continue to be presented to the societies through their organizers.

The reaction of the men is ambivalent. While they may be aware of the desirability of change, they want to retain their traditional status in the family, and many perceive the development of their wives as a threat to themselves. The men need continued reassurance that they have not so much to lose.[7]

The whole program has been carried on within the framework of the cooperative societies in the villages. Without a supporting organization in which the men could consider together new ideas and make a group commitment, it is doubtful whether the program could have been successfully launched.[8]

NEW PROGRAMS

Out of these training courses at the Academy and the classes in the villages there arose two supportive economic activities, namely paddy loans and spinning, and also a health program. By March 1963 the spinning program had placed 88 simple hand *charka* spinning machines in as many village homes. Since experience had indicated that this ac-

[7] McCarthy and Raper, *op. cit.*, p. 33.
[8] *Ibid.*, p. 37.

tivity might result in the women being even more confined to their compounds, it was decided that the machines would be placed only in the villages with a women's program. Also, it was found that at least 15 machines were needed in a village to make it feasible to provide the needed instructions which were furnished by the *Khadi* Association, a government-sponsored spinning and weaving cooperative with a unit in Comilla town. It sold the women the raw cotton they used and bought the thread they made. The women paid one rupee rent a month on the machine, and at the end of ten payments owned it.

The single-thread charka was later largely replaced by the four-thread *ambar charka*. Even the larger machines yield only a few rupees per month, but when money is as scarce as it is in many village homes, these few rupees may be sorely needed. The monthly report of the Academy for November 1968 indicates that the income for the months of October and November totaled Rs. 853. Other income-producing programs for the same period were as follows: screen printing, Rs. 1040; sewing, Rs. 667; and weaving, Rs. 7168. A measure of the increased sophistication of the income-producing activities, as of 1968, is seen in the fact that selected women are sent to Dacca for higher training at the East Pakistan Small Industries Corporation Design Center.

The paddy loan program, which was put into operation in January 1963 provided another means by which a village woman could earn a little money at home. If vouched for by the local cooperative society, a woman could borrow paddy from the central cooperative at around Rs. 16 a maund, process it into hulled rice by the use of the *dheki* (a simple rice-hulling apparatus) in her own yard, and sell it for around Rs. 25. Except for a small service-reserve charge that was set aside, the profit belonged to her. By June 1963 18 women had taken paddy loans valued at Rs. 986; repayments were ahead of schedule. A second loan could be larger, and for other purposes. But to get it, the borrower had first to become a member of the local cooperative society. This requirement resulted in many women memberships, and so represented a first major step towards the goal of making the village cooperative a joint affair for both husbands and wives. Paddy loans were not made after 1964–1965, since production loans, especially for goats and chickens, were proving to be more attractive.

Wheat-use demonstrations were put on in early 1962 at the Academy in cooperation with Wheat Associates, Inc. They were designed to popularize the use of wheat provided by the thana public works program. Beginning in late 1962, and in a much more systematic way, 52 wheat-cooking demonstrations were held in the villages with a total attendance of about 7,000. A program for the use of wheat was also set up in ten rural schools, with 2,400 primary students given an ounce of wheat per day. This tiffin (snack) program was later extended to other schools and the daily ration increased. In 1964, a three-part nutrition program was carried out—the preparation of dishes to popularize the use of wheat, the expansion of the lunch program, and the teaching of a course in balanced nutrition to primary school teachers, midwives, and village women trainees. Wheat dishes were also popularized by serving them to villagers when they came to the Academy, to the women attending village classes, youth clubs, and labor crews. The wheat demonstrations were discontinued in 1965, but interest in nutritional improvement has con-

The Women's and Family Planning Programs 169

tinued. For example, an intensive research project on family nutrition, designed with the assistance of World Health Organization experts, was launched in April 1968.

The program for women in 1965 and 1966 was further expanded to include such varied projects as training village women to teach in the adult education centers and in the primary schools, making and selling garments and silk-screen printed saris and other cloth, caring for poultry in cages, arranging loans from the local cooperative for income-producing projects, increasing family income by the sale of home-produced vegetables and livestock products, purchasing sewing machines, planting seedling trees, installing sanitary latrines at their homes, operating the Abhoy Ashram cafeteria, administering first aid and giving inoculations in villages when floods and cyclones come, and establishing a Maternity and Child Health Centre at Abhoy Ashram that served a total of almost 10,000 mothers and children in 1965. The number served the next year rose to 19,802.

By 1968 the women's cooperative program was more firmly established and was working successfully. The monthly report of the Academy for November 1968, for example, states that in 67 organized societies there were 1,032 women members who had purchased shares worth Rs. 14,000 and had additional aggregate savings of Rs. 23,622. Loans and repayments were correspondingly high and well managed. Since this date the monthly and annual reports available from the Academy indicate no diminution of participation in the program; the annual rally in April 1969 was attended by over five hundred women. A village dai chaired the rally. In addition to the increase in numbers of participants, greater attention is being paid to the quality of

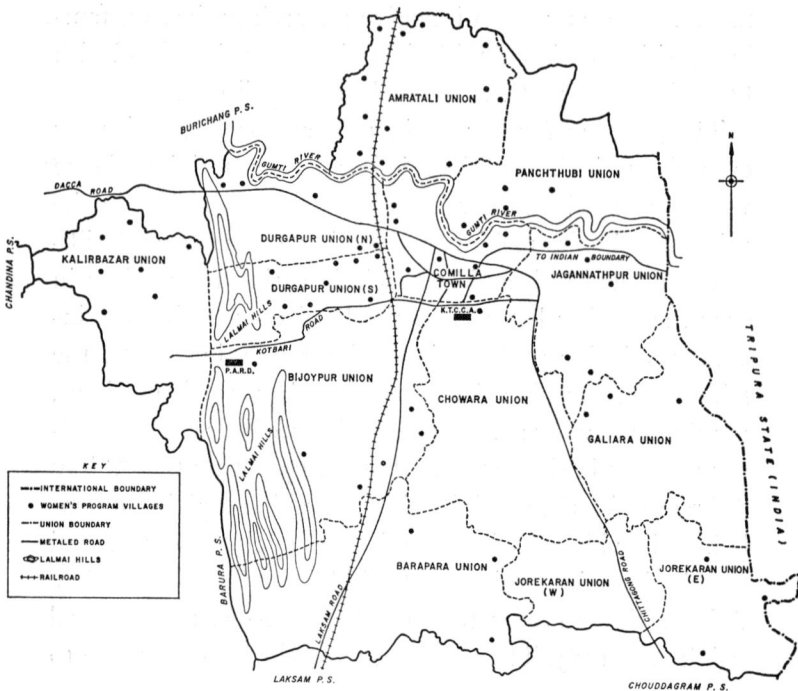

Map 3. Comilla Kotwali thana, villages with women's programs, mid-1966. Developed from information provided by the instructor of women's work, Comilla, PARD, December 1966. Drawn by M. A. Quddus.

the training, to increasing the number of leaders and supervisors for the program, and to the administration of the cooperative and other income-producing activities.

The Pakistani staff of the women's program, not including the women organizers who work jointly for family planning and women's activities, increased gradually from three in January 1962 to 15 in June 1966. A key member of the staff was selected for a year's training at Michigan State University and has recently been made a full-fledged instructor and director of the program.

EMERGENCE OF VILLAGE WOMEN AS INNOVATORS[9]

Given the context of the Muslim culture and village society, it is not surprising that the greatest changes relate to the family's economic situation and to the contacts of the women.

The true innovators are the teachers, organizers, family planning agents, and midwives. They have gained mobility within the village and between the village and the Academy or the town. The matter of having a small fixed income, of contributing to the family support, of being able to help other women are all changes which encourage further change. In many ways the village women who have been trained at the Academy, insofar as they are accepted, are becoming models for other village women to observe and follow, and those who learn in their own villages from these organizers and teachers are also changing. They are especially interested in such income-producing skills as gardening, poultry-raising, and sewing, by which they may help the family to eat a bit better, send a son to school, repay a debt, or even buy some land. Continued progress depends upon the village women's reconciling their new opportunities with traditional values. The function of the Academy's women's program is to give continued support to the village women in an atmosphere conducive to change.

The women's program still has less official connection with governmental departments than have most of the

---

[9] The material in the next two paragraphs was prepared by Florence E. McCarthy, who was a graduate student from Michigan State University at Comilla from January 1966 to April 1967 and had earlier been there as a Peace Corps Volunteer associated with the launching of the work with women.

other programs of the Academy, although there is some indication that the programs in this field are having an influence on regular governmental operations. But it is still sponsored by the KTCCA and remains essentially a pilot project. It is confidently believed by Director Khan and the staff of the women's project that at some time in the future this activity will become a recognized and widely appreciated public program. And when it does, the Academy will provide the training, the most vital part of which will be the living model for this activity that has been created over the years.[10] The most important contributions in the creation of this model have been twofold: the interest and commitment of those Pakistani members of the staff who are finding challenge and fulfillment in their work; and the village women who dared to begin to cast off their confining traditions in search of a better life for themselves and for their families.

The Family Planning Programs

Family planning runs counter to the traditional practices of the villagers. Even so, it is being tentatively accepted by an increasing number of them. This program fits in with the apparent desire of the people to reduce economic stress and the further subdivision of farms, and in some instances to protect the mother's health.

An experimental family planning activity was begun within a few months after the Academy opened, but it was not until March 1961 that family planning began to be fitted into the overall development program of the Acad-

---

[10] In early 1969, women's programs patterned after that at Comilla were begun, upon the request of an international women's organization directed from Amsterdam, in three experimental farm project areas of the East Pakistan Agricultural Development Corporation.

emy. An initial grant of Rs. 5,000 from the provincial Department of Health assisted in getting the program underway. A "Rural Pilot Family Planning Program" was laid out in three parts: action, promotion, and research. Operational from July 1962 it was distinct from the women's program, though closely related.

The action phase of the program was launched in the villages where the women's program was first in operation. It was carried on through the women organizers in the village, the organizers of the village-based cooperatives, the village midwives, and the village doctors. Each of these groups had a three-week training program at the Academy which was continued one day a week thereafter. Each group took family planning supplies from the Academy and distributed them. A record was made of each purchase.

By May 1963, 383 families in 11 villages had purchased supplies one or more times. An effort was made, for purposes of research, to keep the action program confined to the members of the cooperatives in the project villages. But it was soon found that more than half of the participants were nonmembers, and that people from other villages came seeking to purchase supplies. This latter was permitted, with only a record kept of the village of the purchaser. These facts suggest that purchasers prefer a degree of anonymity. In fact, the strict record-keeping of the project affected the operations adversely from the beginning. Later programs of mass distribution of supplies respected the preference for anonymity.

The nonmedical supplies used, condoms and foam tablets, were provided by the government, which permitted them to be sold at a nominal price to retailers and to be retailed at a small profit.

The number of villages in the program rose to 35 in 1965, but was reduced to 22 in 1966 to provide better supervision. The largest number of families participating, up to 1965, was 838.

After the introduction of the government program in July 1965 the Comilla family planning project became an integral part of the larger governmental effort. The Academy, however, continued to supervise the program in Comilla thana and to do research and provide training for the program.

The Academy carried out a considerable promotion effort in the villages. There were discussions of family planning at least twice a year in the weekly meetings of the village cooperatives. A film show was put on in each village once a year, followed up by staff visits. The women organizers, who were in training weekly at the Academy, did continuous promotion work among the village women. Propaganda was also carried on through the union council chairmen and members, model farmers of the local cooperative societies, schoolteachers, and the participants in the women's program. Most family planning meetings were in conjunction with some other Academy-sponsored activity.

The first contacts in the villages, after the interest of the cooperative organizer had been secured, were usually talks to groups of ten to fifteen men. Use was often made of pictures, flannel boards, and flash cards that had been developed by local artists. If interest was shown, the group was told of the possibility of a film show, provided that they would nominate a member of their group to make all local arrangements, assure the presence of a large number of women, and take care of incidental expenses. These film shows, often the first ever seen in the villages, were accompanied by discussions. Other films shown on the same occasion dealt with agricultural mechanization, travel, sanitation, and so on. Two family planning leaflets were produced at the Academy in August 1963, the one *Kaeno Choto Paribar* ("Small Family, Why?"), the other *Zami Chhotto Haowa O-Paribar Parikalpana* ("Fragmentation of Holdings and Family Planning"). In 1964 a family planning film, *Paribartan*, was made by the Department of Health and the Academy.

Concurrently with the action program, the Academy added a research component to the total effort which has served to guide, record, and evaluate the action program and to provide a base for formulating policy decisions. Thus as early as 1960 one of the faculty members made a survey of the attitudes of rural families toward family planning covering such topics as (1) acceptability of various contraceptive methods, (2) the social, emotional, and physiological problems faced by rural people in practicing contraceptive methods, and (3) the importance of local agents in the propagation of contraceptive practices and methods of distributing supplies.[11] The results of this investigation coupled with the wisdom of Akhter Hameed Khan about village conditions and general villager reactions to innovation served to guide the initial efforts.

To carry on this three-pronged program, as well as the later-developed mass distribution and IUD (intrauterine device) programs, the Academy has had assistance from several sources. The East Pakistan Department of Health provided technical personnel when the Academy began its family planning training and action activities, and from mid-1965 has been the official sponsor of the program. The Population Council, Inc., has provided program counsel,

[11] Wiqar H. Zaidi, *A Survey of Attitudes of Rural Population toward Family Planning*, Comilla, PAVD, 1961.

two research associates, and some audio-visual support. In addition, there were two Peace Corps Volunteer nurses, mentioned above in connection with the women's education work, and occasional experts as needed for the inauguration of the IUD program.

SOME REACTIONS FROM THE VILLAGERS

A picture of the day-to-day work of the village women family planning organizers was compiled from the field notes of a Pakistani lady staff member. A village organizer tells how she began her work:

I did it with great trepidation, because most of the men didn't even want to hear about it. I talked about family planning with the women very, very privately, but while the men were at home. But when the men weren't at home I gathered the women together in a group, and I led a discussion among the women. Later, when the classes in sewing, maternal and child health, health and sanitation, and poultry began, then it was even more convenient to have discussions about family planning.

Another organizer explained to some wives whose husbands objected on religious grounds:

Look, if you are two or three months pregnant and you kill the child, then it is a sin. But if you use the medicine, then you won't get a child. So how is that killing? If you have the child, then you won't be able to feed and clothe it properly. You won't be able to treat it when it's sick. Then, if the child dies, it will certainly be a sin. In this way I made them understand.

After this conversation those women who felt the need to use this stuff tried to convince their husbands, and if their husbands were persuaded, they took supplies. And those women whose husbands were not persuaded took no supplies. There are still many husbands who are not persuaded.[12]

A village organizer estimated that half or more of the 60 participating couples for whom she furnishes supplies may believe the practice is against religion, but they accept it anyway, justifying it on the basis of the health of the wives and children. One mother with six children said: "Even if it is a sin, I'll do it! To save (my) life is *foruz* (a commandment of Islam)."

To counteract the fears that family planning is in conflict with the teachings of Islam, Director Khan, who is a scholar of Islamic theology and culture, made a number of speeches in late 1960 on "Islamic Opinions on Contraception." His views were set forth in two articles in the Academy *Journal*.[13] The first was a commentary on the writings of Al Ghazzali and Ibn Kaiyim, two highly respected Muslim theologians and jurists, which indicated that the practice of contraception had been approved by the consensus of the early learned *Ulemas:*

The ancient theologians have freely discussed the question of contraception and an eminent majority have declared it valid and proper.... Al Ghazzali declares that a Muslim may adopt contraceptive precautions for graceful living, to preserve his wife's beauty and vigour, or to escape numerous anxieties caused by a large family.

[12] A. Majeed Khan and Harvey M. Choldin, "Family Planning in Three Villages," (a preliminary report; mimeographed), Comilla, PARD, August 1964.

[13] Akhter Hameed Khan, "Islamic Opinions on Contraception," Comilla, *Journal*, PAVD, Vol. 1, Nos. 3 and 4, August and October, 1960.

The second was a general discussion of the writings of these two ancient scholars in the context of present-day social and economic conditions:

It is fortunate for the Islamic community (so meticulous in its regard for precedents, and so respectful of the ancients), to have such a decisive verdict on the propriety of an individual planning his family. . . .

If the Ulemas of today would study carefully the new economic and social factors and if they would respond properly to the new challenge, they would advise the Muslims to discard the old preference for many wives and children, and to adopt family planning as a policy for the common welfare. The Ulemas of today would find no religious injunctions against this view. . . .

The articles were reproduced in pamphlet form in English and in Bengali, and distributed widely.

By mid-1966 two Imams had become agents for family planning supplies in either the action-research or the mass-distribution program.

Purdah too is slowly yielding to the impact of the women's education and family planning programs. Hundreds of village women appear at the Academy every week now, often with their faces uncovered. The picture is changing —from the shy, burqa-shrouded, noncommunicative village woman of yesterday to the serious and articulate woman of tomorrow. This change is typified by the comely young Bengali mother, a family planning organizer, leaving the Academy with a child in one arm and under the other arm a metal display sign: *Family Planning Supplies Sold Here.*

MASS DISTRIBUTION OF NONMEDICAL SUPPLIES

On the basis of what had been learned in the action-research program, a new widespread distribution system was started in 1964. This facilitated the use of male agents, and provided a ready means for men to purchase contraceptives in near secrecy with no records kept except of the amount of supplies sold to each commercial agent.

This system placed supplies in shops, bazaars, and with individual agents—cooperative leaders, union councilors, midwives, housewives, and others as arranged—throughout the thana. The nominal prices of supplies worked out for the action-research project were applied. Publicity shows to acquaint the people with the new program were put on to attract crowds at the markets and elsewhere that men gathered. Each sales agent was given posters to display on the inside of his shop, and a standard metal sign for outside display.

The staff for the thana-wide mass distribution program was at first housed in a single office at Abhoy Ashram. It was made up of the family planning officer, one male and one female field inspector and two male field assistants. The family planning officer procures the supplies, supervises the field staff, prepares training materials, and arranges for local publicity. The field inspectors and assistants recruit, train, and supervise the sales agents, keep an up-to-date record of supplies left with them, arrange publicity and other meetings in the villages, and make weekly reports to the district family planning officer. The female member of the staff works with the female agents, maintains the register of supplies left with them, sets up village meetings for women, and keeps in touch with the thana office. The family planning officer has a jeep, the male field workers have bicycles, and the female worker uses rickshaws. Within three months 61 male and 51 female agents had taken supplies, and by mid-1966 there were over 600 agents in both rural and urban areas. The 1966–1967 annual report of the Academy indicated that 332 male and 283 female agents sold 50,938 dozens of condoms and 11,287 dozens of foam tablets and assisted in popularizing surgical methods, described below. A recent report shows that in October and November 1968, 572 agents sold 11,152 dozens of condoms, 1,280 dozens of foam tablets, and 31 bottles of Dura-foam tablets.

In early 1965 a system of chief agents was started in Comilla thana. Nine at first, they were later increased to 13. They visit the male salesmen in their zones fortnightly to replenish supplies, and to take them any relevant information learned from their regular visits to the Academy.

After July 1965 when the new national family planning scheme for the Third Five-Year Plan was launched, the mass distribution program was expanded to the whole of Comilla district. The family planning officers of the 21 thanas in the district attend a monthly conference at the Academy; refresher and other courses continue to be given there for thana and district family planning officers. As is typical of programs which have reached some stage of maturity, the Academy has prepared a training manual that makes it possible to train large numbers more efficiently.

PUBLICIZING THE PROGRAM

Various types of publicity are used. Local *zari* singers are employed to learn about family planning and then write and sing songs about it in the market places and villages. Portable tape recorders have recently been used to play some of the songs to the village women who, because of purdah, cannot attend the market shows. The results to date have been encouraging.

Here is an introductory song a family planning team leader, a *sardar*, sings (after each line a chorus chants a repetition of the main thought):

Let me explain why a man should plan in his life, and why family planning is important.

How does God create human beings?

He does it within a plan.

God made a plan, so man should plan in every sphere of his life.

If a man builds a house he has a plan.

The plan is made first of all, and after that the builder is called in.

Then the work can begin.

Such planning is necessary in every sphere of life.

In family life the husband and wife should first make a plan, and then with this plan build a family.

Without planning a man is quite helpless in this world.

A planned family brings happiness to a man's house, to his home.

In April 1966 the Comilla folk-singer team was invited by Radio Pakistan to record some songs on family planning. Three such songs were recorded and since then have been broadcast on different programs. A variety of posters and illustrated instruction sheets are available, too, for use by agents, and province-wide publicity has occurred on the radio along with programs on development; billboard signs are widely displayed throughout the province; and advertisements have been carried in the daily newspapers.

IUD PROGRAM AND SURGICAL METHODS

When it became clear that the intrauterine device would be given considerable emphasis in the family planning section of the Third Five-Year Plan, an IUD clinic was established at Abhoy Ashram. It was equipped and operated in accordance with the recommendation of the National Research Institute for Family Planning, Karachi.

The female staff of family planning and the women's education program informed the village women of the availability at the Abhoy Ashram clinic of this new contraceptive device. The village women showed some interest, and by 1967 a total of nearly 3,000 coils had been inserted, in addition to 857 at a clinic in town.

Attempts have also been made to popularize surgical methods but with considerably less success. The annual report covering the period from June 1966 to May 1967 indicates that no vasectomies were performed and no tube ligations. But a report in late 1968 shows that in October and November there were performed 223 vasectomies and three tube ligations.

FAMILY PLANNING AND THE COMILLA PROGRAM

A national seminar on family planning was held at Comilla in early February of 1966. It was inaugurated by the provincial minister of Health, Labor and Social Welfare. The chief guest was the central minister of Education, Health, Labor and Social Welfare. Numerous papers were presented, and active discussions ensued. By means of this seminar, the training of family planning officers, and research publications, the Academy has continued to assist with this expanding activity.

The relationship of family planning to the Comilla program as a whole was summarized for a United Nations conference in the fall of 1965. The family planning pilot project, it was reported:

> has worked within the context of the comprehensive development project, in close connection with the cooperative and women's education projects. At first, when the approach was more tentative, family planning was introduced only in villages with cooperative societies, through the societies. After it was observed that the villagers were interested in family planning and would not resist efforts to promote it, the project expanded to other villages. Mindful that the cooperatives and women's programmes were not available in most other places in the province, a system was devised working without them.
>
> First ten villages were studied, then 35 villages joined. Then the project expanded to approach all 246 villages of the area (thana) plus three additional areas of equal size (the first three additional thanas with Comilla-like programs).
>
> The method of promotion changed from an intensive to an extensive approach. In both approaches villagers and officers are teachers, the center is utilized, and teaching is repetitive and continuous.[14]

Research on Family Planning

In accordance with the general policy of the Academy, the family planning program utilizes village organizers and

[14] A. Majeed Khan and Harvey M. Choldin, "Application of a Theory of Rural Development to Family Planning in East Pakistan," *United Nations, World Population Conference*, Belgrade, Yugoslavia, August–September 1965, WPC/WP/426, pp. 3–4.

family planning agents who are under constant training and supervision. Extensive records are kept which provide data for analysis and research. In addition to the mass distribution of supplies described above, intensive attention has been given to "research villages" which started with 8 in 1962 and rose to 22 through 1964–1966. Three hundred and fifty-nine families were participating in the program in May 1967. In addition to accurate records of the sale of supplies, records are maintained on reasons for dropouts, age of participants, literacy rates, land holdings of participants, length of married life, total number of pregnancies, and number of living children. The accumulated data have been analyzed by two demographers, provided by the Population Council, Inc., working with Pakistani researchers. The results through 1966 indicated, in the words of the demographers:

First let us assume that the selected villages had a crude birth rate resembling the provincial rate of around 45 per thousand for all five years, and that the pregnancies occurring in these villages (without an allowance for pregnancy wastage) resulted in births. Since the rates of pregnancy reduction obtained, the crude birth rate of the villagers would have been reduced by approximately eleven points in 1964–1965 (allowing for gestation). However, this reduction would drop to approximately eight and six points in 1965–1966 and 1966–1967 respectively. If the rate of 1964–1965 could have been maintained then the national goal of a ten point reduction in the crude birth rate would have been attained. . . . In general the effectiveness or impact of the programme resembles a bell-shaped curve, i.e., in the initial phases the pregnancy reduction increased to reach a plateau and then declined in the remaining phases. However, it should be pointed out that this may represent a cyclical occurrence and that pregnancy reduction may again increase. Continual follow-up research is necessary for an extended time period to analyze any additional trends in fertility reduction.[15]

The authors of the above-quoted study append an interpretive note referring to the comments of Director Khan concerning this study:

Firstly, it has taken over five years for various agricultural practices to be adopted. Adoption of family planning, which involves more radical changes in attitude and behavior, will necessarily take longer, possibly ten years. Secondly, he maintains that perhaps the Academy may be working at cross pressures in promoting affluence (relative to previous depressed conditions in the Comilla area) in the community which in turn has the effect of reducing the rate of adoption of family planning.

These facts and this interpretation perhaps provide a clue to the complexity of comprehensive rural improvement in developing countries.

A more extensive study of fertility trends in Comilla thana collected by ten female interviewers of a sample of 1,600 currently married women, using the Bogue pregnancy history technique, offers the more optimistic conclusion that "fertility has declined by approximately 27 per cent in the thana between 1958 and 1967." The results reflect the impact of the "organizer approach" to family planning as well as the commercial distribution program.[16]

[15] John E. Stoeckel and Moqbul A. Choudhury, *The Impact of the Organization Approach to Family Planning on Fertility in Comilla*, Comilla, PARD, April 1967, pp. 16–17.
[16] John E. Stoeckel and Moqbul A. Choudhury, *Fertility Trends in Comilla Kotwali Thana*, Comilla, PARD (undated).

7. Some Experiments in Rural Education

The historical context for the educational experiments which are described in this chapter was set forth by Akhter Hameed Khan in a speech delivered as one of a series at Michigan State University on "Rural Development in East Pakistan." Director Khan pointed out that the educational system of Pakistan had been a subject of criticism for several decades; but still it remained basically almost the same as it was under British rule—inherently inadequate and irrelevant to the needs of the nation. This system of education, he continued, has a clerical and urban bias, and is a legacy from the nineteenth century and of course a contribution of the foreign rulers. He said further:

The nineteenth century European education did have a clerical bias. If somebody went to high school or to college, it was to get a classical education. It was to become a gentleman. It was to become what was then called a clerk, a person who was not concerned with manual labour, with craftmanship, with technology in general, but a person who held a white collar job. Our educational system was based upon this assumption; the purpose of an education was to make a person a gentleman and not a technician.

In Europe, and especially in the United States, a great evolu-

Some Experiments in Rural Education 187

tion took place because of the growth of science and technology; and education acquired a different bias. . . . In colonial countries that kind of evolution did not take place in the nineteenth century or even in the early part of the twentieth century. . . . We have finally realized that it is a curious type of education indeed which would make everybody a clerk and which would have nothing to do with real life. . . . Eighty per cent of our people are living in villages as farmers, yet you find the strange situation that the syllabus which is being taught in the primary and the high school has almost nothing to do with agriculture.[1]

"The result of this defective system," as stated by the Academy's instructor in education, "has proved to be disastrous for the nation. Those who receive education become necessarily apathetic towards physical labour, as in our curriculum there is little scope for practical work. It is mostly theoretical and abstract study. Because of its urban bias, the educated youths hanker after office jobs, preferably in urban areas. And agriculture is looked upon as a base profession. Thus the education of the dropouts of rural schools does not make them eligible for office jobs and their mentality prevents them becoming enthusiastic farmers. So they become liabilities rather than assets to their poor farmer-parents and their education becomes unproductive."[2]

Another feature of elementary education in East Pakistan was that much of this education was in the hands of the Imams, the religious leaders who conducted the very

---

[1] Akhter Hameed Khan, *Rural Development in East Pakistan*, Michigan State University, Asian Studies Center, Occasional Paper No. 2, Spring 1965, p. 4.
[2] Ali Asgar Bhuiyan, *Youth Work at Comilla*, Comilla, PARD, February 1968, pp. 1–3.

conservative madrassas or religious schools. Quoting Director Khan again:

... for a boy who goes to one of the religious schools, the madrassas, his studies would be based on the Greek astronomy and Greek physiology and Greek anatomy, which were transmitted through Arabic translations about a thousand years ago. A man who learns about the physician's trade in these old religious schools would not know about the circulation of the blood as it was discovered by Harvey. Or a person who has studied astronomy sometimes would not even know about the rotation of the earth around the sun. He would say the sun rotates around the earth. And yet he would be one of those who occupy a position of influence among the common people. Like a fossil, the syllabus in these religious schools has remained almost the same as it was about a thousand years ago. A parallel of our schism would be if, say, at the University of Oxford or the University of Cambridge the same syllabus were being taught today as was taught in the twelfth and thirteenth centuries.[3]

When the Academy started its program in mid-1959, only one-fifth of the population in Comilla thana over five years of age was literate, and the proportion was less than in the previous census. In mid-1966 it was estimated by the Academy's instructor in education that about two-fifths of this age group were literate.

The Comilla experience indicates that education, formal and informal, is an essential part of the development process. Once that process gets under way, unschooled children begin to attend school when facilities are provided for them and when their parents and guardians expect them to go. Adult illiterates begin to learn to read and write and figure when they have a reason to do so.

[3] Akhter Hameed Khan, *op. cit.*, p. 2.

Some Experiments in Rural Education 189

The pre-Academy low rate of literacy was a measure of the people's widespread lack of hope. The rate was lower in the villages than in the towns, and much lower for the women than for the men. Over 95 per cent of the women were illiterate in most villages. Not to be able to read and write and figure seems to have resulted as much from the lack of any everyday need for these skills as from lack of schools and teachers. The teachers in the areas with the lowest literacy rates were the most likely to be tardy or absent. The people in these areas put less value on education. The inspector in turn paid least attention to these "unimportant" schools.

This chapter deals with experimental programs that originated at the Academy. Some of these have already been adopted by the provincial Department of Education, and others are still under its consideration. The four main programs are: (1) introduction of a "rural bias" (farm-life related education) in all of the rural schools in Comilla thana through a pilot school project; (2) the "feeder schools" program (one-teacher village schools for small children and adult illiterates), started in early 1963 in the villages with cooperative societies; (3) the training of village women to teach literacy classes in the villages and to teach small children in government primary schools; and (4) the school plant improvement project launched in early 1964 as a part of the public works program.

A "Rural Bias" Pilot School Project

The need for a rural bias in the school curriculum was among the recommendations of the National Education Commission of 1961 which were accepted by the government. In accordance with these recommendations, the Academy undertook a pilot school project in late 1961. As a beginning the headmasters of 20 primary schools were invited to the Academy fortnightly for half-day sessions on how to relate their schools to the everyday needs of the students. These teachers were at first very much on the defensive and generally unwilling even to consider any changes in the curriculum. After a few months, however, they became tolerant and then actively interested in the experiment. Most convincing of all to them was the eagerness with which their pupils, boys and girls, carried on the individual student projects that were being undertaken.

Youth clubs (*Sabuj Sangha*), with boys and girls as members, were formed in each of the 20 pilot schools. Each club member agreed to carry out a farm- or home-related project during the year. It was hoped that these coeducational clubs would do for the school children of the Comilla area something of what the 4-H Clubs and Future Farmers of America had done for the farm children of the United States. These projects were looked upon as a way to introduce into the Bengali village some improved farming practices, and at the same time show how education should go along with work rather than merely provide an escape from work.

All eleven of the schools in villages with cooperative societies in 1961 were included in this first pilot project. It was hoped by the Academy representatives that in each school there could also be developed one or more groups of community activities, such as a parent-teacher association; a small museum to display local cottage industry products, crops, trees, insects, and soil types; and a cooperative store run by the students.

Some headway was made on each of these goals. By the end of the first half year, scores of student projects had been started in the 20 schools, group projects in seven,

Some Experiments in Rural Education 191

parent-teacher associations in eight, cooperative stores in eight, small museums in 12, and exhibitions of projects in three.

Another accomplishment of this first year was a three-day seminar on "Children's Literature." It was organized by the Academy because of the lack of library books, and often even of textbooks for the pupils. As a result, in the next few months 43 booklets were brought out in Bengali on agriculture, health, sanitation, and the lives of great men. A young woman Peace Corps Volunteer interested in library operations, who had begun to work with the Academy library, assisted in the production of these publications. Two other Peace Corps Volunteers subsequently served in the development of the program.

Early in 1963 the number of pilot schools had risen to 40. Youth clubs were active in all of them. The headmasters served as club leaders, meeting fortnightly at the Academy. An illustrated Bengali booklet, "Modern Village Teacher," was prepared and distributed, telling how the teacher can assist in the all-round development of the students and the community.

HOME AND FARM PROJECTS

The first Annual Youth Rally was held in January 1963 with an attendance of about 2,500 students. More than a thousand of the best of the student projects, selected from the various school clubs, were put on display, including cabbages, fruit-laden tomato vines, squash, and melons, flowers of many kinds, small animals and fowls, paintings and sketches, hand-sewn garments, crocheted pieces, and an assortment of toys—tin, bamboo, wood, and paper. The most common toys were the model airplanes, each of which proudly bore the letters PIA (Pakistan International Airlines). Practical prizes such as kerosene lanterns, jars of insecticide, watering cans, and flashlights were awarded for the outstanding projects in each category.

In 1963–1964, 19 additional primary schools in the thana were brought into the program, making a total of 59. Their headmasters joined the fortnightly conferences at Abhoy Ashram. The assistant teachers, too, began to come for training in student agriculture project work, first aid, and inoculation. In September 1963 the teachers decided to introduce a monthly examination system, the teaching of English, and the development of a school library, and to seek the aid of model farmers in the teaching of agriculture in the schools.

Three thousand students were on hand for the 1964 annual Youth Rally, and nearly 2,500 student projects were displayed; they were chosen from among 15,000 projects entered in the competition at the local schools. Practical prizes were again given, and in addition 100 silver medals, struck by a local silversmith, were awarded to boys and girls who had won first place.

The pilot school project for 1965–1966 was expanded to 68 primary schools in Comilla thana. A total of 3,990 Sabuj Sangha members carried out over 18,000 projects, most of them involving the raising of vegetables.

In mid-1966, 41 schools had small student cooperative stores, with a total capital of Rs. 1,025. Perhaps most promising of all was the growth of the students' savings program, which started with six schools in September 1965 and total deposits of Rs. 83, and by 1966 involved 33 schools with total student deposits of Rs. 2,396. The number of schools with libraries had increased to 62 and the number of books to over 4,000.

By the 1967–1968 year, 69 schools were in the program;

Some Experiments in Rural Education 193

the youth clubs had 5,250 members, both boys and girls, out of 6,148 enrolled students in the participating schools. The officers of the clubs had been elected by the students. Sixty-five simple libraries had been established, with 5,550 books. The 29 "museums" included samples of soils, seeds, fertilizers, insects, insecticides, and other items related to agriculture or of rural interest; these displays were somewhat standardized by a manual on school museums. Some 36 savings accounts totaled Rs. 1,974 made by 956 depositors who followed policies similar to their parents as members of cooperative societies. Twenty-six school cooperative stores had for sale pens, pencils, and paper, with a capital of more than Rs. 1,600. Students were engaged in more than 23,000 home-related or agricultural projects.

ADMINISTRATION OF THE PROGRAM

A major change in the administration of the program occurred in 1966–1967 when responsiblity for managing and funding was shifted from the Academy to the Agricultural Cooperatives Federation of the central cooperative (KTCCA). The change involved a decision on the part of the Agricultural Cooperatives Federation to provide Rs. 10,000 to cover the employment of a supervisor, to pay traveling allowances for head and assistant teachers to attend training meetings at the Thana Training and Development Center; to pay for expenses of conducting annual rallies at ten zonal centers in the thana, and to pay for prizes. A closer linkage was achieved between the major rural modernization programs of the KTCCA and the similar but smaller projects being conducted by the youth club members through their association with model farmers, cooperative leaders, KTCCA officials, and others being trained at the center. And the other way around, the enthusiasm of the youth and their acceptance of cooperative principles and the importance of literacy had a stimulating effect on their elders.

Even though the annual report of the Academy for 1966–1967 identified serious problems related to supervision of the program and continued resistance to it in various quarters, it seemed clear that a working model for replication elsewhere in the province had been created and that a basis for policy changes in the provincial educational system was being formulated. Later reports of the Academy showed no major changes in the program.

"Feeder Schools" and Classes for Adult Illiterates

By late 1962, with the women's education program and family planning activities already well underway, there were more and more reports of opposition from the village religious leaders, especially the Imams. They had been trained in the traditional religious schools and so, unacquainted with modern science and technology, were on the defensive as they saw change being promoted all about them.

The Imam's role as the arbiter of fate was gradually being undermined by the systematic use of sprays to keep down crop and animal pests, by the opening up of drainage canals to reduce the damage of the floods, and the inoculation of the villagers to prevent the spread of the age-old scourges of smallpox, cholera, and typhoid. Some Imams complained to the Academy that members of the village cooperative societies were making less use of their services.

Of all the things that were happening in the villages as a result of the Academy's activities, the family planning and the program for women caused the Imams the greatest misgivings. When the question of the acceptability of family planning to Muslim belief came up soon after the Academy was opened, Director Khan's pamphlet on the subject, previously referred to, provided a temporary answer. But many of the Imams remained far from convinced. Something further needed to be done. The solution was to interest the Imams in the program and to involve them as teachers, first arranging for their training, of course. So at last in the Bengali countryside a bit of reconciliation was introduced in the century-old schism between religious and secular education.

To launch this program the cooperative organizers invited the Imams to the Academy to meet with Director Khan. He reminded them of their ancient and honorable role as teachers and said he thought they would be interested in this proposal as a way for them to perform their rightful role in the community. He told them further that they would need to study to become good teachers of small children and of illiterate adults, and that the Academy would design a one-day-a-week training course for them, which would include instructions to improve their religious knowledge.

Nearly all of the 68 Imams who assembled at the Academy agreed to enter this weekly training program at the Academy and to organize schools. This number rose to 118 by mid-1963. Most of the Imams received a monthly salary from the cooperative society of around Rs. 20; a few received only Rs. 15—small amounts, and not always paid out ungrudgingly. But the societies "after the usual hesitation of villagers about parting with cash regularly for services rendered" agreed to support the program.[4] Rickshaw

[4] *Fourth Annual Report of the Academy, 1962–1963*, Comilla, PARD, June 1963, p. 59.

fares to the weekly training class were paid by the Academy.

The new village school for the young children was called a "feeder school" because it was planned that its graduates would feed into Class II of the regular government primary school. To facilitate this transfer, the standard curriculum of the government schools was used. This was some strain on the Imams, for they had hitherto given religious instruction only. The Academy staff encouraged them in their weekly meetings to share their new teaching experiences. The staff knew that some of them would be more effective than others and that it was these who could best teach the others.

Special training materials were developed for the Imams, including instruction sheets to help them set up and conduct their classes. A circulating library, too, was organized for their use, as was also a four-page weekly newspaper. Later, as will be seen, the Imams themselves produced some booklets appropriate for use by neoliterates.

The books of the circulating library were placed in small plastic satchels, which the Imams took home with them from the Academy for the week. Each satchel had two or three small books in it, which were replaced by new ones upon the Imams' next visit to the Academy. Thus in a six months' period each Imam had carried to his village from 50 to 75 different books. It was a colorful sight—these scores of robed and bearded men coming and going from the Academy with their gaily colored satchels.

The newspaper brought out by the Academy for the Imams and other villagers was called *Jana-o-Jana* (to know or not to know). Written in very simple Bengali and illustrated with line drawings, it was designed to acquaint the villagers with the world in which they live. The first issue,

Some Experiments in Rural Education 197

early in 1963, discussed the relationship between the sun and the earth. Several of the Imams were a bit disturbed about the idea of the world being round. Some of the village women expressed surprise that people in other parts of the world were having daylight when they were having night. The next issue dealt with the continents, then Asia, then Pakistan, then East Pakistan, and then Comilla thana. Other series presented the biological sciences down to germs, agriculture down to the sprouting of the seed and how fertilizer feeds the growing plant, the weather down to the local storm and flood. The paper was published for about 18 months.

In the second year the number of feeder schools was reduced to 86, as the curriculum was standardized and only the better trained Imams could qualify. Each school was set up for three classes, the first two for a half-year each, and the last for a whole year. In mid-March 1965, the first annual rally of the Imams was held at the Academy, at which Director Khan addressed them and congratulated them on their accomplishments. During this year the first booklet of short stories written by Imams was published.

The parents' appreciation for these new schools is reflected in their buying textbooks for their children, in sending their children—about 5,000 of them in 1963—to the classes (especially girls, who were more numerous than boys in the feeder schools), and in many villages arranging for a schoolroom more suitable than the mosque. The adult education activities of the evening classes were also substantial, reaching a total attendance of more than 1,000 that year.

During 1964–1965, the number of schools increased to 88, employing a total of 96 Imams. Because of the hesitancy of some cooperative societies to pay them, it was decided that their salaries would be paid by the KTCCA; monthly salaries were Rs. 25, Rs. 20, and Rs. 15, depending on competence. A First Primer for the feeder schools was published by the Academy and immediately became the standard text. Also a second booklet of stories by the Imams was published. The stories used were selected by competition, with each winner receiving a prize.

In March 1965 a three-man evaluation team, headed by the president of the provincial intermediate and secondary education board studied the feeder schools and found them satisfactorily operated. In the following month the second annual rally of the Imams was held, with an important Muslim leader as the chief guest.

The feeder school program was officially accepted by the provincial director of public instruction in 1965–1966, and his office arranged to incorporate 26 feeder schools, staffed with the best-qualified Imam teachers, into the public school system as "extension primary schools." The teachers became regular employees of the government and received a monthly salary of Rs. 50.

During the year when the use of Imams as teachers was under the supervision of the provincial director of public instruction, nine of the Imams who participated in the Academy-directed program were dismissed, and sixteen other Imams were employed to teach in extension centers. They were paid the regular salaries of primary teachers of one-room schools. This change appeared to have regularized the program, but important differences in the spirit and content of the program had a negative effect, as seen in the following comments by the Academy staff:

> The Academy programme with the Imams was a multipurpose one. It was not just a one-teacher primary school like the government plan. It was aimed not only to eradicate illiteracy,

but also to break the artificial division between secular and religious education. It tried to utilize the services of the Imams fruitfully in carrying out development programs in rural areas. The dismissals of the Imams by the ADPI was considered injurious. Therefore it was felt necessary to revive the programme. In the first phase of the revival, a 16-day training programme was planned and arranged for the Imams. This training programme for the Imam teachers had some new features. Residential facilities of the Academy were made available to them. The syllabus for this training contained both the content of their course and the methods of teaching children and adults. Some guest speakers including the District Judge and the Deputy Commissioner spoke to them on subjects like Western jurisprudence, district administration, education for men, etc. A study tour was arranged and the instructor took them to places of historical importance and to modern industrial units. All these new arrangements were made to broaden their outlook.[5]

The Academy program was resumed the next year (1966) and has continued since on a relatively modest but continuing basis, with problems of quality of performance, attendance at training meetings, and some resistance to the concept persisting. In 1967–1968, 116 Imams taught 2,538 adults and 3,433 feeder-school children.[6] Perhaps it is not too optimistic to stay with the appraisal of 1963 which follows:

This program of universal literacy within a few years, its low cost and the enthusiasm which it evokes in the villagers, holds out great promise. The cost of training 120 Imams one day a week for a year does not exceed fifteen thousand rupees.

[5] *Eighth Annual Report of the Academy, 1966–1967*, Comilla, PARD, November 1967, pp. 72–73.
[6] *Ninth Annual Report of the Academy, 1967–1968*, Comilla, PARD, September 1968, p. 76.

Schoolhouse and pay of teachers is contributed by the villagers. Thus within a year five thousand children and one thousand adults in 120 villages, most of whom otherwise would have remained illiterate, are learning to read and write. Besides, the Imams, instead of enjoying the anomalous position of material neglect and spiritual veneration, have become essential functionaries. Nothing pleases us more than to see their new pride and confidence. When they also call for economic prosperity and social justice it will be an imperious call.[7]

No province-wide extension of the feeder school idea has been put into effect, although a recommendation to this end was made to the East Pakistan Department of Education in November 1965.

Nonmatriculate Village Women Teachers

The introduction of women teachers into the primary schools, it was believed by the Academy, would result in better teaching for the small children and would encourage the enrollment of girls. The program got underway in 1963. "The idea of introducing a female teacher in primary schools working with male teachers is revolutionary," Director Khan commented. "It was possible because of our cooperative villages and also the policy of the recruitment of a lady teacher from the same village where she could work."[8]

As originally worked out, the village women recruited for teachers would have passed Class V, and would generally be between the ages of 15 and 30. Recruitment was to

---

[7] Akhter Hameed Khan and M. Zakir Hussain, *A New Rural Cooperative System for Comilla Thana* (Third Annual Report, 1962–1963), Comilla, PARD, July 1963, pp. 18–19.

[8] *Monthly Report of the Academy, November 1963*, Comilla, PARD, p. 34.

be made of nonmatriculates, because practically no village women had reached the matriculate level (ten years of schooling). It was further thought that only village women would be acceptable, or available, to teach in the village schools.

The village women selected were given a month's training at the Academy, returning after employment for in-service training one day a week. The project began on an experimental basis with 25 women chosen by the village cooperative societies. Three types of teaching appointments, it was believed, would be available for the women: in the government primary schools as assistant teachers to work in the lower grades; in the new cooperative schools that were to be set up in the villages for women and girl illiterates; and in the regular adult village literacy classes. It was assumed that the women teachers who were appointed in the government primary schools would receive a monthly salary of around Rs. 25.

By mid-1965, 39 village women trained at the Academy were serving as teachers in the government primary schools in Comilla thana on an experimental basis, and another 33 were teaching literacy classes for girls and women. In these literacy classes were 844 enrollees.

Despite the apparent success of the program, as of mid-1968 no action has been taken by the provincial educational authorities regarding the introduction of women teachers in other thanas. Meanwhile adult literacy programs had been formed in Comilla, with 45 women teachers and a total enrollment of 1,391, in 45 centers. Eight of these were being conducted by newly literate women teachers who themselves had but recently got their literacy certificates, and in turn had organized centers in their own villages.

In 1967–1968, 811 first certificates, 617 second certificates, and 218 third or final certificates of literacy were awarded, through the efforts of both women and Imam teachers. Contrasted with the slow pace of this phase of the Academy's program is the fact that the women, as indicated earlier, were making substantial advances in the area of handicrafts, cooperatives, family planning, and health activities.

The School Works Program[9]

A school works program was first proposed by Director Khan in a meeting of the headmasters of the government primary schools in October 1963. Each headmaster agreed to submit an itemized list of the basic physical improvements needed at his school that could utilize the labor of students and teachers. By January 1964 work was initiated in 74 schools. The government allotted Rs. 266,000 to the Academy for this purpose.

The program was patterned after the rural public works program, then in its third year in the thana. The objectives of the school works programs were: to involve students in repair and construction work, and to provide them with vocational experience; to involve teachers in welfare planning for their schools, and to enable them to take an active part in work with the students; to provide earning opportunities for students; to involve the community itself in building up the school and planning for its upkeep; to improve the school buildings and facilities; and to find a way of

[9] The next several pages are summarized from two reports by Abdul Muyeed: *School Works Programme, Comilla Kotwali Thana*, 1963–1964, and a similar report for 1964–1965, Comilla, PARD, February 1965 and March 1966, respectively.

implementing the school works program in other thanas based upon the experiences of this pilot project.

Three committees were to administer the program: a new school works executive committee of Academy staff members; a new project committee for each school, chaired by the headmaster, with its membership made up of other teachers, the local union councilor, and influential villagers; and an education subcommittee formed earlier by each union council. The circle officer requisitioned the project money from the government. The chairman and secretary of the school project committee, each of whom signed a bond, received the money from the circle officer and disbursed it against vouchers of purchases made, receipts from employed craftsmen, and the muster rolls of teachers and students who had worked on the project. The union subcommittee visited the projects to see that the program was being carried out as planned.

It was difficult going at first. The 74 original estimates had been presented in all sorts of ways. They were sent back to the headmasters for revision. The new estimates, received in a week, were more understandable, but were still far from what was needed.

The Academy's second request for clarification was accompanied by a set of guidelines for recasting the estimates, which indicated, among other things, the types of projects that would be approved: repair, reconstruction, and extension of school buildings; repair and construction of school furniture; development of playgrounds; construction of sanitary latrines and urinals; repair of existing approach roads; tube well sinking for drinking water; and tree planting.

The estimates were to give a full description of the

work project with a breakdown of expenditures for materials and labor. Only work which could not be done by teachers and students was to be done by outside labor. The estimates submitted for advances were to include the starting date and the probable completion date of the project. After further refinements of submissions, the program got underway in less than three months, as already noted, from the time it was first proposed to the headmasters.

Some of the headmasters set up school project committees without consulting the local people. This resulted in much dissatisfaction. A few of the schoolhouses were located on private land, and so could not qualify for project support until they had been made public property. Furthermore, regular government grants were at this time being made to some schools for new buildings, sometimes larger and sometimes smaller than the Academy's project grant to that school. When the government grant was larger, the project grant for that item was canceled; when the government grant was smaller an amount equal to it was deducted from the project. Funds thus accruing to the thana school works program were reallocated to other schools.

Clearly here was a great deal of detail that needed attention. In order to gain experience, the staff arranged for the program to begin in three schools in December. The other 71 schools would not start theirs until January 1964. Other training in December included all members of the school project committees, in groups of around 40, for a day's instruction. Some supplemental training had to be arranged for the teachers who kept the accounts. In mid-January the members of the union education subcommittees came to the Academy for a day's briefing on the project.

From the beginning it was evident that some village leaders were ill at ease upon seeing the headmaster in a leadership role. So the nonteacher members of the school project committees were called to the Academy along with the headmasters to learn of the functions of the committee.

The pilot school works program was carried on in Comilla thana a second year. The funds available were Rs. 100,000, or 40 per cent of the amount of the year before. The number of schools participating was increased to 83.

It was realized in advance that special care would need to be given to procurement of supplies. Procurement guidelines recommended bulk purchasing through the KTCCA in order to have sufficient materials of good quality on hand when needed, and to prevent price rises as large amounts of some materials were bought. The major purchases were for tools, and materials—wood, bamboo, brick, cement, lime, sand, and metal roofing.

STUDENTS AND TEACHERS WORKING TOGETHER

The expenditures for materials in the first year were nearly two-thirds of the total, the administration cost was 3 per cent, and 32 per cent was spent for wages, of which 18 per cent was for skilled workers, 5 per cent for teachers, and 9 per cent for students. In the second year, with a smaller budget than the first, the proportion of expenditures was much the same as the year before.

The wages paid to the teachers were at the rate of Rs. 2 to Rs. 3 per day. Very few teachers ever worked a day at a time, but rather a few hours now and then throughout the school week. The amount of money earned per teacher the first year averaged Rs. 36 and in the second year Rs. 81. The proportion of teachers participating ranged from a little over half for the high schools to nearly all in the primary schools, where some compulsion may have been used.

The wage paid to a student was arrived at by estimating the proportion of a man's work he had done. The average was about Rs. 0.5 per day. The students were not permitted to work more than two hours at a time, and only two or three times a week. Some few students earned more than Rs. 40 during the project period and were very proud of it. At the other extreme, many boys and girls earned less than one rupee. The average total earned per participating student in all schools the first year was about Rs. 6, and a little less the next year.

The largest amounts were used for student wages in those schools where the guidelines were closely followed, and the smallest where a high value was placed by the school project committee on getting the work done with as little bother to themselves as possible. The Academy staff considered the operation most successful where the students were used liberally.

A sample of teachers interviewed said they thought that most of the students' earnings were used for books and clothes and that some was handed over to their families for food.

BETTER SCHOOL BUILDINGS, FURNISHINGS, AND GROUNDS

During the two year period, the structures of 64 of the 83 schools were improved by new buildings or by repair or extension of existing buildings. The number of structures entirely of brick and concrete increased from nine to 26, and wooden frame buildings with metal walls and roofs from two to 12. Forty-eight schools had projects for the construction of tables, chairs, and desks. These improvements also reflect the funds provided by government grants, mentioned above.

More than half of all project funds were used for construction of buildings. The next largest expenditure was for schoolroom furniture. Nearly two-thirds of all schools had earthwork projects, mainly improvement of playgrounds and access roads. Shade trees were planted at all schools. Sanitary latrines increased from zero to 88. Some of these were of brick and cement, and others partially so. All were of the water-seal sanitary type, made at the Academy after a United Nations pattern. Tube wells for drinking water were available in mid-1965 at 63 of the 83 schools. CARE provided all the materials for 20 new tube wells.

In mid-1965, at the end of the second year, the school works program was closed out for lack of support from the provincial government. It was thought by the Academy staff that if the program could have been continued for a few more years, all the schools would have had brick and cement buildings, vastly improved furnishings, well-developed grounds, clean drinking water, and sanitary latrines.

This two-year rural school plant improvement project had demonstrated that the teachers could take a leadership role in the village. It had also effected a beginning toward the school becoming a community-related institution. The fortnightly meetings of the headmasters and teachers at the Academy served as a forum and a rallying point for their further development.

The students had found that everyday life could be related to education and that they could earn some money while learning about book theorems in actual practice. They learned about mortars and their proportions, how to level floors by a spirit-leveler, how to find out the total volume of earth moved, the total volume of wood used in furniture, how to make geometric designs for furniture, etc.

The school works program caused the villagers to take an interest in the school. The general school attendance increased during the work project period. The buildings and grounds look better. The new tube well is a place to get a drink of water when passing; and the young shade tree his children planted in an area they leveled off is a likely place for a man to stop and rest. Inside the schoolhouse there are furnishings that had best be preserved, even if most of them are of rough lumber and made in part by students. Herewith begins school pride.

Director Khan, in the introduction to the 1964–1965 report on the school works program, stated that this pilot project was ready for replication:

In 1962 the Academy for Rural Development presented a model for rural works to the Basic Democracy Department. Now we present a model of school works to the Department of Education. Whether our sincere efforts should receive careful attention or be ignored is the discretion of the Department. We follow the wise counsel which Hafiz gave to himself: "Hafiz, prayer is your duty. Its acceptance or rejection is not your concern."

As of mid-1968, however, the Department of Education had not taken up the school works project for replication in other thanas.

Although it is quite clear that the experiments and demonstrations in the complex field of education have elements which may be characterized as "breakthroughs," it is, we believe, fair to evaluate the total effort to be less dynamic and successful than the work and achievements in agricultural production, cooperative organization, and mechanization, and less influential on government policy than the works program and other activities of the Academy. But perhaps sustained educational innovations, which are less easily measured than agricultural production, for example, need to be evaluated in longer time intervals and with more sensitive instruments of appraisal.

8. Research and Communications

From the initial planning stage, research has played a vital role in the Comilla program. The need for records, for the analysis of data, and for the publication of tentative findings has been constantly stressed. In a very real sense the whole rural program of the Academy has been a research project. Although research and systematic documentation is, uniquely, an integral part of the whole Academy operation the methods of assembling and analyzing data are still relatively simple—but are becoming more sophisticated as a result of experience, advisory assistance, and staff development programs. Furthermore in several important program areas the research findings are highly tentative and require caution in drawing conclusions as to their validity or application. Nevertheless the fundamental idea of using the results of systematic observations and experimental research for instructional and policy-making purposes as an alternative to speculation or authoritarian directives is making a distinctive contribution to the content and methods of administration of rural development programs.

More specifically, much of the research work has been of the small-scale type, action-oriented, and has served the current needs of the Academy in both its teaching and project dimensions. A constant problem for research efforts has been the fast-moving program developments with their concomitant adjustment of work loads and shifts in personnel assignments which are necessary to maintain momentum. A consequence of these program dynamics has often been that decisions and actions were taken ahead of the evaluative contribution of the researchers.

The Research Program

A research section consisting of several research assistants and enumerators under the direction of a faculty member and a research committee was organized early in the history of the Academy to provide overall guidance and to review research proposals. The research program started with rather elementary surveys to learn first-hand about village organization and the attitudes, practices, and resources of villagers as they related to economic and other developmental programs which were being contemplated. Notes and diaries were kept of all interviews and conferences, and simple questionnaires were designed and utilized. A small publication usually recorded the results of each aspect of rural life which was investigated. Though some of the more academically oriented instructors looked upon these early efforts as hardly respectable, they soon realized how much they didn't know about elementary facts of village life. The instructors were assisted in their research by a field enumeration staff of villagers for whom a weekly training session was arranged. These enumerators, one from each of the 12 unions, were appointed upon the recommendation of the V-AID village worker. It had been found that he himself could not report objectively on the program of which he was a part, so local school teachers and other available literate young men were hired on a part-time basis. This arrangement proved to be a good one, for these village enumerators knew local conditions and thus could readily establish a good relationship with the villagers from whom they sought information.

The research section staff, as commented on by Director Khan at the time, has "discovered that contact with the villagers and their problems soon begins to ramify, that one idea leads to another till such activity develops a momentum of its own. I need not specify the details. I can only say our research activity has become a spearhead and a torch."[1]

TECHNICAL PUBLICATIONS AND OTHER RESEARCH REPORTS

The first three technical publications of the Academy dealt with various aspects of paddy cultivation.[2] The first comprehensive village study was of Dhanishwar, a village near the Academy. The study gave special attention to the historical backgrounds of man-land adjustments, a matter of first importance in the area. It was published by the Academy as *Village Dhanishwar—Three Generations of Man-Land Adjustment in an East Pakistan Village* (Technical Publication No. 5).

Diffusion and Adoption of Agricultural Practices—A Study in a Village in East Pakistan (Technical Publication No. 7) was the first Academy research report to gain widespread recognition. This seventy-six-page publication was a segment of the research on diffusion and adoption of new ideas in agriculture developed at Michigan State University. Productive use of this report continues to be made at Comilla in the promotion of programs to improve village

---

[1] Akhter Hameed Khan, Comilla, *Journal*, PARD, November 1959, p. 95.
[2] For a list of Academy research publications see Bibliography.

living conditions, particularly as influenced by community organizational matters and extension procedures.[3]

Introduction of Tractors in a Subsistence Farm Economy (Technical Publication No. 14) attracted considerable attention because it provided tentative answers to questions such as these: How can a 35-hp tractor be used on two-acre farms, each with several fields, often scattered, and usually separated from adjacent fields by miniature embankments? How were the villagers, most of whom had never seen a tractor, trained to operate them? How were payments for the use of the tractors determined? What were some of the psychological factors involved in tractor use?[4]

In the fall of 1962, at the request of the Agricultural Development Corporation, the Academy conducted a study of the use farmers were making of commercial fertilizers in the production of the amon paddy crop. A total of 1,000 farmers, usually owning two to eight acres of land, were interviewed. These farmers lived in 100 villages in 20 unions of 13 of the 17 districts in the province. The interviewing was done by 20 villagers from Comilla thana who worked on a part-time basis as field investigators for the research section of the Academy. These men had been in training once a week at the Academy for a period of more than two years. For the fertilizer study, they were given a week's intensive training, including the pretesting of a 16-

[3] This early study, by Syed A. Rahim, formed the basis for a later and significantly more sophisticated research undertaking by him for the Ph.D. degree at Michigan State University.

[4] The author of this publication, Anwaruzzaman Khan, was Instructor in Rural Economics at the Academy from 1959 to 1966. Since then he has been with the East Pakistan Agricultural Development Corporation in charge of its farming projects and maintains close contact with the Academy.

item schedule to be filled in for each farmer in the widely scattered villages in the provincial sample.

Other studies which illustrate the range of the Academy's research were: *Studies of Basic Democracy* (1963); *Cooperation as a Remedy for Rural Poverty* (1963), a study of the Balarampur-Deeder Rickshaw Pullers Society; *Experience in Cross-Cultural Living—A Case Study of the Home-Stay Experience of U.S. Peace Corps Volunteers* (in Pakistani homes) (1964); *Communication and Personal Influence in an East Pakistan Village* (1965), which describes and analyzes the contacts the people have outside and inside the village, with emphasis on patterns of leadership; *Imams as Teachers* (1968), which describes and analyzes the contribution of religious leaders (traditional teachers) to a broadly based educational program which is designed to reduce illiteracy and broaden participation of villagers in the development process; and *Rural Credit: Gazipur Village* (1968), which documents sources of credit, extent and causes of indebtedness and related topics. The last report closes with this informative note: "Though the statutory agricultural credit agencies like the Agricultural Development Finance Corporation, Agricultural Board of Pakistan, and the Agricultural Development Bank of Pakistan started working from 1952, they have hardly been able to reach the common farmer. For the last one or two years they have been modifying the terms and conditions and title difficulties in order to make it possible to advance loans to common farmers in the remote parts of rural areas. But these slight and statutory changes are very slow."

Numerous small action-related studies, often dealing with the operation of the cooperatives, or with crops and livestock, have been made since 1964 by the research unit at Abhoy Ashram, and by the members of the research section at Kotbari. The research content of the annual reports of the Japanese experts has been substantial as related to soil types, crop varieties, cultural practices, fertilizer inputs, and insecticides used.

Special mention may be made of a study on costs and returns on irrigated crops made in 1964–1965. It covered 69 plots of winter crops on 67 farms in 21 villages. The research was designed to investigate the relationship between input costs (principally labor, water, fertilizer, and insecticides) and the value of crops produced. Such a study, it was hoped, would "furnish some clue as to why some farmers are using more or less irrigation water than others, and also why more and more farmers are not coming forward to use the tube well water provided by the KTCCA." Intensive cost-return studies were made of 18 plots of potatoes, 20 of boro paddy, and 31 of *shaita* paddy (both winter varieties). The overall study clearly demonstrated that on the average these tube-well-irrigated crops were profitable.

The data for a second and larger cost and return study for 1965–1966 winter crops were collected for three rice crops (Taipei-177, boro, and shaita) and two other crops (potato and watermelon). Farmers were interviewed by trained investigators in 21 villages of the thana in which there were cooperative societies sponsored by the Academy and where deep wells were in operation. A total of 167 plots of cropland belonging to 122 farmers were selcted for the study by stratified sampling. This second study demonstrated in more detail the profitability of irrigated winter crops, including substantial variation in the profit rates of the five crops studied, Taipei rice and watermelon showing much greater return. In addition, the detailed and extensive character of the study allowed comparative analysis of cost inputs, suggesting the requisite rate of fertilizer and insecticide usage for maximum profit of irrigated crops and the tentative conclusion that plowing by rented tractor was less expensive than plowing by rented bullock.[5] A follow-up study for 1969 is currently underway.

Another research report of the Academy is a case study of the Balarampur-Deeder Rickshaw Pullers Society (1965). This report reviews an earlier study (1963) of this same society, noted above.

COLLABORATIVE RESEARCH WITH OTHER AGENCIES

In addition to the Academy's own research activities summarized above, several studies have been carried out upon the request of other agencies, or in collaboration with other agencies. Since fiscal 1964 around Rs. 250,000 per annum have been attracted to finance the Academy's research efforts. The performance of research services for, or with, government departments and other agencies has had the double value of providing an outside appraisal of operations like the public works program or the distribution of fertilizer by the Agricultural Development Corporation, and of strengthening the research capacity of the Academy.

The most ambitious socioeconomic research yet done at Comilla is that reported in a 1965 publication entitled *Modernizing Subsistence Agriculture*, in cooperation with the Bureau of Economic Research, Dacca University.[6] This research project was designed to measure the gains made during one year by cooperative farmers in Comilla thana as

[5] Mahmoodur Rahman, *Costs and Returns: Economics of Winter-irrigated Crops in Comilla, 1965–1966*, Comilla, PARD, March 1967.
[6] This study was made by A. Farouk, Dacca University, and S. A. Rahim of the Academy.

compared with noncooperative farmers in Chandina thana adjacent to it. The field work involved 180 families in Comilla thana and 120 in Chandina. Ten village enumerators were trained for this study. Schedules of information were recorded on labor inputs, uses of credit, production practices, yields, sales of produce, capital formation, investment in agriculture, and other facts. The findings of this study document how complex are the factors involved in economic progress, and how great are the physical handicaps in the Comilla area, but seem to demonstrate that the Comilla families have benefited from the modernization program.

The Academy has had two research projects in collaboration with the Institute of Development Economics, Karachi. One dealt with the scientific measurement of paddy yields, and produced a report entitled "Estimation by Sample Crop-Cutting of Agricultural Production in Comilla Thana," based on studies in 54 villages. This was the first of a series of reports, which is continuing, on crop yields based on crop-cutting samples. These estimates are based on a random sample of cooperative farmers and of noncooperative farmers. The data collected show a considerably higher yield for the cooperative farmers than for the control group. A second project dealing with an economic analysis of alternate methods of irrigation, begun in the summer of 1964, is still in process.

A recent (1969) joint research project has been initiated in collaboration with the United Nations on "Rural Institutions and Planned Change." Also currently (1969) in process is an extensive analysis of the thana irrigation program which is sponsored by the Department of Agriculture and the Department of Basic Democracies and Local Government, the Agricultural Development Corporation, the East

Pakistan Water and Power Development Authority, and the national Planning Commission.

For several years the Academy and the Population Council, Inc., have collaborated in research on various aspects of family planning. As mentioned earlier, the Council has provided two highly trained research workers who have, in association with members of the research staff of the Academy, engaged in basic background studies and in appraisals of operational programs.

Other research projects now in process include studies of the supervised credit system, fertilizer tests, the use of tractors, the economics of tube well irrigation, the role of women in 20 villages, and the effectiveness of publicity in family planning programs. Case studies are being made of the Comilla district public works program, the Sonaichuri irrigation project, and the Comilla motor drivers' cooperative. The research section maintains cumulative records on major programs such as cooperatives, irrigation, women's programs, and agricultural extension in Comilla thana and in the ten thanas under the expanded program.[7]

THE ACADEMY IRRI-RICE VARIETY TESTS

A recent research report deals with the Academy rice variety tests in cooperation with the International Rice Research Institute (IRRI) in the Philippines. This study was undertaken because of the urgent need to find high productive varieties suitable for East Pakistan. The IRRI plant-breeding research holds hope that tropical varieties can be developed that will produce yields comparable to those obtained in the temperate zones. It is the function of the several locality testing projects, of which Comilla was

---

[7] See *Statistical Digest*, Comilla, PARD, May 1968.

the first in operation for IRRI in East Pakistan, to determine what varieties are best suited to each area.

The IR-8 boro variety has been found to be relatively well adapted to East Pakistan conditions in the boro and aus seasons. The Agricultural Development Corporation planned to devote about ten per cent of its irrigation resources, perhaps 300 or more pumps, to the production of this variety in the winter of 1967. The first of the needed seed were produced on the Abhoy Ashram farm and on about 50 acres in five villages in Comilla thana where supervision could be provided.

The cooperative testing of rice varieties with IRRI, and the production of the IR-8 seed for the Agricultural Development Corporation for the 1967 boro crop, were done at the Academy because it was ready to give IRRI the early cooperation needed. Systematic testing of several IRRI varieties, compared with other foreign and local varieties, has continued since this initial beginning under the supervision of an IRRI-trained member of the faculty.

Some Research Problems

The difficulties of carrying on research in an area such as Comilla are by no means resolved when researchers learn what questions to ask. There is first of all the matter of who does the asking. It was learned early at the Academy that the villagers would hardly give an objective answer to a representative of the government. They would either fear him and so try to conceal information, or hope to get help from him and try to please him. This was why, only a few months after the Academy was opened, it was decided that local village teachers and other qualified local people would be trained to interview the villagers. It was these enumerators who collected most of the information from the villagers set forth in the wide range of episodic and program-related research mentioned above. Women enumerators, too, have been selected, trained, and used effectively in the Comilla area.

Then there is the general unwillingness of the villager to give information to anyone about his land, crops, or economic status, lest his taxes be increased. Furthermore, any kind of a sample results in the interviewing of specifically identified household heads. "Why am only I being asked all these questions? Why not also my neighbors?" This necessitates that the "random sample" procedure be explained in full, in simple language.

The assurances that the information given will be kept confidential is not always fully believed. And how can a questionnaire be administered in a village, particularly by an outsider, to say nothing of a high-visibility foreigner, without the contents of the replies being overheard by the people who out of curiosity gather around to see and hear what is going on?

Furthermore there are people in each village, and in each household, who speak for that village or that household. If the random sample happens to select these individuals, well and good. If it does not, there will, at first at least, be almost automatic replies from these traditional spokesmen. When such a spokesman is repressed, he typically takes the attitude that the interviewer may be recording the answers given him, but they are often not the "right" answers. It is a commonplace experience for an outside interviewer to ask the selected interviewee a question, only to have him turn and look behind himself to see to whom the question is addressed. It is not in his experience to have questions addressed to him.

The women interviewers were especially handicapped in

getting information from the village women. First of all, the women were in purdah, unaccustomed to having non-family members in their homes. Furthermore, they were unaccustomed to answering questions about themselves or their families. Such occasional questions as came up from outsiders would tend to be answered by the husband. If he were not present, the eldest son would answer. If no man was present, the eldest woman in the group would answer.

DIFFIDENCE OF VILLAGE WOMEN

The training of the village enumerators, and especially the women because of their more limited contacts outside their own homes, was a tedious matter.

Many women (enumerators) think they already know the answers to the interview questions, especially if the respondents are their friends. They do not understand the importance of asking. . . . They must learn to forget what they know, their preconceptions. Teaching this takes much time and effort.[8]

The problems of interviewing women become yet more complex when questions are asked that relate to family planning. Some of the reactions of village women to the questions asked and to the enumerators who conducted a family planning study are illustrated in the following quotations from a research report:

Some said they were using the Academy's name but that really they were from the government. A rumor arose that they had come to give injections to people with many children to prevent them from having any more. Another rumor was

[8] Begum Hosne Ara and Harvey M. Choldin, "Problems in Field Work with Village Women," Comilla, PARD, Survey and Research Bulletin, No. 12, November 1964 (mimeographed), p. 7.

that the government was going to increase land taxes. Another fear was that the crops of those who were doing well would be seized. One rumor that arose was connected with the Quran, in which it is written—as the people said—that sometimes women will come out of purdah and will go around in the open, and that this will be bad. When the village people saw these women coming they said they had come to destroy the faith.

The enumerators tried to reassure the villagers in several ways. They showed them that they had no injections with them and that they were just women like the village women, wearing burqa; that they were not out to destroy the faith, and they quoted from the Hadiz to show that they were good Muslims. They also pointed out that some neighbouring villagers were members of the Academy programme. Some of the people to whom they talked had kinfolk in neighbouring villages. The enumerators also reminded the villagers of the recent census . . . which had brought them no harm.

Often a group would form, and some people in the group would know about the Academy and support the women. The women showed the questionnaire to anyone who could read to show that there was nothing written about taxation. Some people would say: "These women are our women, they look like us and talk like us, why shouldn't we trust them?"[9]

When agreement had been reached that the prospective respondent would reply to the questions, problems arose with most of the individual questions. When asked about her age, the woman often didn't know "but my parents do." Nor did she know the age of her husband. "Why should anyone want to know our ages?"

Many a woman, especially the very conservative and the newly married one, would not give her husband's name, believing that it was a sin to do so and might shorten his life. Some women couldn't give the exact number of preg-

[9] *Ibid.*, p. 10.

nancies, and some couldn't understand the reason for asking about the number of infant deaths and miscarriages. "Can you bring them back to life?"

FATALISM AND ISOLATION

One of the biggest obstacles to research is that the villager is lacking in initiative and confidence. The psychological residuals of colonialism and an earlier feudalism account, in part, for this reaction. There appear, however, to be more immediate forces—the mounting pressure of the people on the land, the long hot humid summers, and the storms that play havoc with crops and earthen causeways and buildings and lives. The fatalism of the villager is deep seated; it has to do with his estimate of his own power as over against forces he assumes to be wholly beyond his reach. "He is incredulous of all altruistic claims for he does not expect that anybody would be sincerely interested in his welfare. To him the government is a symbol of authority and nothing more. . . . The villager has faith in the Supernatural, would feel lost and insecure without his dependence on it, and is generally resigned to his lot. He has a rigid fatalistic attitude to change."[10]

It is clear that there are formidable problems of research in a traditional society. But, looking at the efforts at Comilla, one wonders if the use of village enumerators, with continuous training and a great deal of field supervision, is not proving that reasonably reliable information about village conditions, including the status of women, can be collected. And what of the new role of the government? Has not the villagers' stereotype of it undergone a consid-

[10] S. M. Hafeez Zaidi, "Social Research in a Semi-Literate Rural Society," Comilla, *Journal* (Special Issue on Rural Social Research) PARD, July 1962, p. 92.

erable change in response to the thousands of local project committees throughout the province that have carried out public works projects that benefit the villagers? The province-wide evaluations of these programs by the Academy indicate the beginnings of a new attitude toward the government and its representatives in the countryside. So, while seemingly almost insurmountable research barriers still exist, at least at Comilla some scaling ladders are under construction.

Research at the Academy has also suffered from two types of isolation. First of all, Comilla is off by itself. There is little normal flow of scholars through it. It is in fact remote, when measured by modern communication facilities, what with unbridged rivers, slow and circuitous water transportation, and a five-hour train ride from Dacca. A redeeming feature is the daily air connection to Dacca and to Chittagong. A second factor is even more limiting, namely that there is on the Comilla staff but one trained specialist in each of several social science fields, although a fairly large number of junior scholars are developing quite rapidly through experience and on-the-job training. Thus, even with the most productive use of the few well-trained people there is limited opportunity for a senior staff member to keep abreast of the research and other developments in his own field. And, besides, there is no ready chance to sharpen the tools of his own particular specialty in his contacts with his associates as occurs in the give-and-take of ideas among the members of a department or college in a larger institution. However, efforts are constantly being made to lessen this isolation through weekly faculty meetings, acquisition of numerous books, annual work-planning conferences, special training seminars, opportunities for study in Pakistan and at Michigan State University and other institutions abroad for several members of the faculty, the presence of graduate students from various institutions, and the visits to Comilla of international scholars and administrators interested in rural development.

Facing the above limitations in research, which are sometimes compounded by needed changes in program emphasis, Director Khan in this as in other areas of activity falls back on what he calls the "rehearsal." Since, in a given instance, there are not the needed resources, or the time, or the mature research design to do the job the way it should be done, the research should nontheless be carried out and the results recorded. This is done in the hope that later in a broader frame of reference some use can be made of the findings, and that at any rate the experience gained will help prepare the staff to perform at a better level.

LACK OF AN OVERALL RESEARCH DESIGN

There are still vast amounts of usable unanalyzed data that have accumulated through the routine recording of what has happened. Voluminous records (often in Bengali) and other data are available on specific items of information related to various programs dealing with the cooperative,[11] the thana council, and the mechanization projects which include irrigation. Smaller, though significant, amounts of unanalyzed data have accumulated for the women's work,

[11] For instance, the assembling and analysis of the weekly cash deposits made by the individual members of the local societies would document and refine such patterns as obtain in the making of deposits as they may be affected by length of membership, size of operations, seasonal variations, age of cooperative society, and so on.

for various education programs, and for family planning. Most of these unanalyzed data are currently being preserved in the documentation section of the library.

Among the problems related to the use of these basic raw data have been the absence of an overall research design that encompassed their use. Such a research design would require more personnel and more data-processing facilities than have been available. Most needed now is a small mechanical data-processing unit and relevant personnel to facilitate the punching, sorting, and analysis of data cards.

Also, there are the continuing problems of upgrading the technical performance and objectivity of the members of the research section and auxiliary personnel such as enumerators. The problem of methodological adequacy is ever present in East Pakistan, where efforts at objective research are new. Then, too, the research work at Comilla, while making considerable headway, remains under something of a handicap for lack of base-line studies of conditions before the modernization effort began.

In the unpublished report of an evaluation team which examined the research program of the Academy up to 1963, the research was criticized as mainly of the "count and divide" type. More analytical research was recommended, with emphasis on case studies and on automatically repeated systematic inquiries, such as crop-cutting surveys. More recent Academy publications reflect substantial improvements on these points.

An important and continuous aspect of the work of Michigan State University's advisors and consultants has been to assist in improving research methodology and standards. Research workshops and seminars continue to be conducted under the deputy director for research and training, Sayed A. Rahim.

The Library

The library was established in 1959. As of mid-1968, the English collection contained more than 14,000 book titles, standard reference works, and bound copies of periodicals, mostly on the subjects of cooperatives, agriculture, economics, sociology, social psychology, education, communications, community organization, public administration, and research methodology. The Bengali collection, started at the library at Kotbari in December 1964, contains more than 1,625 book titles, and a much larger number of pamphlets. One hundred local and foreign journals are regularly received, as are fourteen English, Bengali, and Urdu dailies. Books and other library materials in both English and Bengali are systematically and continuously being acquired by a trained librarian and classified by the Dewey decimal system. All periodicals are regularly bound and filed. Many of the acquisitions in English have been made through the Michigan State University grant from the Ford Foundation. Other sources of new publications have been through Academy funds, exchanges with other libraries and agencies, and gifts.

Since January 1965 the English titles and the new portion of the Bengali collection have been housed in the spacious three-story library building on the Kotbari campus.

Larger Bengali collections of books and pamphlet materials are at Abhoy Ashram. Most of these are how-to-do-it pamphlets, designed for use of the members of the cooperatives, the project committees of the public works programs, and participants in other field activities sponsored by the Academy.

The library now handles the distribution of Academy

publications, in both English and Bengali. These include numerous research reports, and the annual reports of the Academy, of the cooperatives, the rural administrative experiment, women's and youth work, and family planning, plus a variety of special reports on such subjects as the public works program, communications, and training manuals.

To inform the villagers on agriculture, animal husbandry, cottage industry, health and sanitation, and so on, a translation and publication committee was set up in February 1960. By November of that year, the Academy had published 66 Bengali booklets in 66,000 copies and reprinted 38,000 more. More than half of these were sold, and the others were distributed free. Small in size and unique in content and presentation, the booklets attracted the attention of the farmers, union councilors, and the officials interested in rural development. They were also used in other localities for training. Production of these materials has continued and improved in coverage and quality.

Communications

The Academy has had a communications section since 1959. It has been aided in its operations by American Peace Corps Volunteers and British Volunteers. The work of the communications section falls under six major headings: arts and design, photography, tape recordings, films, zari (folk) singers, and translation and editing work.

The artists of the section have prepared special displays of maps and charts for many occasions, including the visits of important people and annual rallies. This section has also prepared sketch illustrations for numerous booklets and posters on agriculture and other subjects.

Photographs have been made of most special occasions, and bound albums have been developed on the public works program and on other major activities. By mid-1966 a fully equipped darkroom was in operation at Kotbari. Many sets of black and white transparency slides have been produced. They deal with model farming operations in the villages, model farmer training at Abhoy Ashram, improved agricultural practices, calf raising, pottery making, youth clubs, child care, midwife training, the operations of the central cooperative office, fish culture, public works, seed selection, soil testing and other program topics. These sets have been shown to many training groups on the Kotbari campus, where dependable electric current was available before it was at Abhoy Ashram. Several unsuccessful attempts were made to work out a flashlight-powered slide projector that could be transported by bicycle to the villages. Many film strips have been produced to tell complete stories of major program recommendations. For the past several years a special illustrated monthly news letter, called "Samajatra," has been published for village cooperators.

The tape recorders used at the Academy have been mostly of the battery-operated type. Recordings are made for village audiences on such subjects as paddy deposits and marketing, cooperative consumer stores, tube wells for irrigation, rural public works, potato production, extension education through the schools, and uses of the tractor. Each tape is introduced by an Academy instructor, and contains a recorded interview with one or more villagers who are participating in the program being discussed.

The use of movie films in the Academy's programs has been intermittent, mainly due to the technical difficulties involved in both production and use. Movies for the Academy staff and their families have been arranged in the evenings especially after the Academy moved to Kotbari, where the electric current was dependable and a better auditorium is available. The evening film showings there feature entertainment, travelogues, and documentaries. Most of the films are obtained without cost from United States Information Service (USIS), British Information Service, and other agencies.

Four Academy program films were made from 1962 to 1964, on the subjects of poultry raising (*Murgi Palan*), on the rural public works program (*Jhankor*), farmers' cooperatives (*Aikyaton*), and family planning (*Paribartan*). The last three were made in cooperation with the Department of Basic Democracies and Local Government, the Department of Cooperatives, and the Department of Social Welfare. The photography was done by professional film crews, on scripts prepared by the Academy staff. Local villagers were used as actors. The USIS made a color film in 1964–1965 entitled "Comilla Shows the Way."

As has been mentioned, the family planning program has made regular use of a local group of zari singers to publicize its activity. The singers studied the program and then developed songs that set forth the economic and social values of family planning, the places where the supplies can be purchased, asserting that they are easy and healthful to use and that it is religiously permissible to use them. A three-hour show at a local market usually attracts 300 to 500 men, and a five-hour show in a village may draw a thousand or more men and children. The songs are tailored to the audience, and new ones are constantly being made up from the cumulative understanding of the program by the song leaders and their associates. The *kabigan* style of singing is generally employed, whereby song leaders present conflicting arguments, one in favor of and one opposing the topic being discussed. The leaders are supported by a harmonium player, a drummer, and three assistants.

By mid-1966, the zari-singing team was being used to publicize other Academy programs also. It was the team's success in publicizing family planning over a two-year period that led to this decision. There were four or five village meetings held each week except during the height of the monsoon. At the meetings use was frequently made of posters, leaflets, and pamphlets prepared by the Academy or available from the provincial and national offices of family planning, agriculture, education, and so on. This enlarged activity involved close coordination with extension personnel, who often attended the performances and made comments to accentuate points raised by the films and songs.

Despite extensive effort, and some decided successes, the use of communications media has been uneven. Considerable attention still needs to be given to a more effective integration of communication techniques into the training and extension work of the Academy.

9. The Impact of the Academy

In the long run, the importance of the Comilla program depends on whether, with adaptations to local conditions, the principles and procedures worked out there can be applied elsewhere in East Pakistan and perhaps in other areas. In the course of the preceding chapters instances of such "extension" of the Comilla program have been described from time to time. A comprehensive review of the expansion of the program in East Pakistan follows.

Three Thana Expansion Programs

By mid-1962, the provincial government was examining the possibility of starting a Comilla-type program in three other thanas, one in each of the other three divisions of the province. This would provide a test of whether the programs could be reproduced under widely differing conditions and without the close supervision of Director Khan. Some people in the government, including the governor, were anxious to expand the Comilla program much more widely, but Director Khan persuaded the government that staff leaders were not then available to extend beyond three additional thanas.

The early discussions about expansion centered around a document, developed over a period of some months by the Academy administration and the chief advisor from Michigan State University, entitled "Proposal for Creation of Three Additional Experimental Demonstrations in Rural Development Based on the Comilla Experience." The major policy themes to be followed in the proposed expansion were:

1. Emphasis will be placed on sustained experimental work for a minimum period of five years, within the general framework of government policies. Freedom to experiment is assured—but the freedom is not to be expressed in the form of extra subsidies to villagers or to cooperative organizations.

2. Cooperative organizations will be expected to repay all costs which are properly attributable to economic investment as contrasted with the costs of educational or research activities.

3. Emphasis will be given to methods of discovering, organizing, and utilizing indigenous leadership and skills within the village rather than in expanding the government establishment to accomplish the work.

4. As "experimental demonstrations" due emphasis will be given to research and documentation, the results of which will be made readily available to any interested person, official, or government organization.

5. All members of the staff concerned with extension education will be expected to measure their performance in terms of adoption by villagers and village organizations of progressive practices and institutions which have the net effect of increased production and generally higher standards of living.

The provincial board of governors of the Academy approved the three-thana proposal in November 1962. A statement of the final plan was finished in late December under the title "Project for the Modernization and Development of the Rural Community in East Pakistan." A project director and deputy project director for each of the three thanas plus two men in reserve were recruited from among a dozen likely candidates assembled for interviews by the provincial registrar of cooperatives. A six-month training period for these trainees was begun at Comilla in January 1963.

This course was organized and conducted by the newly-appointed additional director of agriculture[1] posted to the Academy for the purpose. In collaboration with the eight officials he was training, the additional director worked out segments of the total syllabus a fortnight at a time. Each unit was reviewed by the group upon its completion and then the next one laid out. The training began with topical lectures, but soon moved on to a full review of the Comilla approach to the modernization of the rural community. The additional director and his associates visited the villages, attended training classes in operation, and conferred with faculty and staff members associated with the various field projects. As the weeks passed, more and more time was spent in close study of the operations of the various facets of the central cooperative, the roles of the circle officer, and of the thana representatives of the departments in the various developmental activities underway, and the functioning of the then embryonic Comilla Thana Training and Development Center. In the middle part of

[1] A. Z. M. Obaidullah Khan, later deputy commissioner of Comilla district, and still later secretary of the East Pakistan Department of Basic Democracies and Local Government.

the training program the trainees spent several days in the thanas to which they would respectively be assigned, returning to Comilla with new questions to be answered.

The programs in the three thanas were started in mid-1963 on schedule. The government of East Pakistan provided a launching loan of Rs. 75 lakh at 5 per cent interest per annum plus a Rs. 33.33 lakh grant-in-aid. One and a half lakhs are provided annually for recurring expenses. The project headquarters in each of the three thanas—Gaibandha, Goripur, and Natore—was a former V-AID training institute. Demonstration units were set up in each. The surrounding thana, as at Comilla, served as a project area. The circle officer, the various thana departmental representatives, and the thana council were gradually moved to the project headquarters. In each thana, village-based cooperatives were organized in the first month. Within the next month or two a central cooperative association, patterned after the one at Comilla, was established. These associations soon began to assist in village programs in education, rural youth, women's work, and family planning.

Weekly training for villagers was arranged for, as was also experimentation in the use of farm tractors and low-lift and deep-well irrigation pumps. Some farm machinery was sent on loan from Comilla. Machine shops were established. Regular reporting of all activities was inaugurated. The operation of these various activities was greatly facilitated by the presence of three or four Peace Corps Volunteers at each project headquarters.

Overall supervision for the program in the three thanas, provided by the additional director of agriculture located at Comilla, was done by means of occasional visits and a monthly project directors' conference in which the principal staff member from each of the new areas and representatives from Comilla took part. These monthly conferences rotated among the three areas and Comilla, with more of them held at the latter to take advantage of the greater experience of the staff there. All phases of the program were examined and decisions taken as needed.

The program in each of the three new areas moved ahead from the first month at a faster rate than had the program at Comilla. Marked increases occurred in each thana in the number of local societies, membership in the cooperatives, number of villagers in weekly training, increases in deposits by members, and loans taken by the societies. In each of the three thanas, nonagricultural cooperative societies were organized and have developed along the lines of those at Comilla, but as yet not one of these thanas has a separate federation for the nonagricultural societies.

Some measures of the growth which has occurred in the three thanas is indicated by the following key statistics as of mid-1968:

Number of agricultural societies (in approximately two-thirds of the villages)	641
Number of nonagricultural societies	32
Total membership	16,927
Total amount paid in shares	Rs.247,389
Total savings	Rs.441,891
Total loans (repayment rate: 92%)	Rs.1,152,532
Acres under tractor cultivation	3,575
Acres being irrigated	2,282

Some marketing activities have begun and some emphasis has been given to improving the supply of consumers goods to members. Extension activities focused on increased use of fertilizers, insecticides, and the new rice varieties and other crops, with good results. An oil mill has been started

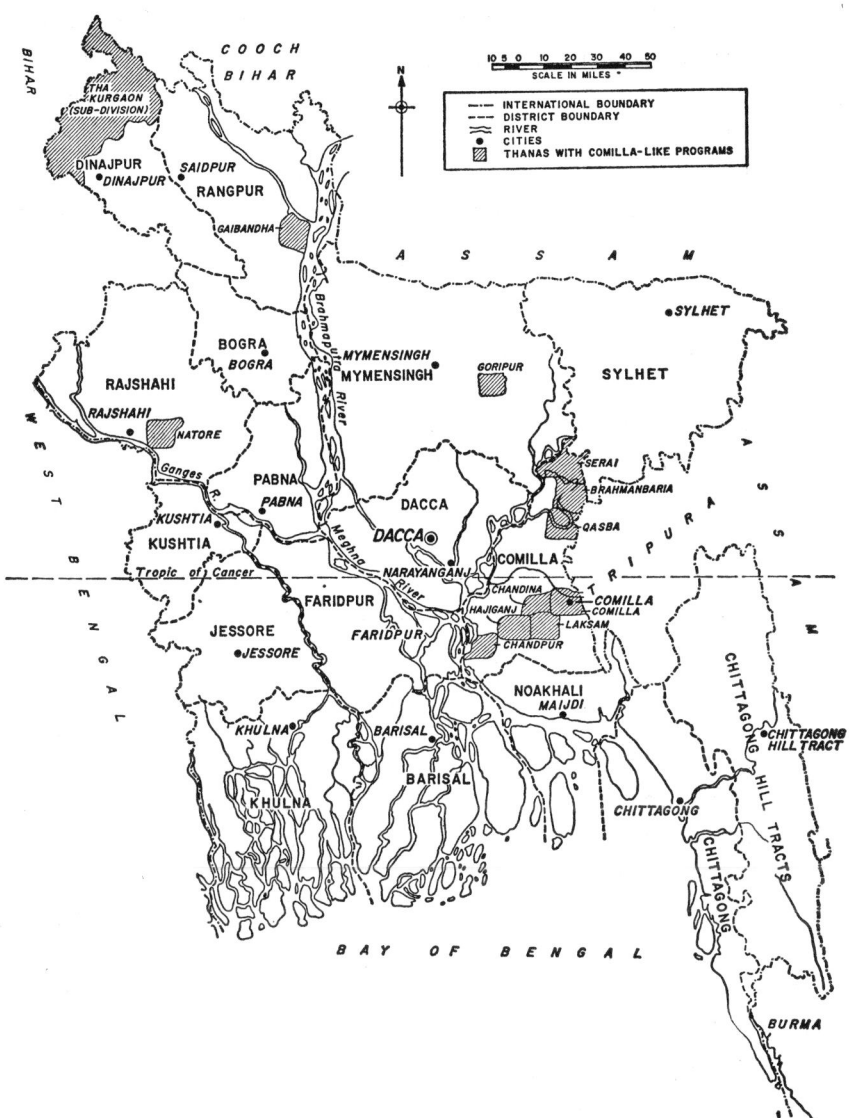

Map 4. East Pakistan, thanas with Comilla-type programs, mid-1966. Based on a map drawn by M. A. Quddus, Comilla, PARD, December 1966.

in one thana. Monthly conferences are continued for project officers at the Academy.

The developments in the three scattered thanas demonstrated that the Comilla program could be replicated in areas far removed (in transportation time) from the Academy.

District Program

Encouraged by successful experience with the three-thana expansion, in January 1965 the government inaugurated the Comilla District Integrated Rural Development Program. Like that of the three outlying thanas, it was initially administered by the Department of Agriculture under the administrative direction of the additional director of agriculture who supervised the three-thana expansion. He continued to be headquartered at Comilla. The program was later transferred to the Agricultural Development Corporation for administration.

The district-wide project was set up on a five-year demonstration basis. It was designed to provide Comilla-type programs in the other 20 thanas of the Comilla district, and to involve the district administration in the support of the various developmental activities in the thanas. Plans were made for the machine shop and tube well sections of the KTCCA to be expanded to provide training and services to all of the thana programs in the district. It was expected, too, that the district farm would later become a research and training center to backstop the agricultural staffs in the thanas.

In essence, the District Program will coordinate and integrate many of the present projects or schemes of the Departments of the Provincial Government as these apply to the Comilla District and the 20 thanas, and will add certain new

The Impact of the Academy 239

institutions which are complementary to the present Departmental schemes. . . .

It is further proposed that, on the basis of experience gained in the launching and operation of the initial District expansion, one or more additional Districts be brought into the program from time to time until all of the Districts in the Province are covered; and that arrangements be made in the Third Five-Year Plan to finance this expansion.[2]

The enlarged development role of the district administration as envisioned in the initial district program proposal was set forth as follows:

As the Thana Councils are the planning and coordinating bodies for the community services at the thana level, the District Council likewise may be used as a supporting institution for the Thana Councils. The District Council will also coordinate the District works program, District water supply program, and other community services.

The Additional Deputy Commissioner, Development, will be the Chairman of the District Technical Coordinating Committee, meeting at least once a month, with all the technical officers as members. . . . In such a system the ADC (Dev.) will through this Committee draw up a district plan for supporting the programs at the thana level, will ensure that each technical officer has all the materials and resources necessary and will supervise the combined operation in the jurisdiction.[3]

The initial proposal emphasized the need for a high quality of training. The key staff of the first seven thanas of the district began their training in the summer of 1964, in a program patterned after the six-month-long training program given the key staff for the three thanas. Included

---

[2] *The Comilla District Development Project*, Comilla, PARD, May 1964, pp. 2–3.
[3] *Ibid.*, p. 16.

were visits to the three thanas to learn first-hand of their experiences in launching and carrying forward their programs.

The program operations of these seven thanas, along with those of the three scattered thanas are coordinated through a monthly project directors' conference, usually held at Kotbari. There is also a quarterly meeting of the agronomists, made up of the agronomist at the district farm and the agronomists in Comilla thana and in the other thanas with new programs. The district policy making group, chaired by the deputy commissioner, with members from the district staff and from the Academy, convenes about twice a year.

Within the first months after the new programs were launched, the organizers of the new village-based cooperatives were in weekly training at the seven thana centers, as were also the first model farmers and the village accountants. By October 1965 machine shops were being set up in each thana in accordance with plans developed by the KTCCA. One 35 hp tractor and one portable pump had been purchased from the KTCCA by each of the seven new central associations. Tractor and pump drivers had been selected in the thanas and were being trained at Comilla. Inspectors and storekeepers were being recruited for training. Also, sites had been selected in each thana for two six-inch irrigation tube wells and ten two-inch tube wells, these latter primarily to introduce irrigated farming.

In the seven thanas of the district there has been generally a regular increase in the number of societies, members, villagers trained weekly at the centers, deposits made by members, and loans. The program in each of these thanas, as in the three earlier scattered ones, developed more rapidly than in Comilla. By mid-1966 five of the central associations had six 35 hp tractors each, and the others had five and four respectively; three had one hand tractor each; two of the associations had sunk two six-inch tube wells, one had sunk one; each of the seven had sunk twelve two-inch wells; two associations had six low-lift power pumps, two had five, two had four, and the other had three. For the seven thanas in 1966, there was an average of 51 acres irrigated, including those served by river-raft pumps.

Some measure of growth in the seven thanas since mid-1966 is indicated by the following statistics as of mid-1968:

Number of agricultural societies	831
Number of nonagricultural societies	117
Total membership (in approximately 45% of the villages)	24,686
Total amount paid in shares	Rs. 698,202
Total savings	Rs. 953,233
Total loans (repayment rate: 82%)	Rs. 4,192,865
Acres under tractor cultivation	5,128
Acres under irrigation	13,309

Some salinity in the water has been discovered in three of the thanas, a situation which has slowed down the expansion of irrigation projects in these areas. Extension activities have emphasized increased use of fertilizers, insecticides, and new rice crops, with good results. Two thanas have started cooperative jute marketing.

Though the operations in the seven thanas have to date been generally successful, problems have emerged in administration, principally between the project directors and the circle officers. This is not surprising in the launching of a new program requiring new administrative relationships, but it is expected that a workable solution will be achieved, in part by the shift of administrative responsibility from project officers on deputation to regular agricultural development corporation employees. These officers, like their predecessors, engaged in a six-month training program at the Academy before assuming their new responsibilities. This should remove the principal remaining administrative hurdle to the further expansion of the Comilla program. Then the programs in the other thirteen thanas in the district can be started, and planning can get under way for the introduction of the program into one or more other districts. It is clear that the thana programs can function best when the district administration is actively interested in performing a supportive role.[4]

Extension of the Public Works Program

Once the Comilla pilot rural public works program and the thana council organization had become operative, there was great interest on the part of the government in expansion to other areas. The national Planning Commission in particular saw in the experience with the pilot public works program in Comilla the possibility of using counterpart funds, generated by the sale of PL-480 wheat, to launch a widespread works program. By duplicating the Comilla program two needed infrastructures could be developed simultaneously, the one physical, the other administrative. The system of canals, embankments, and village roads would be built sooner and maintained better if the people were actively involved in their planning and construction. Also the

[4] For an analysis of administrative and program developments, see *An Evaluation Report on the Progress of the Seven Thana Projects under the Comilla District Integrated Rural Development Programme*, Comilla, PARD, 1967.

The Impact of the Academy   243

sinews of administration would be strengthened in the very process of getting the physical work done.

The potentialities were seen clearly from the outset by Director Khan of the Academy, and by A. M. S. Ahmad, the secretary of the Department of Basic Democracies and Local Government, who had visited Comilla many times while the pilot project was being worked out. The secretary was, as expressed by Director Khan, "the Academy's first trainee in the works programme." The two men early began to plan for expansion. The administrative responsibility would be with the secretary, and the training would be done at the Academy.

In late summer, 1962, the secretary requested the Academy to prepare a training program for the subdivisional officers and the circle officers from the other 53 subdivisional headquarter thanas, as had been recommended by the Academy's report on its pilot project. These officials came to the Academy, the subdivisional officers first for a few days, and then the circle officers, in three groups, for two-week training periods. The training was based on the report and manual prepared upon the completion of the pilot program, visits to the sites of the works projects, and discussions with union councilors and other local leaders. The last half-day of nearly every training period was spent with the secretary, in Comilla.

Before this training program was completed, President Ayub Khan announced that a sum of Rs. 100,000,000 would be available for flood relief for East Pakistan. The government decided to launch a province-wide program patterned after the pilot program at Comilla, to be administered by the Department of Basic Democracies and Local Government. A little more than one-fourth of the Rs.

100,000,000 would be used for the expansion of the rural works program; the remainder went to the district and municipal councils. From the funds for the rural works program, the amount made available to each of the 53 headquarter thanas would be comparable to the amount used in Comilla's pilot project the year before, and about half that much for each of the other 357 thanas. The department forthwith got out a set of comprehensive instructions to the officials who would administer the program, thana by thana. The time was short, but the Academy agreed to give an intensive three-day training program for the remaining circle officers, who came in groups of around 50. A total of 284 circle officers, some of whom served two thanas, reported for this short course.

The three-day training was a condensed version of the two-week course that had been given the first 53 circle officers. Even though the training period was short, Director Khan, the village leaders of Comilla thana, and the secretary had some time with each group. The circle officers were urged to pay close attention to what the village leaders had to say about how they had carried out their projects the year before, and to supplement their brief stay with yet further study of the report and the manual.

On the last afternoon, the secretary met with each outgoing group. He listened to their questions and gave them every assurance that the department put a very high priority on this works program. He said each circle officer would be expected to organize the work in his thana along the lines of the Comilla pilot project of the past year. He said further that they were being asked to do a hard job with minimum time for planning, but that the work must be done well so the program could be further expanded next year.

The Impact of the Academy

In retrospect Director Khan had this to say about the accelerated training of the circle officers in late 1962:

The presence of a model, of a living model, made all the difference in this training. When the officers came they said, "This is all talk. This cannot be done." Their main arguments were that the people were stupid and dishonest, that they would steal all the money. Another argument was that the officers at the top were not interested in doing anything. "They would not let us do anything. Even if we tried to do anything they would stop us." It was very funny for us because when we talked with the officers at the top, the Deputy Commissioner or the Subdivisional Officer, they said, "This is all right but the officers at the thana level are all incompetent and dishonest and they would not do anything." When we talked with the Union Council Chairmen they said, "This is all very good, but you know the officers would *never* allow us to do these things." It was terrific, this complete distrust. But when we brought the officers to Comilla I said, "You said that the people are dishonest and incompetent. Okay. Now you have seen the work in Comilla for these days. You have talked with these people. You have been to the villages. Have they done it properly?" They said, "They seem to have done it in Comilla." I said, "Are these some special kind of people in Bengal, the people of Comilla, or are they just like the people in your area?" And they would scratch their heads and say, "Yes, well, they seem to be the same sort of people." I said, "Then why can't you do it?" They said, "Possibly we can." And they went and did it.[5]

The high point of the public works program was reached in 1964 when Rs. 200,000,000 were allocated on a province-wide basis. The rural portion of this work was carried

[5] Akhter Hameed Khan, *Rural Development in East Pakistan*, East Lansing, Michigan State University, Asian Studies Center, Occasional Papers, No. 2, Spring 1965, p. 50.

out by 25,000 local project committees. In preparation for this program, 343 circle officers were trained at the Academy for seven days, in eight groups, plus assistant directors, divisional commissioners, and other officials of the Department of Basic Democracies and Local Government for shorter courses.

Political and international problems no doubt accounted for the drop to Rs. 142,200,000 in 1965 and Rs. 110,990,000 in 1966. The greatest decreases occurred in allocations to the district councils and the municipal and town committees, each of which received a smaller amount than for any year since the works program began. Only the thana councils and the thana training and development centers were allocated larger funds in 1966 than the year before. Later, public works funds were largely allocated to the province-wide irrigation program.

When the public works program was being inaugurated in West Pakistan in 1963, President Ayub paid tribute to the leadership of East Pakistan:

You would be surprised how much happiness has been given to the people of East Pakistan by the expenditure of a mere ten crores (100,000,000) of rupees, and how much they really feel thankful to the Government for that. It is amazing how much value they have obtained out of that ten crores. The amount of work they have done would be worth 20 crores, because there was no middleman, no contractor. . . . They rehabilitated their roads, their wells, their means of communication, and so on. Wherever you go you get the spontaneous word of thanks from even the ordinary villager for our efforts in East Pakistan. We are going to continue that system.[6]

[6] From a speech by President Ayub Khan to the Staff Seminar on Basic Democracies at Lahore, May 29, 1963 (East Lansing, Michigan State University, Pakistan Project files).

The Impact of the Academy 247

Other Influences of the Comilla Approach

Though it is difficult to make definitive estimates of the effect the Comilla effort may have had upon various other public activities, they cannot be considered negligible. A key factor in facilitating the influence of the Academy on governmental policies and operations affecting the rural sector is to be found in the organization and membership of the board of governors of the Academy. This board, as indicated previously, is chaired by the chief secretary of the government of East Pakistan who has occupied the position since 1964. The members of the board are made up of the chief representatives of the nation-building departments, Agricultural Development Corporation, EPWAPDA, and the national and provincial finance offices. Each of these officials thus is informed about the Academy's program, and most of their departments or agencies are cooperating in some phase or another of the work.

AGRICULTURE AND COOPERATIVES

The Department of Agriculture, in addition to administering the expansion of Comilla-type programs to other thanas (from 1963 to 1968), has sent to the Academy for two weeks' training nearly a hundred of its senior officials from throughout East Pakistan, in groups of around a dozen. The department has also been influenced by the research design for regular crop-cutting work being done by the Academy's research section in cooperation with the Institute of Development Economics. Numerous agricultural extension booklets prepared at Comilla have been printed and distributed throughout East Pakistan by the Department of Agriculture, which has also prepared and distributed booklets of its own, generally similar to the

Comilla publications, with an emphasis on the illustrated lesson sheet.

The Academy's village-based cooperative system, the most complex program of the Academy, is becoming known to more and more village leaders and to officials throughout the province. The rigorous standards of the system require patient development of leadership, which is a relatively slow process. The Academy has resisted pressure to expand the system without proper training of the leadership, as evidenced in the three thana and district expansion programs previously described.

MULTIAGENCY IRRIGATION PROGRAMS

EPWAPDA and the Academy have been associated in many activities, including the public works program, irrigation, and the rural electrification experiment in Comilla thana. Just what use EPWAPDA may be able to make of what is being learned from its cooperative rural electrification experiment with the Academy in Comilla thana is not yet clear. But experience is being gained in the use of electricity for irrigation pumps on deep tube wells and on river rafts, as well as for food storage and processing. Insights, too, may gradually emerge as to the attitude of the villagers toward the later possible use of electricity for lighting of local markets, for small business enterprises, and for use in village households.

In mid-1966 the Academy offered to assist a multiagency ten-thana intensive boro rice production project (Chapter 5). The needed supplies and technical inputs were provided by the Department of Agriculture, the Department of Basic Democracies and Local Government, the Agricultural Development Corporation, and EPWAPDA. The

The Impact of the Academy

training and evaluation functions were performed by the Academy. Village farmers from Comilla thana were sent to the ten thanas to assist the farmers there, and farmers from the ten thanas observed the work being done in the Comilla area.

From this pilot multiagency effort of 1966–1967 there emerged in 1967–1968 a bold plan for a "Thana Irrigation Program" to make irrigation water available throughout the province within a four-year period, by installing 40,000 pumps. More than Rs. 161 million ($34,000,000) were allocated by the government of East Pakistan: one million for the pilot project, 30 million for the 1967–1968 program, 60 million for 1968–1969, and 70 million for 1969–1970. A summary of the accomplishments of the program for 1968–1969, as reported by the Academy's thana irrigation program evaluation team, follows.

Against a target figure of 11,500 pumps, 10,880 were in use during the year. A little more than four-fifths of them were in the two eastern divisions, Dacca and Chittagong, where the rural population density is greater than in the other two divisions of the province. More than half (57 per cent) of all pumps were delivered in December 1968 to the local groups of farmers organized to use them; a month later, 93 per cent of the groups had received their pumps. A little more than a fourth of the pumps were put into operation in December, more than four-fifths by January, and the remainder in February.

The irrigation groups averaged 51 members and irrigated approximately 40 acres per group. (This average of less than one irrigated acre per participating farmer should be seen against the fact that the average size of farms in the province is only a little more than three acres, and that, in the two divisions where the irrigation pumps are concentrated, farms are even smaller.) Nearly half of the groups consisted of members from one village or part of one village, and a little over half were from more than one village.

More than three quarters (78 per cent) of the irrigation pump groups planted IRRI-rice varieties on 37 per cent of the acres irrigated by them. The average yield reported by the managers and model farmers on fields planted with IRRI varieties was about 60 maunds per acre in contrast to half that amount per acre on fields planted with local varieties.[7]

The per acre cost of irrigation water was nearly Rs. 50 without taking into account the subsidy for pumps and direct costs (fuel and oil) to the farmers. (This cost compares with Comilla thana project costs of Rs. 71 for tube well water, Rs. 21 for water from the Sonaichuri project, and Rs. 31 for water provided by pumps on river rafts.)

Supervised credit was supplied by the Agricultural Development Bank in five districts and by the cooperative directorate in 12 districts. Approximately two-thirds of the amount of credit applied for was made available.

The basic organization of 91 per cent of the pump groups was initiated by union council chairmen. More than three-fourths of the detailed plans for these groups were submitted to the thana councils through the union councils. Of the plans submitted, four-fifths were approved by the

---

[7] For a knowledgeable discussion of the prospects and problems of the widespread use of the new high producing varieties of rice, etc., see Clifton R. Wharton, Jr.', "The Green Revolution: Cornucopia or Pandora's Box?" *Foreign Affairs*, New York, April 1969, pp. 464–476.

The Impact of the Academy 251

thana councils, and allocations of pumps were made shortly thereafter. The basic policy of involving the lowest level of local government in the planning process, with coordination at the thana level, was thus accomplished to a high degree. An estimated 2.3 per cent of the groups failed, half because of insufficient water, and the other half from organizational, mechanical, and other problems.

The Agricultural Development Corporation reported training 765 mechanics and assistant mechanics in zonal centers and 7,900 pump drivers in 78 centers to handle the pumping equipment. Eighty-one per cent of the pump drivers were from the thanas examined by the thana irrigation program evaluation committee. Throughout the year training and review sessions continued to be held for circle officers, thana agricultural and cooperative officers and thana irrigation officers. Review sessions alone were attended by 937 officers.

The program was guided by many documents: 9 working papers on plans for the programs, 46 working papers and circular letters from the Department of Basic Democracies and Local Government, 2 circular letters from the Department of Agriculture, 1 circular letter from the cooperative directorate, and 1 circular letter from the Agricultural Development Corporation. The Academy produced 6 reports and training manuals.

Thus the 1968–1969 program accomplished more than 90 per cent of the target objectives for installation of pumps, with almost 600,000 farmers involved in the irrigation of almost 500,000 acres of land.

Yet another outreach of the Academy's work in irrigation is assistance in organizing Comilla-type cooperatives in the Thakurgaon tube well project in the northwestern part of the province. This project was developed in the early 1960's under the sponsorship of EPWAPDA by a loan and technicians from West Germany, at a cost of about Rs. 140 million ($30,000,000). A total of 380 wells of 2 to 3½ cubic feet per second discharge were installed; the project extends over several thanas. As stated by Director Khan of the Academy:

> In 1965 the EPWAPDA Chairman was puzzled and worried by the absence of any enthusiasm on the part of the farmers to take advantage of this new resource. Very few acres had been irrigated even when water was being offered free of cost. The Chairman came to see for himself the extensive use of tube-well water in the cooperative villages of Comilla. . . . He then invited the Director of the Academy to visit the Thakurgaon project and suggest an effective organizational pattern. . . . Finally in July 1966, the EPWAPDA invited the Academy to include Thakurgaon along with the 11 thana projects under its guidance. Taslimuddin Ahmed, who had successfully organized the Natore project area since 1963, was deputed to organize a central cooperative association and assist in establishing village-based cooperatives in Thakurgaon. . . . EPWAPDA will continue to provide all technical and financial support. If the village cooperatives could be organized as successfully around the Thakurgaon tube wells as they have been organized in Comilla, Thakurgaon may well become the richest and most progressive area in East Pakistan. In that case the Comilla Academy will have a good example of physical engineering having been consummated by social engineering.[8]

Effective cooperative organization work among the farmers in the Thakurgaon project is gradually being

[8] Prepared for the author in October 1966 (East Lansing, Michigan State University, Pakistan Project files).

The Impact of the Academy   253

achieved. In 1967–1968 five officers of the project were in training at Comilla for 60 days each, four engineers and mechanics for eight days, and five accountants for fourteen days. Director Khan in October 1969 expressed satisfaction with the progress being made.

FAMILY PLANNING ACTIVITIES

Family planning activities in East Pakistan and at the national level have been affected by the Academy's work. The Pak-Swedish-American Family Planning Research and Study Group convened at Comilla for a day's conference in November 1963 to hear firsthand of the work there. In September 1964 Director Khan, upon the request of President Ayub Khan, met with the national commissioner of family planning to discuss ways and means of introducing and promoting the IUD (intrauterine device) program. After a thorough discussion, it was agreed that IUD insertions would likely be relevant in localities where medical services were available, but that in the extensive rural areas the mass distribution of nonmedical supplies as worked out in Comilla thana would be promoted.

Thus Comilla's influence on family planning in East Pakistan centers mainly around the extension of the nonmedical program to all the thanas in the Comilla district, and then to the thanas of the remaining 16 districts in the province. Also, valuable information is being assembled at the Academy from the family planning research underway. This research until recently dealt largely with the use of nonmedical supplies but now also gives attention to the procedures by which the IUD program and surgical methods can be speeded up. The Academy serves this activity as a training, research, and advisory institution.

A few doctors have come to Comilla to see the work of the maternity and child health clinic at Abhoy Ashram, the systematic mass distribution of nonmedical family planning supplies throughout the thana, and more recently the experimentation with other methods. Lawyers, judges, and others come primarily out of interest or wonderment—what is this that is going on at Comilla?

At the national level, there seems to be, as a result of the family planning work sponsored by the Academy, an added emphasis on the use of local leaders at the planning stage. The work at Comilla emphasizes the involvement of villagers themselves in carrying out the program in a modified version of the organizer system, by which the supplies are received, distributed, and accounted for by a local agent. Many of the procedures found workable at Comilla have been incorporated in the Third Five-Year Plan. The family planning research done by the Academy seems to have given added impetus to this activity.

EDUCATION PROJECTS UNDER REVIEW

As of mid-1966 the Department of Education had accepted for review the pilot school project, which introduces a "rural bias" into the schools by sponsoring boys' and girls' individual farm- and home-related projects. But there are problems involved in the extension of this type of project to other thanas due to the vastness of the undertaking and the paucity of education officials who have the inclination to experiment with new activities.

The Comilla pilot project in adult education (Imam teachers, women teachers, publications, and so on) is operative in the three scattered thanas. In the fall of 1965 it was accepted for further possible expansion by the Department of Education. This department earlier created the post of assistant director of public instruction for adult education and posted the newly appointed official at Comilla. Since August 1965 the department has also had under consideration the duplication of the school works program in other thanas in collaboration with the thana council. Yet more recently, upon Director Khan's recommendation, the department has under advisement the appointment of thana boards of education.

UNIVERSITY TEACHERS, STUDENTS, AND OTHERS

The Academy has also reached and influenced private groups and individuals. College and university teachers became interested in the work of the Academy as soon as the programs got underway. Some of these teachers have used Academy publications in their classrooms and have made use of ideas and programs they observed firsthand in the Comilla area. Many East Pakistan university students visit the Academy.

Four Dacca University students have worked out their M.A. theses under the instructors at the Academy, as have also students from the East Pakistan Agricultural University at Mymemsingh. The subjects of these theses have ranged from social and economic theories to such practical matters as the growing and cooperative marketing of potatoes and other vegetables. In recent years, too, degree students of the Social Welfare College, Dacca, have done their required field work training at Comilla. In these and other colleges and universities in East Pakistan, numerous papers by graduate students have been prepared on one aspect or another of the work of the Academy.

Many volunteer social welfare workers have also come to Comilla to study its activities. They are especially interested, as have been several groups of missionaries, in the cooperatives, in the work with women and with youth, in literacy training, in the work of the clinic at Abhoy Ashram, and in the lunch programs for school children.

PRIVATE BANKING AND BUSINESS

Some business and professional people, too, have been influenced by the Academy's programs. The financial transactions of the KTCCA relate to many private enterprises in Chittagong and Dacca, as well as in Comilla. The purchase of automotive vehicles, farm tractors, irrigation pumps, power spray-pumps, motor scooters, cold-storage equipment, and the like, attract equipment dealers. And naturally enough, the purchase and operation of trucks and buses by the Comilla cooperative societies have been noted as something new by the trucking and bus companies. The United Bank, Ltd. has set up a branch bank at each of the headquarters in the thanas with Comilla-type programs, and has expressed a desire to do so in any other thanas where programs are launched. The National Bank of Pakistan has made a similar offer.

INFLUENCE ON GOVERNMENT POLICY

The Academy's action and research programs taken together have had considerable influence on policy in the government of Pakistan. This is best seen in the references to the work at Comilla in the Third Five-Year Plan. The plan describes how the rural public works program was piloted in Comilla thana, and how it "vitalizes the local bodies and gives opportunity to local talent for leadership, organization and administration. . . ." The report continues:

Comilla is used as the experimental area in which model operations are tried out on the basis of which the provincial programme is organized. . . .

The Impact of the Academy 257

Thana/Tehsil Training and Development Centres should be established all over the country to organize comprehensive training in administration and skills and servicing and coordinating the activities of the cooperative village units. These centres should be on the Comilla model which consists of a strong central cooperative federation to organize and service village multipurpose cooperatives and a team of departmental officers working as teacher-trainers, and which ensure the closest association of the cooperative structure and training organization and the Basic Democracies. This model can be duplicated with necessary adjustments to local conditions. The Training Programme at the Academy for Rural Development and the Basic Democracy Institutes should be coordinated with the training programme of the Thana Training and Development Centres.[9]

By 1969, all but about 20 of East Pakistan's 411 thanas had constructed Thana Training and Development Centers patterned on the center at Comilla. There have been expenditures of public works funds for these centers of around Rs. 100,000,000 ($21,000,000).

INTERNATIONAL INFLUENCE

The international dimension at Comilla deserves at least brief mention. One or more groups of people, mostly officials, have come to the Academy to study its programs from more than a score of developing countries, including Afghanistan, Brazil, Ceylon, Ecuador, India, Iran, Iraq, Kenya, Laos, Malaysia, Morocco, Nepal, Nigeria, Philippines, South Rhodesia, Somalia, Sudan, Thailand, Tunisia, Turkey, Uganda, and the United Arab Republic. It seems probable that some effects on the planning and execution of

[9] *Outline of the Government of Pakistan's Third Five-Year Plan.* Rawalpindi, Government of Pakistan Printing Office, Aug. 1964, pp. 231–232.

rural development programs in these countries will come out of the visits. Furthermore, the Academy's publications have been received with interest in these and many other countries, a number of papers have been presented on one phase or another of the Comilla program at international conferences, and Comilla materials are being used in graduate studies at numerous universities in the United States, Europe, and Asia.

The Role of Akhter Hameed Khan

In speculating about the future of the Comilla approach, it is necessary to ask, first of all: How dependent is the program upon one man—Akhter Hameed Khan? That man himself answers the question with characteristic modesty:

Now, here is the question which I am most frequently asked: "It's all right. You can do these things in Comilla, because you are doing it." Which, of course, is wrong. It's not I who am doing it, as I emphasize again and again. It's not the Academy which is doing all these things. It is the normal cadre of officers who have been there. What the Academy is doing is sitting with them, advising them sometimes, but most of the time it's just analyzing the research. But the real question is, how do you extend all this activity? What is the use of all these pilot projects? Are they really going to affect the working of the government? . . .

When we have a pilot project we ask [the government] to nominate a young officer from among the elite, young in age but senior in status, to be put in charge of the pilot project. Then he . . . learns to work at the thana and the village level. This remedies the greatest weakness of our people who now sit in the policy-making positions. . . . Then, after two or three years, he can go back to Dacca or to more important positions.

The Impact of the Academy 259

In this way we would be sure that the influence and the methods would spread.[10]

Yet almost everyone who has been exposed to the program would agree that without Akhter Hameed Khan there would be no Comilla program in its present form. The Comilla approach is largely the product of this man who has worked insightfully and hard and long at one place. He encourages, stimulates, and to a large extent dominates his staff. He commands the respect and cooperation of government officials and the representatives of aid-giving agencies. He is a plain man, studious, articulate, and poetic. He is strict and demanding of himself and of his associates, and is capable of an occasional outburst of anger when faced with inaction, ineptitude, or procrastination.

Director Khan likes to teach. Hardly a training group has been at the Academy when he was on campus that he has not spoken to at least once. Hardly a rally of villagers has been organized that he has not addressed. He likes to get policy statements defined and in writing. These policy statements range widely over the activities of the Academy.

He is also a good listener. When he comes upon an operational problem he does not know the answer to, he listens intently until he has secured all the information he can get. He often seeks out the reactions of members of his staff, local officials, provincial or national officials, or an advisor or consultant. He characteristically outlines the question to which he wants an answer, and holds the discussion to the point.

Before formally proposing to the government a new

---

[10] From a speech at Michigan State University, October 1966 (East Lansing, Michigan State University, Pakistan Project files).

project, he carefully canvasses the reactions of key government officials, particularly the chief secretary of East Pakistan, and relevant members of the Academy's board of governors. If they are interested, he has thus secured their early support for the proposed program, or at least he has removed outright opposition. If they are not interested, he has spared himself a potential "No." Also, he may have found that more educational work needs to be done with this official or that one, who perhaps had best come to Comilla and study the programs underway there to see for himself. Or maybe some point of view should receive greater emphasis in the Academy's training to satisfy a new administrative dimension that is emerging.

But, whoever else's advice Director Khan seeks, he leans most heavily upon the reactions of the villagers in the Comilla area. They are the sounding board for new programs to be undertaken, and for the methods being considered to carry them out. He assumes that the answers to the developmental problems lie with the people themselves. He goes to them for answers. He encourages the villagers to share with him their estimates of their problems. He thinks with them about how they can go about solving them.

When weary or discouraged, Director Khan turns to the village. He walks village paths to renew his strength. When a prestigious visitor arrives he tells him of the Academy and its activities. He then maneuvers to get him into his Jeep to go to the villages to see what is being done there. A visitor's question about this or that phase of the village program may not be answered promptly. Rather he stops upon meeting some farmer along the way. "Now," he says to the visitor, "let me interpret for you, and you ask this man your question."

The Impact of the Academy

Director Khan has remained at the Academy in spite of many attractive opportunities to work elsewhere. He was invited to accept the directorship of the Agricultural Development Corporation, and to become the vice chancellor of Dacca University. Early in 1965 a concerted effort was made to get him to serve as coordinator of agricultural programs in East Pakistan. He chose to continue to work at Comilla. For Akhter Hameed Khan the great challenge has been to find a workable way to meet the needs of the villagers. If this can be done, he thinks, the wider constructive programs can follow.

We must conclude then, despite Director Khan's disclaimers, that the Comilla program has been heavily dependent upon him. He has been wise enough to prevent it from becoming a one-man show. Important as this man is, yet more important are the viable development procedures that are being worked out by him and his associates.

A first effort to shift some of the burdens of work and responsibility of the directorship was made in 1964 when a new director, K. M. Shamsur Rahman, was appointed to the Academy, with Akhter Hameed Khan taking on a newly created position as vice chairman of the board of governors while retaining the chairmanship of the managing committee of the KTCCA. After approximately a year he resumed the directorship of the Academy. In 1968 he again relinquished the directorship of the Academy to A. H. M. Azizul Huq, while retaining the other two above-named positions. The transition in leadership of the Academy now appears to be assured. Furthermore, the relationships and integration of the work of the Academy with the work of the KTCCA and the expanded programs has been thoughtfully documented. The understandings reached serve as guidelines for assuring the continuation and collaborative effort for operations and further policy development.

The Faculty of the Academy

Working with Director Khan is a faculty of growing competence and a managerial staff in the cooperatives who are becoming more skilled in business methods essential to the operation of the economic organizations on which so much of their common welfare depends. The first five years of the Academy's work was characterized by a deliberate effort to learn by doing, by trial and error, to find out what would work with Comilla villagers. Everyone's nose was kept to the grindstone in the pursuit of indigenous answers; academic principles from textbooks which had questionable relevance to the needs of Comilla villagers were deliberately shelved. Some members of the faculty discovered that this kind of rigor and mission was not for them and were released from their commitment of working under a five-year bond, but several of the original group stuck with the task. Two factors now make it easier for the Academy to select and retain new staff members. These are: (1) a clearer conception of the nature of the programs and requirements for staffing, and (2) the more firmly established prestige of the Academy.[11]

As the early experiments took root, the work was seen in ever wider contexts, and the need for continuous staff development was more clearly recognized. As an outgrowth of this recognition a staff development policy was created by the Academy, the Ford Foundation, and Michi-

---

[11] See Appendix II for a list of the major staff at Comilla, 1959 to mid-1969.

gan State University, under which several staff members have been sent to nondegree courses and conferences in Europe, Asia, and the United States, and four members of the faculty sent to Michigan State University, two for the Ph.D. degree and two for the masters degree. But most of the staff development still takes place in the learning experiences inherent in the creative work of the Academy itself, aided and abetted by supervision, assistance of foreign advisors, association with Peace Corps Volunteers, British Volunteers, and visiting scholars, through association with colleagues and through specific training sessions organized by advisors and short-term consultants.

Comilla has been seen from the beginning as an institution-building operation, and not as a one-shot performance or a brilliant instance of development without continuity. The emphasis on research, on record keeping, and on training, have, among other things, pointed up the fact that Comilla was to be built with the long-range future of rural life in Pakistan in mind. As has been made clear at a number of different points in this narrative, great care has been taken to integrate the operations into the lives of villagers and into the structure of Pakistan public administration and to inform and educate, continuously, the leaders of government, as well as others, as to what Comilla is all about. Especially important from the government side is that every group of probationers of the Civil Service of Pakistan and of the East Pakistan Civil Service is sent to Comilla as a part of their training.

The recruitment and retention of personnel for Comilla itself, and for the extension to other thanas and districts, has of course involved plenty of problems. Yet the dynamic nature of the program has by and large attracted highly qualified people (young, for the most part) despite the lack of amenities in many a rural thana. Almost all of the enlarging activities in Comilla thana have been staffed by persons recruited from within the projects. This has been the case with the new cooperative system, the reorganized thana council, the work with women, family planning, youth activities, and the irrigation and agricultural processing programs. Capable men and women have been attracted to the Academy from inside and outside the civil service. The turnover rate is somewhat high, due to the relatively rigorous standards of the Academy, and the requirements for fitting into a team effort.

It is encouraging to note the high quality of officials who have become available to work in the expansion program. The largest number of those posted at the Academy and in the expansion thanas have been connected with the Department of Agriculture and the Agricultural Development Corporation. There have been three additional directors of agriculture in charge of the expansion program since 1962. Each has been a member of the Civil Service of Pakistan and interested in the work.

Nevertheless, with all of the achievements and involvements of capable government officials and leaders, faculty members, and others, the principal limiting factor in expanding the basic lessons of Comilla to other areas in Pakistan is the shortage of highly motivated, creative, and skilled personnel. The early skepticism about the validity and workability of the hard requirements laid down by the director and early associates for successful rural development work has given way to enthusiasm and applause as the various programs have succeeded to a remarkable degree. This change in attitude has made it possible for the Academy and the KTCCA to attract a much larger number of persons who are eager to be associated with and to be trained by the now prestigious organization, but there is still an acute shortage of capable people commensurate with the vast needs and opportunities which every new development breakthrough creates.

10. Reflections

To get at the roots of rural development problems; to formulate tentative approaches to their solution; to test these hypotheses in experimental programs involving the motivation and instruction of hundreds of decision makers under conditions of free choice; to record, document, and analyze the record of successful and unsuccessful approaches; and to utilize these records of the experiments as the primary instructional materials for the administration of rural development programs—all of these add up to the complex story that we have attempted to tell in this short book.

The training part of the Comilla Academy's program was from the outset focused upon the reorientation of officials trained in law and order administration toward the new responsibilities assigned in developmental programs. Thus the academic phase of the project started and has remained in the official records of the government as a project in public administration.

A second focus, which began to emerge early, was on the assembling of first-hand information about local conditions, and along with this the training of villagers to serve as extension agents to their neighbors. This innovative work with the villagers—hardly envisioned in the original plan

—soon began to yield training materials highly relevant to the Academy's function as a teaching institution for officials with development responsibilities. Furthermore, new reservoirs of village leadership have been found and utilized in the process.

Working thus directly with the villagers, the Academy inevitably began to direct its attention to their primary needs: increased agricultural production, cooperatives, credit, mechanization, water control and irrigation, agricultural processing, warehousing, and extension methods. Since better organization and a higher quality of public service was found to be central to the achievement of these objectives, a new and improved pattern of rural organization, the Thana Training and Development Center, was created. Also out of this context came the programs for women, youth, and family planning. Each of these is an integral element in what became a comprehensive approach to rural development in a thana-size laboratory. The limitation of the basic experimentation to this small area has been a central working concept and is worthy of being elevated to a general principle of advice to any who may hope to utilize the essence of the Comilla experience elsewhere. As for its applicability to other areas, the Comilla approach is not so much a formula for development as it is a formula for *finding* a formula for a development program to fit a particular area.

The rural pilot experiments got underway in the laboratory area as the withdrawn and fatalistic small farmers began to express themselves and as the skeptical officials began to realize that something might be done. At first this meant above all else that the Academy staff members and officials needed to listen, and to listen, and to remember what was said, and to know and to care what it meant.

Listening to villagers with respect and understanding has been a condition of getting anything done.

Often in the launching stage, a handicap was taken as a spur to action. This approach led to programs intended to solve the difficulty of too much water in one part of the year and too little in the other, and to programs planned to cope with widespread illiteracy, ill health, nonparticipation, and the toll that poverty takes. It was the low incomes and near absence of money among the villagers that led the Academy staff to the conclusion that the villagers had to become creditworthy, even though this could be achieved only through the painful regular saving of small amounts by very poor people. It was the isolation of the village that made it a socioeconomic entity, and so the locale of the new cooperative society. It was the low rate of literacy coupled with lack of mutual trust among the villagers that made necessary the weekly meeting of the full membership of the group. It was the weakness of the undernourished bullocks, and the lack of bullocks on some farms, that first made the custom-hire of tractors attractive. The fact of no year-round communication by land or water vehicle in extensive areas resulted in dependence upon head- and shoulder-load transportation, and so motivated the effective participation of villagers in local road-building projects. The flood led to drainage efforts, and the bleak dry season led to irrigation programs.

Positive uses have been made of cultural factors. The Friday meeting of the men at the local mosque is the precedent for the weekly training of village leaders at the Academy; and traditional folk singers who make up their own songs are being used to promote family planning and other programs.

Many of the development procedures at Comilla have

indigenous roots. The process of institution building underway there deals realistically with local conditions and takes care to hold the interest and cooperation of villagers and officials. Such, in summary, is the "Comilla Approach." It is yielding these basic results: a steady flow of factual materials for the training of officials and village leaders, a viable voluntary cooperative unit (society) at the village level that has broken the cycle of fatalism, a strong central (thana) cooperative association, a vitalized local administration that emphasizes development activities, a continuing educational activity for villagers that does not disrupt farming, and a formula for the expansion of proven programs to other parts of the province.

Four important tests of the soundness of a rural development program are: the extent to which it succeeds in introducing technical advances; the volume and quality of training for needful new types of work and for essential traditional tasks; the observable improvements for participating families in production, incomes, and levels of living; and the prospect for permanence of any gains.

First, the Comilla program stacks up well as to technical advances: on the Academy farm in early 1966 new strains of rice from IRRI were field-tested in East Pakistan for the first time, and it was on the farms of members of five of the new cooperative societies in the Comilla area a few months later that tested seed from the Academy farm was first mass-produced for other farms. These things happened because the strict conditions for testing could be met earlier on the Academy farm, and on the farms of cooperative members, accustomed to organized ways of proceeding and to accepting the advice of trained agriculturists. Seed testing and multiplication were then shifted to the experiment stations and district farms of the Department of Agriculture and, under supervision, to some of the larger private farms.

Antecedents of these recent technical advances at Comilla include: the increased use of practices early recommended by the Japanese experts and later taught by thana officials (e.g., seedbed preparation, fertilizing); the introduction by the Japanese of new crops and of improved varieties (e.g., watermelons, potatoes); the introduction and use of machines (tractors, irrigation pumps, power sprayers); the establishment of agricultural processing units (e.g., cold-storage plants, creamery); and the fuller use of soil and water resources through the construction of drainage canals and irrigation facilities. Technical advances have been safeguarded by administrative and social advances, such as revitalizing the union and thana councils, setting up local project committees for public works, creating new types of cooperatives and "feeder schools," furthering education and home improvement work among village women, introducing the idea of "rural bias" in the regular schools, and persevering in careful research and evaluation.

Second, the extent and quality of the training done at Comilla is generally adequate, as amply set forth in earlier chapters: the new mechanical skills (tractor drivers, pump operators, well drillers, repairmen), the new organizational activities (cooperatives, public works, irrigation, processing units), the new development responsibilities given to provincial and thana officials and to traditional local leaders, the new opportunities for rank-and-file farmers and nonfarmers (weekly meetings of cooperative societies, regular training classes, annual rallies). In recalling the above array of training activities it is important to remember that recruits for practically all of the new jobs at Comilla have

Reflections 271

been from among persons already involved in Academy-sponsored programs.

Third, as related to improvements in productivity, family incomes and levels of living, the Comilla performance cannot be so specifically documented. Even so, some clear gains emerged early. Rice yields were moderately increased by seedbed preparation, line sowing, weeding, more fertilizer, and better insect control; rice prices to the farmers were raised by cooperatively keeping the crop off the market in the low-price harvest season; production credit was secured at less than a third of the annual cost formerly prevailing; encumbered land was redeemed from the moneylenders as debts owed them were paid with cooperative loans. Family incomes and levels of living began to rise as production increased, prices improved, and the debt burden shrank. In the meantime, the Academy's programs for women and youth had begun to operate in the villages, the thana officials were adding teaching of villagers to their other functions, and the thana pilot works program had become a model for East Pakistan. All of these things taken together were bringing to the villagers and the officials a new spirit of confidence and adventure which pointed to further experimentation.

So, naturally enough, in more recent years use is being made of the new varieties of rice from IRRI, which can be produced successfully only under farming conditions, including irrigation, which are more advanced than obtained in the Comilla area during the first years of the Academy's work. With the greater inputs have come more substantial economic returns to the participating farm families. This is a truism, for except for better incomes and levels of living, the Bengali farmers would not be interested in increased production. Comparable gains, too, have been made by the members of the nonfarm cooperative societies through loans and group action in producing and marketing goods and services.

Fourth, the permanence of Comilla's gains is inherent in its extensive and realistic training activities based on research and evaluation and on the changes being effected in the attitudes of the people toward innovations. The Academy's leaders continue to explore new ways of doing things, and of developing further the interrelationship between physical and social engineering. History may well record that Comilla's greatest contribution has been its social and administrative pioneering that have encouraged sustained efforts in modernization. The energizing of old institutions and the creation of new ones as needed are not ends in themselves; they are the means of assuring the ongoing of the gains that are made.

The diverse programs at Comilla exhibit intersupportive qualities. For instance, a cooperative loan can be the more easily repaid when, as a result of the public works program, the damages from floods are reduced, the supply of irrigation water is increased, and there are more village roads that connect with the larger market. Then, the other way around, too, for the initial rural public works project could be launched more easily in areas where the local people were already working together in the new village-based cooperative societies. Or again, it was the effective working together of officials and villagers in achieving the physical infrastructure of canals and village roads that yielded an administrative infrastructure of concerned officials and a supporting citizenry. To realize the importance of a supporting local citizenry, one need but remember how often development efforts have failed for lack of local people being able and willing to work together.

The quality of intersupportiveness permeates the Comilla program as one activity leads to or strengthens another, and so each enhances the other. One soundly based early physical innovation (use of low-lift pumps) facilitated the introduction of tractors, and this in turn of tube well irrigation, and then a cold-storage plant and a second one. These cumulative physical innovations are paralleled by and integrated with the equally basic social and administrative innovations described. For instance, the thana representative of a nation-building department, in becoming a teacher of village cooperative managers and model farmers, comes to have more respect for the villager and more confidence in himself, and so he is the readier to enter into the various facets of the modernization program. So too, with the village woman, traditionally limited by purdah, who becomes a teacher of other village women, of small children in the local school, a taker of loans from the cooperative to buy a milk cow or goat, or who uses a sewing machine to make clothes to sell or for her family, or learns silk screen printing. She will encourage her children to take part in other innovative activities.

There is little need to portray the intersupportive factors in the growth cycle of the Comilla farmer, for this is already well documented. But think of the school youth, who each year carry on thousands of individual farm- and home-related projects, culminating in an annual rally where they meet one another, look at one another's exhibits, and where the best performers line up to receive their prizes: flashlights, bars of soap, small cans of insecticides, and for the top winners, small silver medals struck for the occasion by a local silversmith. These youths are sensing the interdependent relationships among themselves and between themselves and their environment, and with their elders and the government men; for they know their fathers are involved in cooperatives and the public works project committees, and their mothers are doing and saying new things.

In short, here is an integrated interdependent ongoing set of activities which has encouraged innovation and created within the people a sense of newness and hope. As yet, the concept of "chain reaction" is perhaps too strong, but compared with the starting point, one naturally thinks of it. At any rate, *in toto*. Comilla's comprehensive development program may be seen as one of the most effective community development efforts that to date has been made in a depressed area of a developing country.

The account of these first years of the Academy's work sets forth only the beginnings of a development process. Much of what has been discovered and demonstrated can properly be attributed to the dedicated spirit, energy, and seminal insights of one man—Akhter Hameed Khan—augmented by the collaborative work of his associates, the support of his government and to a degree by assistance from external agencies. But government policies can and do vacillate; development processes can and do suffer setbacks; officials can and do find the discipline of development tiring; and countless other hazards will no doubt continue to intervene in the achievement of an ordered and sustained solution of rural problems in East Pakistan.

Yet the Academy and the Comilla program, though still experimental, have successfully passed through the initial stage of institutional development in Comilla thana itself and in other thanas in which the basic principles learned in

Comilla have been applied. The program has gained acceptance from the government of Pakistan as a constructive force for demonstrating new techniques and providing tested information for the formulation of policies and programs of rural development more generally. It has shown its ability to attract promising young men and women to its staff, and to advance their competence as professional development workmen. There is a long road ahead from here to widespread improvement in the living standards of the thousands of villagers in East Pakistan, but a way is being shown how that road might be successfully traveled.

There may well be elements in the Comilla experience that will be useful in other parts of the world. If so, the villagers of the world—the majority of mankind—will be the beneficiaries.

APPENDIXES

1. "*A Light in the Darkness*"*

Yesterday I came back from visiting West Pakistan and Dacca. There I met with many officers, Pakistani and American. I was astonished when I saw that everyone knows about Comilla—I never thought that news of the little job we are doing here would spread far and wide. Now I think that in Comilla you have lit a light in the darkness.

All around us there was darkness—the darkness of envy and the darkness of fear. Everyone thinks that nothing can be done in our country. When it is said that some work must be done in the country, the answer is always: "Who will do it, when everyone is a thief?" This, then, is the darkness of envy. And the darkness of fear. So the poor people of the village are all agitated and fearful—they don't know who will help them, or how. People in our country thought that no work would be done, that our situation would not improve at all.

Amidst this darkness you have lit a lamp. You have kindled a light. If we light a tiny lamp, its rays will cover a great distance. After returning from ten days of travel outside I am able to understand that this little light of Comilla can be seen from far away. And many people saw this light in the darkness, and their hearts have filled with hope. Here among us a kind of courage and a kind of hope has been born.

---

* A speech by Akhter Hameed Khan at a rally of the Comilla Cooperative Societies, October 14, 1962; translated by Marianna Tax Choldin.

Last year in this month of October we called the members of the Association together. Then five or six hundred members came. Today, one year later, we have again called the members together. You see how many people have come. One of us was saying that next year we won't be able to have a meeting here. So many people will come that there won't be room for us all here. In the space of two years such a thing has happened.

Let us see what else has happened. Last year we had no Central Association. We hoped that if we could save money we would be able to give the members of the Association a loan from our own bank. We had difficulties. When members of the village cooperative society needed money they couldn't get it in time. They had to make applications here and applications there. They had to butter up these people and those people. There was every kind of difficulty. Today, one year later, our Central Association has given more than two lakh rupees in loans. And we have saved more than ten lakh rupees. Now we can buy as many tractors as we want. As many as we need.

The Central Association has become so strong that some of our big banks have come to us saying that they want to open a branch here. The National Bank wanted a branch. The United Bank also wanted a branch. Why? I showed them our accounts, and they themselves also made calculations—where is our country's wealth coming from? Where are these lakhs and lakhs, crores and crores of rupees coming from? Where is our country's wealth being created? Not in Dacca, where there are thousands and thousands of automobiles. But in the villages where the paddy and the jute grow. I made calculations and showed the bankers that the people of this one thana alone—there are about 300 hundred villages here—if they stick together and learn things, can keep the money in the bank instead of keeping it themselves. When we need money we will take it out of the bank, and when we get money we will put it in the bank. When the crops are harvested we won't take

Appendix I 281

them to market in separate bundles. We will put them together in a big bundle and take them to a big market like Hajiganj or Doulatganj, and sell them there. Then do you know how much money will come into this bank, how many rupees' worth of business there will be, how many rupees' worth of jute and paddy sales? You think you are very small and weak. If this one single thana among East Pakistan's 411 thanas works together, we can have a business concern here of more than one crore.

Last year there were only 40 village societies. Now about 100 villages have societies. I hope that within the next year there will be 200 societies. What else have these societies done?

When a poor farmer in our villages needed money and took a 100 rupee loan, he also had to give land, he had to give two maunds of rice, he had to bow and scrape and be afraid. These little societies of ours have united you and having united, you have begun to work. Now in many places people don't have to go to the moneylender at all—the fear that you used to have of the moneylender is gone now. The society has saved you. Another thing has happened—for so long each of you worked alone. This was very expensive for you farmers. You weren't able to buy machines. Many people don't have cows. And those people who do have cows but have only two or three *bigha* of land incur losses by keeping cows. The farmers' expenses are great and their earnings small. Where the society did a good job—made a plan and brought machines, made a plan and arranged for water—the farmers' expenses decreased and their earnings increased. Moreover, members of your societies are now learning improved methods of farming and are profiting greatly.

Now you can see what kind of changes the society can bring about in one year. Your situation was bad; now it is gradually improving. I want to say that it can become far better yet. You have been oppressed by the moneylender—you will be no longer. How will you do this? By accepting the terms of the deposit, by saving money every week and depositing it, and by continuing to do this. If you don't stop, your condition will gradually improve. You will accumulate your own capital. You won't have to go to anyone else. You will have machines, you will be able to do all your work in a better way. Bear in mind that these days the running of the world is completely dependent upon money. It is dependent upon capital. He who has no money has no worth. He has no place in the world. He who has money and capital has power.

Please do not think that this is a new principle, and that previously things were better. This is not so. Five hundred years ago a Persian poet made this observation about money: "Money, although you are not God, although you are not Allah, still you have two qualities of Allah." Allah's two qualities are *chattare aiub* and *kajiul hajat*. The first means covering up or concealing crimes and wrongs. The second means meeting all demands and needs. The poet is saying that money possesses these two qualities of Allah, chattare aiub and kajiul hajat. Remember that if you don't make money deposits, if you don't make the society strong, nothing can be done. The society will be destroyed.

Another thing: if you work together—as you are doing now—have meetings, prepare plans, try to change our situation, you are on the path of progress. Because now each person has a little bit of land; one or two acres, four or five bigha. Suppose you want to plant a winter crop; then you have to make some arrangement for water. A tube well can irrigate 40 to 50 acres. So one person can't do very much with a tube well. But if 40 to 50 householders get together, make a plan, and work together, they can use all these machines and increase their gains—the more you work together, the more you will see that your expenses are decreasing and your incomes increasing.

You have seen that this year in several societies where members have stored their paddy together. At the time they stored their paddy together the price of paddy in the Comilla market and all the little markets was only 13 or 14 rupees. Then, when June and July came, they sold their paddy all together. In trailers or boats they took the paddy to the large markets. There they got a price of 18 or 19 rupees. Moreover, in the little markets of Comilla the merchants weigh 82 tolas to a seer. This is cheating. When they weigh the paddy they take too much from you. We saw how the moneylender takes a share of your earnings. The merchants also take a share of your earnings. But just as when the society worked as one unit the oppression of the moneylender was stopped, in the same way you yourselves get that share of your earnings which the merchants used to take. You sold your paddy for 18 or 19 rupees instead of for 13 rupees. And you sold your paddy at a weight of 80 tolas, not 82 tolas, per seer. In South Rampur, for example, it was seen that when they collected their paddy and weighed it, they had 609 maunds. But when they sold it at Hajiganj it turned out that they sold 623 maunds of paddy and still a little was left.

So you see, first of all, that the society will save you from the moneylender. If you accumulate capital, your condition will improve. Secondly, if you join together, make a plan, and work, you can decrease your expenses and increase your earnings. Thirdly, if you store your paddy or other crops together, you can get a good price for it at the market, and you will have for yourselves that money which you are now giving the merchants. Your income will increase by at least one-third.

Now you can see that the society is able to bring about a big change. It can improve your situation very much. But for this to happen you must make even greater efforts. Remember: if you are hoping for your situation to be improved by the efforts of outsiders, you are mistaken. That will not happen. You must make the effort yourselves. Those of you who are Muslims can read in the Quran that Allah says: "Allah does not better the condition of any nation until that nation makes the change in its heart." That is, if there is envy, lack of faith, factionalism in men's hearts, then you will see that their condition will not improve. Gradually it will worsen. But if the state of mind and heart changes, the external state will also change. Bear in mind that neither the Central Association nor the Government of Pakistan, nor American aid will be able to better your condition. Let me give an example. When you plant a tree you put a fence around it to protect it. We were, I was, that fence. You were that tree. We have formed a Central Association. This Central Association received government aid. It received Ford Foundation aid. We also took aid from other institutions. But if the tree itself is not strong, what good is the fence? You were a garden. We were only the gardener. We do a gardener's work. We give help where it is needed. But if there is no strength in the soil, if the tree is not strong, what good is the gardener, and what good is the fence? The Central Association can do nothing, the Government of Pakistan can do nothing either; even with aid from America and the Ford Foundation nothing will happen if you yourselves do not make the effort.

What is your own effort? I'll tell you again. It's a very simple thing. First of all, you have to save your money. You must take some trouble—even if you don't eat, you must save your money. If you don't make your own capital, this whole society will vanish like the mist. Not a trace will remain. Money is the basis of all this work. And all this money will come from your hands. It will not come from outside. It will come from your efforts. Now if you work wisely, you can keep all this money in your own hands. The first principle is—please don't ever forget this—if you stop saving money, if you stop making deposits, all this work will never, never be finished. But if you keep saving money, if you keep increasing your capital, your strength will gradually grow. And a tremendous change will come about in your lives. Remember the words of the poet: that money possesses two qualities of Allah. The second principle is this: now you are separate, each man for himself. For example, I say: "I will save, I will take whatever I can from my neighbor." If you continue to follow this kind of principle you will all perish. What is going on in the village now? Some people have become rich. How? They give a 10 rupee loan and take two maunds of rice as interest. They have become well-off. But in their hearts there is fear. I went to one place. I asked a rich man: "I see that you have lots of land; why don't you make a garden?" He answered: "How can I make a garden? The thieves don't leave anything. They take the coconuts from my trees; they steal the fish from my pond." He has gotten rich, but he is plagued by fear, and the poor people are plagued by envy. So I say: As long as this kind of situation remains, where each man is alone and is concerned only for himself and envies his neighbor, everyone will perish. But if you all unite, join together, have a meeting every week and concern yourselves with the problem of how to better your situation together, you will see that everyone's condition will improve.

The principle of a cooperative society is "All work for each, and each works for all." If you work this way, you will see how much *barkat* will come. Barkat is the mercy of Allah. Making a little thing big. This is the fruit of united effort. If I envy you, if I want your destruction, then I'll be in a bad way and you will be too. But if you help me and I help you and all the time we work together, Allah's mercy will be upon us; and a little thing will become big. Plans, meetings, sitting down together every week in common goodwill—this is the basis of a cooperative.

I, as a Muslim, must consider what is said in the Quran about this: I can say that there is a verse in the Quran, addressed to those who have just become Muslim. Allah, who knew of their condition, said: "Remember how you were separate, each group hostile to the others, and how Allah united your hearts. In Allah's goodness and kindness you all became like brothers. Before it was as if you stood on the brink of a fire and were about to fall in. Allah led you away from the edge of the fire." Such is the meaning of this verse.

If we all unite, sit down together and help one another, if the poor and the well-off sit together, if those who have money unite, if those who have wisdom unite, if they get machines and seeds and all other necessities together, if they pool their rice and sell it at the big markets—then you will see how Allah's mercy will be upon you. And the fruit of this mercy will be that your external conditions, the condition of your villages, all will improve.

In addition there is in this unity, in this love, in this working together a kind of pleasure, and when you experience it you will see that there is nothing in the world like this love, this working together, this unity. One derives a kind of pleasure from envy. When you quarrel with someone you feel fine because you really showed the fellow a thing or two. But there is another kind of pleasure. For example, let us say I helped someone and worked together with him. When you experience this pleasure you will see that it is greater by far than the pleasure of envy. This is the second principle. The first one is to save money, make deposits, collect things together. Then sit together and make a plan, that the mercy of Allah may be upon you. The strength of love, the strength of mutual help, will be great in your hearts.

The third principle is: remember, our old methods of farming are now outdated. We can't use the same methods we used 100 years ago. The reason is that then the population was very small. The land was more fertile. They used to get 15 maunds of paddy from one bigha of land. But now the population is so large that you have to get 30 maunds out of land which used to yield only 15. If you don't, people will die of starvation. If you want to produce more, you must learn new methods. Another aim of the cooperative society is for you to learn these modern methods and work according to them. If you don't, your income will not increase. If your income doesn't increase, how can you make deposits? And if you don't make deposits, where will your capital come from? No more capital will be brought from America. The government of Pakistan won't give you any more capital. You must make all your own capital. This capital will come when you farm well, when you learn the new methods.

I will say another thing. Remember that this cooperative society will rescue you from much danger. But if you do not make this cooperative society strong, nothing will happen. Perhaps you have heard this story: a farmer had a goose. This goose laid a golden egg every day. The farmer thought there must be many eggs in the goose's stomach. Now the goose was giving an egg per day. He thought if he could get all the eggs at once he could make a good profit. So he killed the goose and began to look for the eggs inside its stomach. But there were no more golden eggs in the stomach. Your society is a goose. It will give you your golden eggs. Golden eggs! But if you want all the eggs at once and you kill the society, you won't get anything at all. Remember—if you lose your honesty, if you don't repay all the loans you take on time, you will be killing the goose.

Before, I said that the Central Association is also yours. Here we have formed a Central Association which is not a government agency. This association has officers, it has a staff. The sole aim of this Association is to be of service to you. I was able to bring in some money. This money is now deposited in the bank. Don't think that I am keeping your money in my pocket, or that it is going into Zakir Hussain's pocket, or that anyone else is taking it. That money isn't going anywhere. That money is being kept to be of service to you.

I said that the Central Association is like a fence. If you break the fence, the little trees inside will be eaten by the cows. Plenty of cows want to eat those trees. You must also keep the Central Association strong. Many people think that it would be better if they could rent a tractor for five rupees instead of nine rupees. But this isn't sensible thinking. Why? If the Central Association can't run its business, how can it endure? If it is always incurring losses, how can it keep running? And if the Central Association ceases to function, how long will your village societies last? The Central Association is also your society. Protect it. And strengthen your village society, too. The rule for strengthening it is: make deposits. If you only take out, how long can it last? You must give. If you don't put manure into the ground, if you only want to take the crops out of the ground, what will happen? After a while you won't get anything at all from that land. Remember that the Central Association, the village society, all are dependent upon your efforts. Upon your deposits, upon the increase in your earnings.

I have no more to say. Just bear in mind that this institution which you have founded is for your own good. Here you had darkness. No path could be seen. Now you have lit a light. You have shown a path. One year of effort has yielded this kind of fruit. I hope that you will continue this kind of effort. Make the village society strong. Make the Central Association strong. Having learned all these advanced methods and procedures you will better your condition. As a result your financial situation will improve, and strength will enter your hearts. Peace will come to you. And I think that this is the road to success.

I am praying for you. I hope this work which we are doing will be an ideal for the whole country. People from other places will see this work and learn. And we will always remain two or three years ahead of them.

II. Principal Personnel Associated with the Academy through March 1969

Pakistan Academy for Rural Development Staff

Directors
Akhter Hameed Khan, Director, 1959–1964 and 1965–1968; Vice Chairman of Board, 1964——
K. M. Shamsur Rahman, Director, 1964–1965
A. H. M. Azizul Huq, Director, 1968——

Instructors and Other Principal Staff
Taherunnessa Ahmed, Women's Work, 1963——
A. M. Akhanda, Agricultural Extension, 1966——
Ali Asghar Bhuiyan, Education, 1966——
A. Mannan Bhuiyan, Training Officer, 1968——
M. Z. Hussain, Chief Training Officer, 1959——
A. B. M. Nurul Huq, Librarian, 1963——
Ameerul Huq, Sociology, 1968——
Anwarul Huq, Research, 1968——
M. Nurul Huq, Rural Business Management, 1959——; Deputy Director (Admn.), 1967——
Serajul Islam, Coordinator of Training, 1959–1964
A. Majeed Khan, Sociology and Anthropology, 1959–1964
Abdul Aziz Khan, Agricultural Economics, 1964——
Anwaruzzaman Khan, Rural Economics, 1959–1966

Shafia Khatun, Women's Work, 1962; Education, 1964–1966
M. A. Mannan, Communication, 1964——
A. K. M. Mohsen, Training Officer, 1959——
Abdul Muyeed, Community Organization, 1959——
M. A. Quddus, Education, 1959–1964
Syed A. Rahim, Research Specialist, 1959——; Deputy Director (Research), 1968——
A. T. R. Rahman, Public Administration, 1959–1966
Mahmoodur Rahman, Rural Business Management, 1963——
K. M. Tipu Sultan, Public Administration, 1964——
S. M. Hafeez Zaidi, Social Psychology, 1959–1962
Wiqar H. Zaidi, Research Specialist, 1959–1963

Research Assistants and Others

Badaruddin Ahmed, Tawfique Ahmed, Manjur-ul-Alam, Hazrat Ali, Fazlul Bari, Miss Ummul Ara Begum, A. Wadud Chowdhury, Moqbul Ahmed Chowdhury (Family Planning), Z. H. Chowdhury, M. S. Gazi, Mrs. Naseem Ara Hoque, Shahjada Mahboob-e-Ilah, Khairun Nessa Islam, Md. Rezaul Karim, Rezaul Karim, Ali Akhter Khan, A. K. M. Obaidullah, Miss Maya Rani Saha, Syed Ali Sher, A. R. Tarafder

KTCCA, Senior Personnel

Akhter Hameed Khan, Chairman, Management Committee, 1962——
M. Zaker Hussain, Chief Training Officer for Projects, 1959——; Project Director, KTCCA, 1962–1965; Senior Vice-Chairman, KTCCA, 1969——
Shafique Hossain, Director, Special Cooperative Societies Federation, 1969——
A. K. M. Mohsen, Training Officer for Projects, 1959–1964; Project Director, Special Cooperative Societies Federation, 1964–1965; Training Officer (PARD), 1966——

Shamsul Haq, Special Cooperative Officer, 1959–1964; Project Director, Agricultural Cooperatives Federation, 1964–1967; Vice-Chairman, KTCCA, 1967——

Q. H. Kazi, Seed Multiplication and Certification, 1967——

Mariam Khan, Director, Budget and Accounts, 1968——

Mohammadullah, Project Director, Special Cooperative Societies Federation, 1965–1968; Director, Agricultural Cooperatives Federation, 1968——

A. S. M. A. Rouf, Vice-Chairman, KTCCA, 1968——

A. B. M. Wajihullah, Director, Cold Storage, 1966——; Secretary, Industrial Cooperative, 1969——

Additional Directors of Agriculture in Charge of the Comilla Expansion Program, Posted at Comilla

A. Z. M. Obaidullah Khan, 1963–1964
A. F. M. Yahya, 1964–1965
Quazi Azher Ali, 1965–1967
M. Z. Hussain, 1967

Additional Director of Public Instruction for Adult Education, Posted at Comilla

M. A. Quddus, 1964——

Additional Director for the Department of Basic Democracies and Local Government, Posted at Comilla

Taslimuddin Ahmed, 1966
S. R. Khan, 1967–1968

III. Curriculum Vitae of Akhter Hameed Khan, Director of the Academy

Akhter Hameed Khan, born October 1914, in Agra, India, son of a police official in the Government of British India. Married in 1939 to Hamida Mashraqui (deceased 1966), daughter of Allama Inayatullah Mashraqui; three daughters and one son. Married in 1967 to Shafeeq Qamar; one daughter.

Education
B.A., Meerut College, 1932, history, philosophy, and English literature.
M.A., Agra University, 1934, English literature.
Competed successfully for Indian Civil Service, 1936; attended Cambridge University, Magdalene College, as part of Indian Civil Service training, specialized in history and English literature.
During the summer vacations of 1944–1947, studied Arabic and Islamic Jurisprudence at Deoband, Madrasatul-Ulum (a center of Islamic learning famed throughout the Muslim world) United Provinces, India.

Occupational history
Indian Civil Service, first posted at Comilla, Tripura State, as Assistant Magistrate, 1938.

Appendix III

Resigned from Indian Civil Service as a subdivisional officer, Netrokona (Mymensingh District), 1944.

Moved with his family to Aligarh (United Province) where he worked as a locksmith apprentice for about two years (1944–1946) to learn how the working man lives; during this time he organized a cooperative workshop to manufacture locks and buckles.

Moved to Meerut in early 1947, just prior to Partition; there he organized Khaksar students, and with younger brother edited weekly Urdu and English newspapers, organs of the Khaksar Party.

Moved to Okhla (Delhi) in mid-1947 to become headmaster of the Secondary School of Jamia Millia, and a bit later lectured in Islamic history in the College section of Jamia Millia.

Moved to Islamia College, Karachi, Pakistan, August 1950, to take post of lecturer in Islamic history and English literature.

Appointed Principal of Comilla Victoria College, December 1950.

Served as V-AID Administrator in East Pakistan, 1954–1955.

Returned to Principalship in Comilla, 1956–1958.

Appointed first Director of East Pakistan Academy for Village Development in mid-1958. Attended Michigan State University, with other newly appointed staff members of Academies, from June 1958 to March 1959. Director of Academy at Comilla 1959–1964 and 1965–1968; since 1963 has been Vice-Chairman of the Academy's board of governors.

Honors received

Awarded the Sitara-i-Pakistan, March 1961, for distinguished public service.

Ramon Magsaysay Award for Government Service, Manila, August 1963.

Honorary Doctor of Laws Degree, Michigan State University, June 1964.

IV. Acknowledgment of Assistance Received by the Academy*

The Academy has been exceptionally fortunate in obtaining support from important quarters. From the very beginning the government of East Pakistan was an enthusiastic patron. All the Chief Secretaries, Mr. M. Asfar (1958–1961), Mr. Qazi Anwarul Huq (1961–1964), and Mr. Ali Asghar (1964——), have been unfailing friends, as have been the secretaries of the Department of Basic Democracies and Local Government, (Mr. A. M. S. Ahmad), and of the Department of Agriculture (Mr. Hussin Haider, Mr. H. R. Malik, and Mr. A. M. F. Rahman). President Mohd. Ayub Khan, publicly praised the Academy several times and kept himself informed of its work. Ministers and officials of the central and provincial government have been helpful at many times. Mr. I. U. Khan, the secretary of Agriculture in 1961, sponsored the Comilla cooperative project and personally pleaded for its approval before the Pakistan Planning Commission. In the Planning Commission also we have many memorable friends. Dr. Richard V. Gilbert, chief of the Harvard Advisory Group, first initiated the works program pilot project and then promoted its adoption as a national program. Mr. Richard Patten, advisor in East Pakistan, is a frequent visitor and a stimulator and conductor of ideas

* As expressed by Akhter Hameed Khan in published and unpublished documents provided by him to the author.

Appendix IV

between the government departments (Basic Democracies, Agriculture, Education) and the Academy.

If I mentioned all the persons who have helped the Academy, the list would be very long indeed. The following extracts are taken from the acknowledgments I wrote in the introductions to two of the Academy's annual reports.

From the Third Annual Report, 1961–1962 (pp. 3–4):

I gladly acknowledge the great contribution made by the Ford Foundation and Michigan State University during the course of the third year as in the previous two years. Dr. Schuler and Dr. Fairchild were closely associated with every stage of thought and work and their influence was vital. Mr. Niehoff laboured unceasingly for the development of the Academy, bringing new resources, better administrative arrangements and new prospects. The Academy owes a deep debt of gratitude to Mr. Richard O. Niehoff and to Dr. Harry L. Case, Representative of the Ford Foundation. What it may accomplish in the coming years would be due to the material support and wise guidance given by them in the uncertain initial period of trial and testing. The Ford Foundation grant of eight hundred thousand dollars has made the Comilla Cooperative project one of the most soundly financed and well-planned projects in Pakistan. The villagers of Comilla thana and myself will never forget this great generosity.

Acknowledgment is also due to the instructors and other staff of the Academy. Evidently the maintenance of a high standard of performance depends entirely upon them, and if the Academy's work has been praised the credit belongs to them. As for the villagers of Comilla, their response to and their identification with the Academy's experimental programmes are growing with the years. We are now bound to them by strong and unbreakable ties and we and they are embarking on the long journey towards progress and prosperity with mutual esteem and confidence.

From the Fourth Annual Report, 1962–1963 (pp. iii–iv):

Though not without periods of strain, the Academy has made good progress for which the credit is due to the several partners in this endeavour. For truly it is a joint endeavour. The staff deserves the foremost mention. I am only one of them, but on account of my office too often praised for the work done by all of us. I keep this praise as a trust.

Secondly, the Academy owes much to the senior Government officials—the Chief Secretary, the Additional Chief Secretary, the Secretary of Agriculture, of Basic Democracy, of Health, of Education, the Registrar of Cooperatives—whose generosity towards the Academy is almost unlimited. Equally we continue to receive support from the district, the subdivisional and thana officers of Comilla, a support which is essential for the success of the experimental projects.

The third partner in the Academy effort is the Ford Foundation and Michigan State University. Our appreciation of the investment that the Ford Foundation has made is even greater now that the investment has begun to pay dividends. Looking back we can see clearly how great an advantage it was to possess the resources for making experiments freely and fearlessly. The presence of the advisors has been helpful. I want to acknowledge especially the debt we owe to Dr. Fairchild . . . Dr. Raper took the place of Dr. Schuler in July 1962, and his wide experience, balanced advice and dedication are most welcome. Mrs. Raper has been a remarkably devoted and able editor, and most of the instructors have benefited from her labours. Mr. Martens is helping to improve our agricultural extension efforts both in Comilla and the new areas. Dean Taggart and Mr. Niehoff visited during the year, and have continued to promote the interest of the Academy with farsightedness and determination. It is heartening to know that we have staunch friends at Michigan State University.

Our fourth partners are the people of Kotwali thana. The success of the "Comilla-approach" is mainly their achievement. They have taught us as much as they have learnt from us. There have been difficulties and failures, but there has been no wavering in the desire to go forward. They have responded to every call. It is no easy task they have undertaken—to adopt new ways, to become a model, to create a new order. That they find pleasure and satisfaction in this ordeal is a measure of their spirit. . . .

Even in this brief acknowledgement, I must mention the great help Robert D. Havener (November 1964 to July 1966) gave us in the reorganization of our cooperative setup, the added dimension in research emphasis that accrued from Robert D. Stevens' brief stay (November 1964 to February 1965), and the overall assistance that Michigan State University advisor, Nicolaas G. M. Luykx, II, provided for the operations of the Academy and our expanding field programs.

Then, too, there have been the contributions of the Japanese farm experts from early 1960, and of U.S. Peace Corps Volunteers, more than a score in all, who came in two groups, in October 1961 and June 1963. These young men and women assisted us greatly in our experiments.

After 1964, British Volunteers worked in the tractor section, the machine shop, and the communication section. In 1966 the Danish government deputed an expert for the creamery and in 1968 three more experts for poultry, machines, and marketing. The presence of these experts together with their gift of equipment has greatly strengthened the processing and marketing programs of the KTCCA.

V. Foreign Personnel Associated with the Academy

Michigan State University Advisors and Consultants

CHIEF ADVISORS FOR PAKISTAN ACADEMIES

William T. Ross, anthropology, July 1957–July 1960
Richard O. Niehoff, public administration, January 1960–July 1962 (coordinator of the Pakistan project, East Lansing), July 1962——

RESIDENT ADVISORS AT COMILLA

Edgar A. Schuler, sociology, July 1959–July 1962
Henry W. Fairchild, agronomy, January 1960–July 1963
Arthur F. Raper, sociology, July 1962–September 1964
Martha J. Raper, editorial associate, July 1962–May 1964
Delvin W. Martens, agricultural extension, October 1962–May 1965
Robert D. Stevens, agricultural economics, October 1964–February 1965
Robert D. Havener, cooperative management, November 1964–July 1966
Nicolaas G. M. Luykx, II, agricultural economics, February 1966–June 1968

Appendix V

SHORT-TIME CONSULTANTS AT COMILLA
Hideya Kumata, communications, April–June 1960
Charles P. Loomis, sociology, May–June 1962
Howard F. McColly, agricultural engineering, September 1962
Leyton V. Nelson, crop science, January–April 1967 and November 1968–March 1969
Henry E. Larzelere, agricultural economics, March–September 1967
Robert Carolus, horticulture, October 1967–April 1968

Peace Corps Volunteers Who Have Worked at the Comilla Academy

FIRST GROUP OF U.S. PEACE CORPS VOLUNTEERS
(OCTOBER 1961 TO JUNE 1963)
  Robert Burns, engineer
  Kenneth Clark, machine and maintenance
  Jean Ellickson, librarian
  Floyd Goodson, machine movement
  Roger Hord, masonry
  Florence E. McCarthy, women's work
  Peter McDonough, communications
  David Phillips, youth work
  Robert Taylor, dairy
  James J. Bausch, sociology
  William Gold, construction
  Sandra Houts, nurse

SECOND GROUP OF U.S. PEACE CORPS VOLUNTEERS
(JUNE 1963 TO JANUARY 1965)
  Ellen Agenbroad, nurse
  Peter Babcox, communications
  Deborah Babcox, women's work
  William R. Bridges, youth work
  Lyman Chancellor, construction

Ray Elsenbreck, construction
Erwin Lemmons, dairy
Robert Lindley, machine maintenance
Roger Lumbra, machine movement
Gary Morley, rural administration
Peter Orr, forestry
Frederick Wend, civil engineer
Carthel Williams, construction

In addition, there were 11 Peace Corps Volunteers during the second period in the three scattered thanas with Comilla-type programs; in these thanas the Peace Corps Volunteers did about the same types of work as at the Academy.

Advisors Provided by the Danish Government

J. Riis, dairy, 1966——
Paul Hvenegaard, poultry, 1967——
Ole Christensen, marketing, 1968
John Hanson, machine shop, 1968

British Graduate Voluntary Service Overseas Personnel

Edward Burch, mechanical engineer, 1965–1966
Peter Felix, communications, 1965–1967
James Cordiner, mechanical engineer, 1966–1967
Barrie Ward, communications, 1967–1968
David McHutchison, engineer, 1967–1969
John Evers, communications, 1969——

Japanese Farm Experts (Colombo Plan)

Isao Matsuda, 1960–1963
Nasuo Ryushu, 1960–1962
Katsuo Ito, 1960–1961
Toshio Fumoto, 1960–1961
Kaname Tsueike, 1961–1963 & 1965–1967
Tamakazu Ohmori, 1961–1963
Tatsuaki Miyasaki, 1963–1965

Kiyto Yoshizumi, 1963–1966
N. Koike, 1966–1968
M. Watanabe, 1966–1968
Jun Adachi, 1968——
T. Misawa, 1968——

Researchers from the Population Council of New York

Harvey M. Choldin, sociology, January 1964–August 1965
John E. Stoeckel, sociology, September 1966–April 1968

Fellows of the Africa-Asia Program of Syracuse University

Arthur Osteen, public administration, April–July 1962
John Elmer, international law, August 1963–January 1964
Elliot Tepper, public administration, September 1964–September 1965
Blake W. H. Smith, economics, September 1965–September 1966

Michigan State University Graduate Research Students

Florence E. McCarthy, January 1966–April 1967
Peter Bertocci October 1966–December 1967
Jean Ellickson, July 1968–August 1969

Others

Phillis Johannes, Laubach Literacy Fund, November 1963–June 1967
John Roak, University of Pennsylvania, graduate student, November 1964–November 1965
Richard Wheeler, Fulbright scholar, University of Michigan, January–August 1965
Maria Thoger, UNESCO, literacy expert, August 1965–April 1966
Monika Krohmenn, cooperative expert from Germany, March–May 1966

VI. Statistical Tables

Table A. Selected data on Pakistan, East Pakistan, Comilla district, and Comilla thana, as related to other Asian countries*

Item	Japan	Taiwan	Philippines	Thailand	Pakistan	East Pakistan	Comilla district	Comilla thana
Estimated population (mid-1964) (in millions)	96.9	12.1	31.2	29.7	100.8	51.5	4.4	0.2
Population density per square mile (1964)	669	860	269	148	271	922	1,693	2,031
Per cent of population that is rural (1960)	36.5		64.7	88.2	75.5	94.8	96.8	67.1
Inhabitants per physician holding a professional degree (1965)	920	2,400	1,700	7,600	7,000		11,312	
Per cent distribution of farms by size (1960)								
Under 0.5 acres						13	23	
0.5 to 1.0 acre						11	20	
1.0 to 2.5 acres						27	34	
2.5 to 5.0 acres						26	16	
5.0 to 7.5 acres						12	4	
7.5 to 12.5 acres						7	2	
12.5 to 25.0 acres						3		
25.0 and over								
Per cent of land irrigated (1960)						7	5	
Per cent of farms (1960)								
With milk cows						38	27	
Using manures						23	61	
Using fertilizers						4	4	

	(1)	(2)	(3)	(4)	(5)	(6)	(7)	(8)
Per cent of population (1961)								
Muslim					88.1	80.4	86.0	84.6
Caste Hindus					4.9	8.6	9.0	12.9
Scheduled classes					5.8	9.8	4.4	2.6
Christians					0.8	0.3	0.1	0.7
All others					0.9	0.8	0.5	0.8
Per cent by distribution of farms by tenure of operator (1960)								
Owner farms						61.0	80.0	
Owner/tenant farms						37.0	20.0	
Tenant farms						2.0		
Illiteracy, per cent at 15 years of age (1960)								
Total	2.2	46.1	28.1	32.3	81.1	78.5	79.7	72.7
Male	1.0	29.9	25.8	20.7	74.7		70.2	61.1
Female	3.3	62.5	30.5	43.9	88.3		89.7	85.9
Land holdings in acres (1960)								
Average size	2.9	3.0			5.0	3.5	1.8	1.7
Per cent under one acre	29.6				18.4	24.0	43.0	

* Sources: *Demographic Yearbook, 1965*, United Nations, pp. 113–115; *World Population Data Sheet*, Washington, D.C., Population Bureau, Information Service, December 1966, *Statistical Yearbook*, UN, 1965; *Production Yearbook, Food and Agriculture Organization, 1965*; *UNESCO Statistical Yearbook*, UN, 1965; "Gross National Product," Agency for International Development, Office of Program Coordinator, Washington, D.C., June 1966; *Economic Survey of Asia and the Far East, 1965*, UN; *World Crop Statistics—Area, Production and Yield, 1948–1964*; Rome, Food and Agriculture Organization, 1966; *Pakistan Population Census, 1961, East Pakistan and Comilla District* (reports), Karachi, Office of the Census Commissioner; *Pakistan Census of Agriculture,1960, Volume I, East Pakistan*, Karachi, Ministry of Food and Agriculture, 1962.

Table B. Provincial and other nonproject trainees with three or more days of training, serviced by the Academy, by year, from 1959 to 1966*

Type of trainee	1960	1961	1962	1963	1964	1965	1966	Total
			Pakistani officials					
V-AID personnel								
Development officers	26	55						81
Supervisors	55	3						58
Other V-AID personnel		24						24
Circle Officers	127	137	48	358	397	363	232	1,662
Civil Service probationers		39	25	52	24	44	79	263
Other general administrators	10	37	19	90	104	67	28	355
Department of Agriculture		2	10	59	69	46	40	226
Department of Education		4	62	69	18	47	33	229
Department of Health		8			16	32	19	75
Department of Social Welfare			24	26	32	10		92
Cooperatives		4	21	94	7	41		167
Three-area expansion program				8	6	6	3	23
Comilla district expansion program						8	12	20
All others		7	26	54	163	118	97	465
Total, Pakistani Officials	218	316	235	810	836	782	543	3,740

			Nonofficials					
Pakistani								
Professors and students	40	18	17	80	305	91	258	809
Ansar leaders	13	87	28	10				138
Volunteer cooperative leaders			21	54	106	378	300	859
All other Pakistanis			55	30	24	4	164	277
Non-Pakistani								
Christian missionaries			12	35	62			109
U.S. Peace Corps Volunteers			25	32	99	7		163
Conference participants					35	25		60
Seminar participants				24		115		139
Other foreign trainees				2	34	67	9	112
Total, Nonofficials	53	105	158	267	665	687	731	2,666
Grand Total	271	421	393	1,077	1,501	1,469	1,274	6,406

* Figures for 1966–1967 and 1967–1968 are not available in "Pakistan officials" and "nonofficials" categories listed above. However, the Eighth and Ninth annual Reports of the academy show the following courses offered and number enrolled. For *1966–1967*: 5 rural development courses, 118; 10 orientation courses for officials, 224; 5 orientation courses for nonofficials, 94; 10 in-service training courses, 408; 11 conferences for model farmers on IRRI rice cultivation, 567; 6 groups for supervised study for students from colleges, 127; 11 groups of foreign trainees (6 countries), 34; 31 conferences and seminars, 1,130 (Total enrolled = 2,702). For *1967–1968*: 5 rural development courses, 88; 33 job training courses, 774; 49 conferences and seminars, 3,656; 10 groups of foreign trainees (5 countries), 62; 10 orientation courses for teachers and university students, 200 (Total enrolled = 4,780).

Table C. Villagers trained at the Abhoy Ashram campus of the Academy by year, from 1959 to 1966*

Type of training	1960	1961	1962	1963	1964	1965	1966†	Total
In weekly training at end of year (Comilla projects only)								
Cooperative organizers	7	25	46	131	167	183	216	775
Model farmers			25	112	122	139	0‡	398
Imams ("feeder schools")				115	93	91	32	331
Accountants				45	45	51	36	177
Village "doctors"				36	39	27	1§	103
Village midwives (dais)				8	12	34	61	115
Schoolteachers					59	95		154
Research enumerators		14	20	26	20	20	22	122
Family planning workers		10	16	24	32	20	99	201
Women teachers				30	29	26	45	130
Other women trainees				173	196	159	30	558
All others		10	35	109	118	125	14	411
Total	7	59	142	809	932	970	556	3,475
In fortnightly training at end of year								
Primary school principals and teachers			20	75	78	80	136	389
Village midwives (dais)	15	60	105	15	10		101	306
V-AID workers	30	33						63
Youth leaders and others	12	12	12					36
Total	57	105	137	90	88	80	237	794
In monthly training at end of year								
Enlightened farmers	30	30						60
Model farmers							94	94
Thana council members			25	25	25	25	23	123

Chairmen of cooperative societies	12	12	12		167	183	216	566
Secretaries of union councils	12	12		12	12	12	12	84
Agricultural extension workers				4				28
All others	32	54		10	104	48	21	279
Total	86	108		51	308	268	366	1,234
In short courses during the year								
Camps	227							227
Midwives (dais)		59		42	112	229	52	24	459
Schoolteachers	125						104	288
Other women			78	100	125	149	78	530
Tractor and pump drivers and mechanics			105	85	30	12	115	347
All others	30	47	68	44	31	40	165	425
Total	382	106	293	341	415	253	486	2,276
In intermittent training during the year								
Schoolteachers & college students	12	93	90	84	91	94	102	566
Union councilors		18	120	120	120	120	128	626
Chairmen and members of local project committees	108	191	204	136	134	128	166	768
All others	108	191	158	247	264	331	148	1,447
Total	120	302	572	587	609	673	544	3,407
Grand Total	652	680	1,195	1,874	2,352	2,244	2,189	11,186

* The training categories are not mutually exclusive; the table shows the number of individuals, by activities, by year.

† Training for villagers in Comilla thana for 1967 and 1968 was carried on in the same general fields and at about the same rate as for the period from 1964 to 1966.

‡ Extension work was taken over by the model farmers, who met monthly: see later entry in this table.

§ When the village "doctors" formed themselves into a cooperative unit, only the organizer (manager) of the society came to the Academy each week. The village "doctor" would be an unlicensed practitioner, of the kind commonly referred to by Westerners as a "paramedic."

Table D. Status of cooperatives in the Comilla thana affiliated with the KTCCA, June 30, 1961 to June 30, 1968
(all figures are cumulative)*

	June 1961	June 1962	June 1963	June 1964	June 1965	June 1966	June 1967	June 1968
Societies enrolled†								
Agricultural	11	70	127	162	202	216	292	339
Agricultural	8	59	110	122	152	158	225	261
Nonagricultural	3	11	17	40	50	58	67	78
Number of members (net)†	670	2,474	4,260	6,018	7,297	7,771	11,552	15,454
Agricultural	376	1,860	3,156	3,833	4,910	5,161	8,462	11,518
Nonagricultural	294	614	1,104	2,185	2,387	2,610	3,090	3,936
Deposits (Rs.)‡								
Agricultural societies								
Total deposits		38,504	123,244	219,503	304,959	415,901	551,052	1,102,724
Net savings deposits		27,601	82,450	150,825	170,020	202,290	286,814	553,616
Net share purchase		10,903	40,794	68,678	134,939	213,611	264,238	549,108
Nonagricultural societies								
Total deposits		2,328	13,003	39,803	97,677	221,827	261,406	349,654
Net savings deposits		1,832	7,222	21,672	21,490	26,171	30,903	40,064
Net share purchase		496	5,781	18,131	76,187	195,656	230,503	309,590
Loans (Rs.)								
Total issued		238,664	671,328	1,479,753	2,892,092	4,190,051	6,110,215	11,384,325
Total repaid		60,162	321,554	657,823	1,483,611	2,409,904	3,677,509	6,011,302§

Agricultural societies							
Loans issued	235,664	621,328	1,141,117	1,866,393	2,662,377	4,333,028	8,577,505
Loans repaid	60,162	276,754	563,510	1,115,579	1,775,120	2,746,699	4,548,426
Nonagricultural societies							
Loans issued		3,000 ‖	50,000	338,536	1,025,699	1,527,674	1,777,187	2,806,820
Loans repaid			44,800	94,313	368,032	634,784	930,810	1,462,876

* From "A New Rural Cooperative System for Comilla Thana . . . , Eighth Annual Report 1968," Comilla, PARD, April 1969.
† Number of societies/members enrolled at beginning of period minus societies/members dropped during the period.
‡ Amount deposited during the period minus amount withdrawn.
§ The bulk of the short-term loans were not due for repayment until the end of the calendar year; also there were medium and long-term loans.
‖ This figure and the two in the next column are estimates arrived at after the agricultural and nonagricultural societies began to be separately supervised.

Table E. Expenditures (in rupees) for public works in Comilla thana, by year, from 1962 to 1966

Type of project	1962 and 1963	1964	1965	1966	1962–1966*
	Regular works projects				
Road construction	155,838	156,475	53,096		365,409
Road maintenance		11,412	19,619	70,400	101,431
Brick surfacing		58,107		7,426	65,533
Bridges (new)	98,304	120,043	46,445	9,339	274,131
Bridges (repairs)		4,059			4,059
Culverts for embankments and roads	38,817	179,673		47,049	265,539
Big culverts			16,176	2,400	18,576
Flap gates		30,000	5,000	3,300	38,300
Embankments (new)	15,461	68,863	16,320	3,052	103,696
Embankments (repairs)		19,444	940	1,999	22,383
Drainage, khals and canals	134,856	32,135	18,090	48,678	233,759
Sand erosion dams (new)	22,930	7,056	2,726		32,712
Sand erosion dams (repairs)		2,427	250	1,299	3,976
Regulators	34,148	20,000			54,148
Regulators (extension)		306			306
Grants to 12 union councils		50,000		100,000	150,000
Construction of community halls				18,300	18,300
Contingencies	16,198	40,000			56,198
All other expenditures	19,034			3,000	22,034
Total	Rs. 535,586	800,000	178,662	316,242	1,830,490
	Special works projects				
Irrigation		600,000	400,000	312,462	1,312,462
Rural electrification			400,000		1,000,000
Grand Total	Rs. 535,586	2,000,000	978,662	628,704	4,142,952

* In 1966–1967, Rs. 65,000 were allocated to the union councils and in 1967–1968, Rs. 328,000. For details see, A. K. M. Mohsen, *The Comilla Rural Administration Experiment, Annual Report 1963–1964*, Comilla, PARD, October 1964; K. M. Tipu Sultan, "Comilla Rural Administration Experiment," Third and Fourth Annual Reports 1964–1965 and 1965–1966, Comilla, PARD, 1966 and 1967;

Table F. Training for village women at the Abhoy Ashram campus and in the villages of Comilla thana, by designated periods, from 1962 to 1966*

Period, and subjects taught	At Abhoy Ashram		In the villages	
	No. of courses	No. of participants	No. of training centers	No. of participants
March 1962–March 1963				
Maternity disease and family planning	1	11	7	77
Child care	1	12	6	97
Home sanitation	1	14	8	104
Kitchen gardening	1	8	6	85
Spinning	1	4		
Poultry	1	15	5	60
Sewing	1	17	11	94
Literacy	1	19	1	18
Cooperative movement	1	12	6	72
Total	9	112	50	607
April 1963–June 1964				
Child care			7	105
Maternity			6	80
Home sanitation	2	24	15	425
Poultry raising	2	28	9	172
Garment making	1	15	13	74
Silk-screen printing	1	4		
Gardening	4	25	21	311
Village women teachers	1	30	28	390
Spinning	2	14	7	54
First aid	2	49	20	175
Enumerators	1	84		
Savings			3	15
Total	16	273	129	1,801
July 1964–June 1965				
First aid	1	25	34	540
Forestry	2	40		
Poultry	2	17	34	1,548
Gardening	2	27	34	1,764
Sewing	1	16	13	324
Silk-screen printing	1	9		
Adult education	1	15	33	891
Maternal and child health	1	42	12	396
Enumerators	1	22		
Spinning			21	840
Total	12	213	181	6,303
July 1965–June 1966				
Adult education	2	25	45	1,023
Spinning	1	8	7	29
Silk-screen printing	1	4		
Organizer's course	3	33		
Total	7	70	52	1,052
Grand Total	44	668	412	9,763

*Although comparable statistics have not been compiled for the period beyond 1966, training classes at Abhoy Ashram continued to be well attended as indicated by the fact that in 1966–1967, 180 women were enrolled in ten different subjects for periods varying from one week to one year. For the 1967–1968 year, thirteen different courses were attended by 406 women. During these same two years, the number of women trained in the villages remained at about the level of the two preceding years (Eighth and Ninth Annual Reports of the Academy, 1967 and 1968).

Table G. Status of cooperatives in Gaibandha, Goripur, and Natore thanas from 1963 to 1968 (cumulative basis except as otherwise indicated)*

Reporting items	1963–64	1964–65	1965–66	1966–67	1967–68
Gaibandha					
Number of local societies (agricultural and nonagricultural)	49	90	164	209	210
Membership of local societies	1,568	3,189	4,474	4,801	4,999
Share purchases (Rs.)	6,160	14,590	45,450	61,677	76,830
Savings deposits (Rs.)	27,555	97,249	52,079	93,887	125,503
Loans issued (Rs.)	59,706	178,363	370,592	158,585	221,336
Loans repaid (Rs.) (end of reporting period)	4,965	82,564	181,517	124,881	80,188
Loans overdue (Rs.) (end of reporting period)			17,549		14,305
Interest and fees received					11,921
Goripur					
Number of local societies (agricultural and nonagricultural)	50	79	140	184	279
Membership of local societies	1,269	1,995	3,275	4,122	5,842
Share purchases (Rs.)	12,376	33,010	49,590	61,548	104,615
Savings deposits (Rs.)	21,578	54,560	62,412	102,259	156,735
Loans issued (Rs.)	110,642	341,992	610,458	285,279	656,901
Loans repaid (Rs.) (end of reporting period)	20,405	178,420	349,253	179,206	291,978
Loans overdue (Rs.) (end of reporting period)					170,735
Interest and fees received					28,331

	Natore				
Number of local societies (agricultural and nonagricultural)	43	63	90	148	183
Membership of local societies	1,658	2,680	3,174	4,503	6,086
Share purchases (Rs.)	9,822	23,451	36,220	42,472	65,944
Savings deposits (Rs.)	25,488	73,703	122,754	115,579	159,660
Loans issued (Rs.)	91,012	264,539	485,606	106,400	274,295
Loans repaid (Rs.) (end of reporting period)	10,266	85,204	212,189	135,921	109,899
Loans overdue (Rs.) (end of reporting period)			13,344		54,140
Interest and fees received					17,508

* From *A New Rural Cooperative System for Comilla Thana . . . , Eighth Annual Report, 1968*, Comilla, PARD, April 1969 (source of data: records of the office of the Additional Director of Agriculture and PARD).

Table H. Status of cooperatives in seven thanas in the Comilla district from 1965 to 1968 (cumulative basis except where otherwise indicated)*

Item	1965–1966	1966–1967	1967–1968
Number of societies (agricultural and nonagricultural)	282	550	948
Membership of societies	8,724	14,625	24,686
Savings deposits (Rs.)	189,728	394,375	953,233
Share purchases (Rs.)	174,632	320,638	698,202
Loans issued (Rs.)	735,299	1,510,233	4,192,865
Loans repaid (during reporting period) (Rs.)	95,842	605,810	1,546,406
Loans overdue (during reporting period) (Rs.)		239	107,990
Interest and fees received (Rs.)	10,806	82,373	216,802

*The seven thanas are: Laksam, Chandina, Sarail, Habiganj, Quasba, Brahmanbaria and Chandpur. Source of data: *A New Rural Cooperative System for Comilla Thana* . . . , Eighth Annual Report, 1968, Comilla, PARD, April 1969.

VII. Principal Sources of Financial Support

(primary source of funds is shown without parentheses; equivalent value is shown in parentheses in totals)*

Activity	Source of funds	Year†	Amount‡ Rupees	Amount‡ U.S. dollars	Remarks
Operations of the Academy	Government	1960	249,365		Salaries, research, etc.
	Government	1960	132,000		Temporary buildings, equipment, etc.
	Government	1961	318,743		Salaries, research, etc.
	Government	1962	398,214		Salaries, research, etc.
	Government	1963	459,202		Salaries, research, etc.
	Government	1964	570,524		Salaries, research, etc.
	Government	1965	556,779		Salaries, research, etc.
	Government	1966	871,925		Salaries, research, etc.
	Government	1967	824,900		Salaries, research, etc.
	Government	1968	850,000		Salaries, research, etc.
Subtotal			5,231,652		
Development of the new campus	Government	1960–1965	5,100,000		Buildings, roads, grounds, etc.
	Ford Foundation	1960–1965		200,000	Architect's fees and foreign exchange for building materials and equipment

Principal sources of financial support (continued)

Activity	Source of funds	Year†	Amount Rupees	Amount U.S. dollars	Remarks
Training, demonstrations, and research	Government	1961–1966	936,000		Training, demonstrations, and research
	Ford Foundation	1961–1966		810,000§	Promotion of cooperatives and use of farm machinery on a demonstration basis
Comilla's prorated share of the MSU contract with the Ford Foundation for the Pakistan project	Ford Foundation	1957–58		60,008	Planning the Academies, selecting and training the staff, etc.
	Ford Foundation	1958–59		90,221	Advisory services, library and audio-visual support, staff development, etc.
	Ford Foundation	1960		138,881	Advisory services, etc.
	Ford Foundation	1961		138,652	Advisory serivces, etc.
	Ford Foundation	1962		113,589	Advisory services, etc.
	Ford Foundation	1963		99,138	Advisory services, etc.
	Ford Foundation	1964		66,712	Advisory services, etc.

Principal sources of financial support (continued)

Activity	Source of funds	Year†	Amount‡ Rupees	Amount‡ U.S. dollars	Remarks
	Ford Foundation	1965		55,000	Advisory services, etc.
	Ford Foundation	1966		70,581	Advisory services, etc.
	Ford Foundation	1967 and 1968		92,300	(Figures are approximate)
Subtotal				925,082	
Total government			11,267,652 or (9,210,990) or	(2,367,153) 1,935,082	
Total Ford Foundation					
Grand total ‖			Rs. 20,478,642 or	$4,301,429	

* In addition to these rupee and dollar figures, the provincial Department of Agriculture has made available twenty-one 35 hp. farm tractors, about forty 15 hp. diesel irrigation pumps, and some smaller equipment, and grants from several departments for research; CARE (midwife kits and some foodstuffs); UNICEF (medicines and other supplies for the Maternity and Child Health Centre at Abhoy Ashram); Population Council of New York (two researchers; a mobile audio-visual unit); Danish government (several advisors and equipment items); Laubach Foundation (one advisor); Wheat Associates (commodities); U.S. Peace Corps and British Volunteers. The public works program was largely funded from counterpart PL-480 funds.

† The fiscal year is used in this table; accordingly, 1960 refers to the year ending June 30, 1960.

‡ Throughout the period under consideration, one Pakistan rupee was valued at approximately $0.21, and one U.S. dollar at approximately 4.76 rupees.

§ This grant was made to the government of East Pakistan for the use of the KTCCA for the Comilla thana modernization project. The grant specified that a certain percentage was to be repaid by the KTCCA into a revolving fund for further modernization. Other amounts were to be used for research, training, and documentation.

‖ Dollars and Rupees converted and combined.

VIII. A Brief Chronology of the History of the Academy

January 3, 1953. The Ford Foundation joins the government of Pakistan and the U.S. International Cooperation Administration in constructing and staffing the Village Agricultural and Industrial Development (V-AID) Training Institutes.

July 22, 1955. The V-AID program is made an integral part of the government's 5-year economic and development plan.

October 13, 1955. First Five-Year Plan reads: "The Academies are designed to radically improve the quality of training and administration of V-AID and in the supporting nation-building and administrative departments."

January 4, 1956. Floyd W. Reeves of Michigan State University is asked by George Gant (Ford Foundation, Karachi) to recommend individuals and institutions to provide advisory assistance to the government in establishing the Academies.

June 1956. Reeves and three other MSU professors arrive in Pakistan to conduct a survey and develop a scheme (plan).

August 26, 1956. The plan of the four-man MSU team is submitted to the government [it was discussed, and accepted].

June 1957. Memoranda of agreement are reached between the government of Pakistan, the Ford Foundation, and MSU, with the latter to provide advisory services to the Academies.

July 1957. A second four-man team, again headed by Reeves, comes to Pakistan to further the plans for the Academies.

Appendix VIII

July 1957–April 1958. The staffs, a Director, and ten social scientists for each Academy, are recruited in Pakistan, England, and the United States; Akhter Hameed Khan is made Director of the Comilla Academy and Md. Raja Afzal the Director of the Peshawar Academy.

April 1958–May 1959. The staffs of the Academies are trained—6 weeks in Pakistan, 9 months at MSU, and 6 weeks in European and Asian countries.

May 1959. Upon request, Akhter Hameed Khan prepares for the chief secretary of the government of East Pakistan statements on "Reorganization of Local Government" and "Integrating Basic Democracies and V-AID."

August 1, 1959. First training course begins at the Academy, with 10 East Pakistan civil servants present.

August 1959. Director Khan of the Academy determines that the staff make systematic observations of the work of local officials and of village conditions, record what they see and hear; and that the Academy's research be partly statistical, of sociological significance, and of immediate use.

September 1959. Agreement is reached with relevant officials that the V-AID development area in Comilla thana, 80 square miles, may be used by the Academy staff for observation and study.

October 29, 1959. President Ayub Khan announces the Basic Democracies Order.

November 21–24, 1959. Training procedures for officials of the Department of Basic Democracies and Local Government are agreed upon in Dacca; Academy staff begins at once to prepare syllabi for training courses.

November 1959. Many "camps" (day or two conferences) are held at the Academy for village groups—enlightened farmers, youth leaders, schoolteachers, rural artists, etc.

January 1960. Chief secretary of East Pakistan makes the whole of rural Comilla thana (107 square miles) a laboratory area for the Academy, with "full responsibility for policy determination."

February 1960. A team of four Japanese farm experts, arranged by the Colombo Plan, arrives at the Academy and begins its work in paddy and vegetable production—first on the Academy's 6-acre farm, and then in the villages.

May 1960. Village-based cooperatives are organized at South Rampur, Monshasan, and Tongirpar villages; a low-lift irrigation pump is the nucleus around which the cooperative is organized in each instance. Three 35 h.p. tractors and eight 1½ cubic foot per second diesel irrigation pumps are supplied to the Academy by the provincial Department of Agriculture.

January 25, 1961. Twenty-five new-type cooperative societies are organized; 20 of these are village-based agricultural societies, the others are made up of weavers, potters, vegetable growers, village women, and rickshaw pullers.

March 31, 1961. A Yugoslavian team, upon the request of the Minister of Food and Agriculture, visits the Academy to study the village-based cooperatives; the team recommends that the Comilla cooperatives be further developed and expanded.

March 1961. Pilot family-planning program is started in six villages that have cooperative societies.

April 1961. I. U. Khan, secretary of Ministry of Food and Agriculture, visits the cooperatives at Comilla to prepare a plan for the expansion of this movement into other areas.

August 1961. Comilla thana council is approved by the provincial government as a model for training and research.

September 1961. A total of 21 35 h.p. tractors and 77 irrigation pumps are now available (from the provincial Department of Agriculture) at the Academy.

Mid-October 1961. Government approves (final action Jan. 11, 1962) the plan for a 5-year (1961–1966) modernization project for Comilla thana, with emphasis on cooperatives and mechanization.

October 1961. First group of U.S. Peace Corps Volunteers arrives.

November 1961. Plans are underway for the launching early in 1962 of the Comilla thana pilot public works project.

January 26, 1962. Comilla Kotwali Thana Central Cooperative Association, Ltd. (KTCCA) is registered.

February 1962. Women's program is underway—96 village women come to the Academy for a one-day orientation.

March 18, 1962. Academy begins its first two courses for village women on child care and on maternity disease and family planning.

May–June 1962. Provincial government examines possibility of launching Comilla-type programs in three scattered thanas (this was done, with the key personnel trained at the Academy during the first half of 1963).

May–November 1962. Plans are underway to extend the rural public works program to the 54 subdivisional thanas (later extended to all 411 thanas; the expanded program is fashioned on that of the pilot project in Comilla thana with officials from all over the province coming to the Academy for training).

Late August 1962. Additional chief secretary (Dev.) calls a meeting in Dacca to discuss the Comilla thana "absorption test"; this program involves the Sonaichuri gravity-flow project, deep large-bore tube wells, pumps on river rafts, rural electrification, and an intensified regular rural works program.

October 13, 1962. Provincial board of governors for the Academy is officially constituted, with the chief secretary, government of East Pakistan, as its chairman; the name of the Academy is changed from *Village* to Academy for *Rural Development.*

November 1962. The first 6-inch tube well for irrigation is completed at the village of South Rampur.

The 100th local cooperative society is organized.

January 23, 1963. Youth rally is held with 3,000 school children present; prizes are given for best individual farm- and home-related projects.

February 1963. The KTCCA purchases the 17-acre Abhoy Ashram campus.

March 5, 1963. Women's rally is held with about 400 village women present; prizes are given for work done.

April 1963. Academy moves to new campus at Kotbari; East Pakistan Cooperative College also moves from Dacca to the Kotbari campus.

May 1963. Director Khan prepares a paper on "The Public Works Program and a Development Proposal for East Pakistan" for President Ayub Khan and for members of the National Economic Council and the Planning Commission.

June 1963. Second group of Peace Corps Volunteers arrives.

July 1, 1963. Comilla-type programs are launched by Department of Agriculture in three scattered thanas.

Late August 1963. At the end of the second month of operations, the three scattered thanas have 85 cooperative societies with 2,621 members.

November 1963. The evaluation study by the Academy of the 1962–1963 province-wide rural works program is off the press.

Early January 1964. Director Khan writes out for Finance Minister Shoaib why it is relevant now that a program be launched in Comilla district, and why the family planning activities should be greatly expanded.

Mr. K. M. Shamsur Rahman of the Civil Service of Pakistan is appointed Director of the Academy. Mr. Akhter Hameed Khan becomes vice chairman of the board of governors. (Mr. Rahman resigned a year later.)

January 1964. A 75-page report, "Comilla-US AID conference" arrives; it summarizes discussions at the Academy with nine US AID officials, June 11–14, 1964.

February 4, 1964. Excavation is begun through the levee of the Gumti River for the intake of up to 200 cubic feet per second of water into the Sonaichuri basin for irrigation.

Late February 1964. The mass distribution of nonmedical

family planning supplies is launched, through the use of numerous sales outlets throughout the thana.

March 5, 1964. The first rally of the Imam teachers of the feeder schools is held.

April 1964. Foundations are laid at Abhoy Ashram for new dairy processing unit.

June 1964. A maternity health clinic is set up at Abhoy Ashram.

August 27, 1964. Outline of Pakistan's Third Five-Year Plan refers to Comilla "as the experimental area in which model operations are tried out on the basis of which the provincial program is organized."

October 8, 1964. Experimentation begins at the Academy in the use of the intrauterine device (IUD) for family planning.

October–November 1964. A bone-meal production experiment for chicken and cow feed is started by the butchers' cooperative society.

November 1964. The Special Cooperative Societies Federation is set up to handle the operational affairs of the then 48 nonagricultural societies.

Late November 1964. A World Bank team of three (Kenneth Jones, Food and Agriculture Organization; Frank Beck, consultant from U.S. AID, Iran; and Horst Von Oppenfeld, World Bank) visits Comilla with reference to the later possible financing of the expanded program.

December 1, 1964. Government approves the Comilla district program.

January 1965. Six thousand people attend the annual cooperative rally.

February 1965. Seventeen miles (of a projected 60) of overhead electric lines are completed by East Pakistan Water and Power Development Authority (EPWAPDA).

March 11, 1965. To date, the Balarampur-Deeder Rickshaw Pullers Cooperative Society has supplied 2,150,000 bricks to the Sonaichuri gravity-flow project.

June 1965. Training is completed for the project directors for seven thanas in Comilla district where Comilla-type programs are being started.

August 9, 1965. The cold-storage plant of the KTCCA is put into operation—ice is being made, and potatoes are being stored on an experimental basis.

October 1965. After a little more than three months in operation, the seven thanas with new programs in Comilla district have a total of 157 Comilla-type cooperatives with a membership of 4,337.

November 1965. Seminars are held at the Academy on "Primary Education" and on "Agricultural Research and Extension."

January 1966. KTCCA becomes the apex cooperative association in the thana; the Agricultural Societies Federation is set up to handle the operational affairs of the agricultural societies (then about 157).

February 1966. Director of the International Rice Research Institute (IRRI), Manila, visits the Academy; arrangements are made to test more than 300 rice varieties on the Academy farm.

Newly formed coordinating committee of the Academy replaces the old training and research committees.

One hundred water-seal latrines are ordered by village women for installation at their homes.

March 29, 1966. Special faculty meeting is called to discuss, and plan for training and research work of each instructor for 1966–1967.

April 18–21, 1966. Farmers' seminar is held at Comilla, with the central and provincial Ministers of Agriculture present.

April 28, 1966. To date, 29,200 maunds of potatoes are stored in the KTCCA cold-storage plant.

May 2–7, 1966. A province-wide writers' seminar is held at the Academy to discuss the production of literature for neoliterates.

May 25, 1966. The deputy commissioner of Comilla district calls a meeting to improve the relations between civil administration (circle officers and subdivisional officers) and the new projects (project and deputy project directors).

May 1966. The KTCCA has applications in for an operating loan of Rs. 3,000,000 ($630,000) from the State Bank of Pakistan, and for a foreign exchange loan of Rs. 6,000,000 ($1,260,000) for mechanization from funds loaned to Pakistan by the World Bank. (Both loans were subsequently received.)

June 1966. Nineteen hundred IUD coils are inserted at the Abhoy Ashram clinic, and the sale of nonmedical contraceptives averages more than 3,000 dozen pieces a month.

Plans are being worked out by Department of Basic Democracies and Local Government, Agricultural Development Corporation, Department of Agriculture, EPWAPDA, and the Academy to demonstrate winter paddy production in early 1967 with low-lift irrigation pumps in 14 thanas. Training outline and manuals are now being developed.

July 1966. The Thirteenth All-Pakistan Economic Conference is held at Comilla.

August 1966. The Academy develops a standard four-week course in rural development, the first of which courses is given in September 1966.

October 1966. The first week-long faculty planning conference is held which defines research, teaching, and extension objectives for the year.

December 1966. The position of deputy director for administration is approved by the board of governors.

February 1967. The zari singers are now employed as a regular part of the communication section program to popularize improved methods of agriculture, cooperatives, family planning, and other programs of the Academy.

A new cooperative for women sweepers is formed as part of the women's program.

The field inspection staff reports that 2,201 acres of land are under tube well irrigation and 474 acres under pump irrigation.

March 1967. An all-Pakistan seminar on the rural works program is held at Comilla.

April 1967. Winter vegetable-growing competitions are held in 68 youth clubs. Youth club rallies are held in ten village centers.

Detailed plans for the new Thana Training and Development Center are prepared.

Ten new six-inch tube wells are projected for completion by October 1967.

June 1967. Fifty-five thana family planning offices with 6 team leaders attend a one-week training course.

Eight tube wells are electrified and 15 more are projected for completion by December 1967.

Two thousand fifty maunds of improved rice seeds are procured.

July 1967. IR-8 and Panjam-2 seeds are harvested from the Christy seed multiplication farm. Crop-cutting records indicate that 84 maunds (green weight) per acre were produced from IR-8 seed and 55 maunds from Panjam-2 seed. "Elite" seeds were harvested from 300 selected hills.

September 1967. Seven hundred seventy thana-level officers are trained in the organization of irrigation groups for the expanded irrigation program.

October 1967. Visitors to the Academy include: three teams from the World Bank, a group from the Royal Iranian delegation on Agriculture, a Japanese industrial survey team, an advisor from the Bank of England, Indonesian lay doctors, the executive director and director of inspection from the State Bank of Pakistan, and representatives of the Friends (Quakers) Community Development Service and the Church World Service.

Final preparations are made for the second cold-storage plant.

Appendix VIII 327

A Danish poultry expert arrives.

Ten primary cooperative societies are selected for multiplication of seed potatoes.

March 1968. Training programs include: 25 civil service probationers, 10 students from the College of Social Welfare and Research Center, University of Dacca, 12 community development officials from Thailand, and 6 groups of model farmers, managers, and union assistants with 623 participants.

The annual meeting of the KTCCA is held; a review of the year's progress is made, and an election is held of an eight-man management committee.

The cold-storage plant receives 3,312 maunds of seed potatoes and 18,152 maunds of table potatoes.

April 1968. The board of governors reviews the program of the Academy and makes decisions with reference to financial, personnel, and other items on the agenda prepared by the Director who serves as member secretary.

Five irrigation pump houses are constructed; there are now 50 electrified pumps.

November 1968. Mr. A. H. M. Azizul Huq is appointed Director of the Academy. Dr. Akhter Hameed Khan continues to serve as vice-chairman of the board of governors and chairman of the KTCCA.

The Academy enters into a contract for Rs. 60,000 with the Department of Basic Democracies and Local Government to undertake an evaluation of the thana irrigation program.

The library receives in the past five months 839 volumes in English, 108 volumes in Bengali, and 178 periodicals.

As now planned, one hundred twenty-five deep tube wells and 65 low-lift pumps will be in operation in Comilla Kotwali thana for the boro season (in early 1969).

Seven research projects on rice varietal trials and insecticides are underway plus research on potatoes, corn, sorghum, chilies, and tomatoes.

The construction of a poultry slaughterhouse has begun. Almost 6,000 eggs and 526 dressed chickens are marketed during the month.

Two women trainees are sent to the Design Center in Dacca for training in dying cloth.

December 1968. A sample of twenty-seven thanas involved in the thana irrigation program are selected for intensive study.

The thana council advances Rs. 43,950 to project committees under the public works program; 1,135 persons are vaccinated against smallpox; 3,300 pounds of insecticides are distributed; and the thana fisheries officer inspects 10 tanks (ponds).

Reports on the family planning program include the sale of 6,640 dozen condoms, 740 dozen foam tablets, 22 IUD insertions, 22 vasectomies, and 4 tube ligations.

January 1969. Two hundred eighteen adult education centers enroll over 5,000 adult males and females. Literacy certificates are issued to 91 first level students, 48 second level, and 46 full literacy.

The seed-testing laboratory is completed and begins operations.

A separate marketing section for all KTCCA products is established.

The service section of the Karkhana repairs 133 pumps, tractors, and other vehicles during the month.

February 1969. The evaluation committee of thana irrigation program reviews the work of four research assistants and nine field investigators.

Spraying campaigns in selected societies are made to offset unusual damage by insect attacks.

Intensive work on the potato-seed-multiplication program is undertaken by a member of the faculty recently returned from an intensive training program abroad and by an MSU consultant.

Over Rs. 2,000 is realized from the sale of fruits, garden products, and plants from the Academy gardens.

A special report of the KTCCA shows that since 1963–1964 grants of over Rs. 2,725,000 have been received for tube wells from the Department of Basic Democracies and Local Government.

Over 500 village women attend the annual rally of the women's program.

April 1969. KTCCA establishes a new department of agricultural research and extension.

Six varietal and other research projects are underway on rice crops and seven research projects on nonrice crops.

The consolidated balance sheet of the KTCCA for the ten months ending April 30 shows assets of Rs. 24,290,076 and a profit on operations of Rs. 142,206.

GLOSSARY, BIBLIOGRAPHY, AND INDEX

Glossary

Ambar charka, an improved hand-operated machine for the spinning of four cotton threads at once; it was introduced and promoted by Gandhi (see *charka* below).

Amon paddy, the seasonal rice crop grown in the late summer and fall.

Ansar, a member of the local home guard, which is a defense unit in the village; not on the regular police or army payroll.

Aus paddy, the seasonal rice crop grown in spring and early summer.

Barkat, continuing benefits, or blessings.

Bigha, approximately one-third of an acre of land.

Boro paddy, the seasonal rice crop grown in the winter months. In most places irrigation is necessary for this crop.

Burqa, a full length all-covering garment for women, with a peep hole for each eye.

Charka, a single-thread hand spinning machine (see also *ambar charka*).

Crore, 10,000,000 punctuated thus: 1,00,00,000. One hundred lakh.

Dai, midwife.

Dheki, a simple machine by which paddy is husked and partially polished; this is accomplished by a perpendicular peg on the end of a pole dropping into a steep-sided stone or wood container.

Eid-ul-Fitr, a Muslim holiday period at the end of the month-long Ramazan fast.

Foruz (Fardz), behavior enjoined by the Quran.

Hāt, a local public market held at a scheduled time, usually once or twice a week.

Imam, the prayer leader of a mosque, commonly a local lay person in rural East Pakistan (see *mullah*).

Jamma, small pieces of brick, usually broken by a hand hammer in the Comilla area; it is used in concrete making in lieu of gravel.

Kabigan, a style of singing in which two song leaders take opposing sides of a question.

Khadi, hand-woven cloth made of hand-spun yarn.

Khal, a canal, or drainage channel.

Khichuri, a dish of whole wheat, rice, pulse, and spices.

Kotwali, headquarters; usually refers to the thana (county) in which the district office is located.

Lakh, 100,000 punctuated thus: 1,00,000.

Madrassa, a traditional Muslim school where much of the instruction is based on the Quran.

Maund (or md.), a unit of weight, approximately 80.5 lbs., sometimes 82.5 lbs.

Mullah, a man who is the head of a mosque; ideally, he has had training in Muslim law and doctrine (see *Imam*).

Paddy, unhulled rice.

Pan, a mascatory green leaf, commonly chewed with betel nut and lime in East Pakistan.

Purdah, seclusion of women from public observation, common among the rural Muslims of South Asia.

Quran, the sacred book of the Muslims, the Koran; the Bengalis prefer this old spelling.

Ramadan (sometimes spelled *Ramazan*), the ninth month of the Muslim (lunar) year, with fasting practiced from dawn to sunset.

Glossary

Rupee, unit of currency in Pakistan. It is made up of 100 *paisa*. A *rupee* has been valued at about U.S. $0.21 for the entire period covered by this study. For rough approximation, therefore, rupees may be converted to dollars by dividing by five.

Sabuj Sangha, a youth club of school children, generally similar to the 4-H Club or the Future Farmers of America.

Sardar, a recognized leader of a village.

Sari, a woman's garment of about six yards of cloth. It is draped so that one portion forms a skirt and the other end a covering for the waist and head.

Seer, approximately two pounds; one fortieth of a maund (see *maund*).

Shaita paddy, a seasonal rice crop grown in the winter; it is usually sown broadcast in the Comilla area.

Thana, original meaning, police station; pronounced "t'ana"—ä as in father. Similar to a county.

Ulema (or *Ulama*), the mullahs as a group; orthodox Muslim religious teachers.

Zamindar, a collector of land revenue in an area for the government. The system formerly operated in Bengal.

Zari singers, folk singers in Bengal. These performers often compose songs for special occasions, and may answer a question by improvising a song.

Bibliography

Major Works in English Published by the Pakistan Academy for Rural Development, 1959–1966[1]

The Academy as a Whole

Annual Reports of the Academy, 1960———.
The Academy at Comilla: An Introduction (illustrated), April 1963.
Monthly Reports of the Academy, 1961———. Mimeographed.

Cooperatives

A New Rural Cooperative System for Comilla Thana, 1961, and subsequent annual reports under the same title.
Hussain, M. A., "A Field Investigation into the Management of Village Cooperatives in Comilla Experimental Area," 1965. Mimeographed.
Huq, M. Ameerul, *Five Years of a Workmens' Cooperative* (case study of the rickshaw pullers' cooperative), December 1965.
Huq, M. Nurul, *Cooperation as a Remedy for Rural Poverty,* 1963.

---

[1] For a complete listing of bibliographic items for the Comilla and Peshawar Academies through 1964 see Edgar A. Schuler and Raghu Singh, "*The Pakistan Academies for Rural Development, Comilla and Peshawar, 1959–1964: A Bibliography,* East Lansing, Michigan State University, Asian Studies Center, Occasional Paper No. 1, Spring 1965.

Rahman, Mahmoodur, *Comilla Cooperative Cold Storage*, December 1967.

Rural Administration

The Comilla Rural Administration Experiment, 1963, and subsequent annual reports by different authors under the same title.

Rural Public Works

A Manual for Rural Public Works, August 1962.

Mohsen, A. K. M., *Report on a Rural Public Works Programme in Comilla Kotwali Thana*, June 1962.

Rahman, A. T. R., et al. *An Evaluation of the Rural Public Works Programme, East Pakistan*, 1962–1963, 1963, and *ibid.*, 1963–1964, 1965.

Sultan, K. M. Tipu (editor), *The Works Program in Comilla Thana: A Case Study, 1962–1966*, November 1966.

Women's Program

Women's Education and Home Development Programme, 1963, and subsequent annual reports under the same title by different authors.

Family Planning

Choldin, Harvey M., *Comilla Pilot Project in Family Planning*, August 1965. Third Annual Report.

Khan, A. Majeed, *Rural Pilot Family Planning Action Programme, May 1962*. First Annual Report.

——. *Pilot Project in Family Planning—Progress to May 1963*. Second Annual Report.

Mannan, M. A., *The Comilla Pilot Project in Family Planning*. Fourth Annual Report, March 1967, and Fifth Annual Report, April 1968.

"The Supply of Family Planning Contraceptives to Different Unions of Comilla Kotwali Thana," March–August 1965. Mimeographed.

Education and Youth Work

Bhuiyan, Ali Asgar, *Imams as Teachers*, May 1968.
Khatun, Shafia, "Feeder School Experimental Programme," 1964–1965. Mimeographed.
Mohsen, A. K. M., *Youth Work at Comilla: Backgrounds and Annual Report for 1963–1964*, August 1964.
Muyeed, Abdul, *School Works Programme, Comilla Kotwali Thana*, 1963–1964, Feb. 1965, and *ibid.*, 1964–1965, March 1966.
Quddus, M. A., *Education for Illiterate Adults*, 1963.
Teacher School Club (Sabuj Sangha) Manual, 1964.

Project Proposals

The Comilla District Development Project, May 1964.
The Comilla Pilot Project in Irrigation and Rural Electrification, November 1963; Revised edition, October 1966.

Technical Publications and Other Research Reports

"Annual Plan for Training and Research, 1968–1969," June 1968. Mimeographed.
An Evaluation Report on the Progress of the Seven Thana Projects under the Comilla District Integrated Rural Development Programme, September 1967.
Ara, Begum Hosne, and Harvey M. Choldin, "Problems in Field Work with Village Women: A Preliminary Report," 1964. Mimeographed. (This paper was further developed and appeared in *Demography*, Vol. 3, 1967, under the title "Cultural Complications in the Fertility Survey," by Harvey M. Choldin, A. Majeed Khan, and Begum Hosne Ara.)
Khan, Ali Akhtar, *Rural Credit in Gazipur Village*, April 1968.
Khan, A. Majeed, *Experience in Cross Cultural Living: An Evaluation of Home-Stay Experience of Twenty-nine U.S. Peace Corps Volunteers in East Pakistan, 1961*, November 1963.

Bibliography 339

Khan, Anwaruzzaman, *Introduction of Tractors in a Subsistence Farm Economy: A Study of Tractor Introduction on a Cooperative Basis in Comilla Kotwali Thana, East Pakistan* (Technical Publication No. 14), 1962.

———. "Trial of 302 IRRI Varieties of Rice, 1966, Abhoy Ashram Farm," July 1966. Mimeographed.

Luykx, Nicolaas G. M., II, "Terminal Report on Introduction of Mechanized Farming in Comilla on a Cooperative Basis, 1961–1966," June 1967. Mimeographed.

Mannan, M. A., *Knowledge and Interest of Farmers in Winter Irrigation* (Technical Publication No. 20), 1966.

Matsuda, Isao, *Annual Report of the Japanese Farm Experts, January 1961–February 1962*, 1963. (A similar comprehensive report has been prepared by the Japanese Farm Experts each year. Only this one, however, has been published in English. The others are available in unedited English to the Academy staff. All have been published in Japanese.)

McColly, Howard F., *Special Report on Introducing Farm Mechanization in the Cooperative Project* (Technical Publication No. 15), 1962.

McDonough, Peter, *An Interim Report for the Communications Section* (Technical Publication No. 16), 1963.

Qadir, S. A., *Village Dhanishwar: Three Generations of Man-Land Adjustments in an East Pakistan Village* (Technical Publication No. 5), 1960.

Rahim, S. A., *A Comparative Study of Improved and Country Methods of Paddy Cultivation in the Comilla Development Area* (Technical Publication No. 1), 1960.

———. *Voluntary Group Adoption of Power Pump Irrigation in Five East Pakistan Villages* (Technical Publication No. 12), 1961.

———. *Diffusion and Adoption of Agricultural Practices: A Study of the Pattern of Communication, Diffusion and Adoption of Improved Agricultural Practices in a Village in East Pakistan* (Technical Publication No. 7), 2nd edition, 1963.

———. *Communication and Personal Influence in an East Pakistan Village* (Technical Publication No. 18), 1965.

———. and A. Farouk (Dacca University), *Modernization of Subsistence Agriculture—An Experimental Survey in Comilla* (Preliminary Report published jointly by PARD and the Bureau of Economics Research, Dacca University), 1965.

———. and Anwaruzzaman Khan, *A Follow-up Survey on Seed Multiplication Scheme* (Technical Publication No. 4), 1960.

Rahman, A. T. R., *Basic Democracies at the Grass Roots: A Study of Three Union Councils in Kotwali (Comilla) Thana* (Technical Publication No. 13), 1962.

Rahman, Mahmoodur, *Irrigation in Two Comilla Villages*, June 1964.

———. *Cost and Return: A Study of Irrigated Crops in Comilla Villages* (Technical Publication No. 19), October 1964.

———. *Costs and Returns: Economics of Winter-irrigated Crops in Comilla, 1965-1966*, March 1967.

———. *Live Stock Population: A Survey in Comilla Kotwali and Chandina Thanas*, June 1968.

Statistical Digest (compilation of basic statistics on Comilla activities) May 1968.

Zaidi, S. M. Hafeez, et al., *Annual Evaluation Report 1960: An Evaluation Survey of the Academy's Extension Projects* (Technical Publication No. 11), 1960.

Zaidi, Wiqar H., *An Investigation into Factors Related to the Adoption of Improved Methods of Amon Paddy Cultivation in the Comilla Development Area* (Technical Publication No. 2), 1960.

———. *A Survey of Cottage Industries in the Comilla Development Area* (Technical Publication No. 3), 1960.

———. *Adoption of Improved Methods of Paddy Cultivation in Comilla Development Area II (Amon, 1960)* (Technical Publication No. 6), 1961.

———. *A Survey of Attitudes of Rural Population toward Family Planning* (Technical Publication No. 8), 1961.

———. *Adoption of Improved Methods of Paddy Cultivation in*

Bibliography

Comilla Development Area III (Amon, 1960) (Technical Publication No. 9), 1961.

———. *Adult Education Center in Comilla Development Area* (Technical Publication No. 10), 1961.

Varietal Trials and Related Studies

Akhanda, A. M., "Fertilizer Trials on IR-8, IR-9-60 and Taipei-Boro, 1966–1967, Abhoy Ashram Farm," November 1967. Mimeographed.

———. "Study of Insecticides for Rice," May 1968. Mimeographed.

———. "Tests of IRRI Selections" (Amon, 1967), May 1968. Mimeographed.

———. "Tests of IRRI Selections" (Boro, 1967–1968), September 1968. Mimeographed.

Bari, Fazhul, "A Comparative Yield Trial with Different IRRI Selections," June 1969. Mimeographed.

"Cultivation of IR-8 and Irrigation Prospects and Problems: A Report on the Farmers' Seminar" (March–May, 1968), August 1968. Mimeographed.

Huq, M. Azizul, *Training Report on Organization of Irrigation Groups and Cultivation of IR-8*, November 1967.

Khan, Anwaruzzaman, "Trial of 302 IRRI Varieties of Rice, 1966, Abhoy Ashram Farm," July 1966. Mimeographed.

Safiullah, M., "Aus Crop Survey in Comilla Kotwali Thana, 1967," May 1968. Mimeographed.

———. "Winter Crop Survey in Comilla Kotwali Thana, 1968," September 1968. Mimeographed.

Journal of the Pakistan Academy for Rural Development, Comilla

The *Journal* was published from 1960 to 1965, at first on a bimonthly basis, and then quarterly. It carried reports on program operations and on the research and evaluation efforts by faculty members, and most issues contained also one or more articles contributed by others in the field.

Other Reports, Papers, and Articles in English about the Academy and Its Work

Berelson, Bernard. "Pakistan: The Rural Pilot Family Planning Action Programme at Comilla." New York: The Population Council, 1964. Mimeographed.

Bertocci, Peter J. "Patterns of Social Organization in Rural East Bengal." Unpublished Ph.D. dissertation, Michigan State University, May 1968.

Choldin, Harvey M. "Urban Cooperatives at Comilla, Pakistan: A Case Study of Local-Level Development," *Economic Development and Cultural Change* (Chicago), Vol. XVI, No. 2, January 1968.

———. "The Development Project as Natural Experiment: The Comilla Pakistan Project," *Economic Development and Cultural Change*, Vol. XVII, No. 4, April 1969.

Datta-Ray, Sunanda K. "Integrated Plan for Rural Uplift in Comilla: Lessons to be Learned from the Pakistani Experiment," *The Statesman* (Calcutta), April 4, 1966.

Dupree, Louis. "The Comilla Experiment: A Scheme for Village Development in East Pakistan." Reports Service, *American Universities Field Staff*, South Asia Series, Vol. XIII, No. 2 (Pakistan), January 1964.

Fairchild, Henry W., and Shamsul Haq. "Cooperative vs. Commune: Pakistan's Comilla Thana Villages Start a Momentous Experiment," *International Development Review*, Vol. IV, No. 1, March 1962.

Gilbert, Richard V. "The Works Program in East Pakistan," *International Labour Review*, Vol. LXXXIX, No. 3, March 1964.

Hussain, A. F. A. "The Comilla Cooperative Experiment," *Review of International Cooperation*, Vol. LVII, No. 2, March 1964.

Khan, Akhter Hameed, and A. K. M. Mohsen. "Mobilizing Village Leadership: The Kotwali Public Works Project

Taps a Reservoir of Latent Ability," *International Development Review*, Vol. IV, No. 3, September 1962.

Khan, A. Majeed, and Harvey M. Choldin. "New 'Family Planners' for Rural East Pakistan," *Demography*, Vol. II, 1965.

Khan, A. Z. M. Obaidullah. "An Experiment in Modernization of Rural Community in East Pakistan," *Indian Quarterly* (Indian Council of World Affairs, New Delhi), Oct.–Dec. 1963.

McCarthy, Florence E. "Bengali Village Women Mediators between Tradition and Development." Master's thesis, Michigan State University, 1968.

Millikan, Max F., and David Hapgood. *No Easy Harvest: The Dilemma of Agriculture in Developing Countries*. Boston: Little, Brown and Co., 1967.

Neal, Ernest E. "Program of Community Development Assistance: A Report to the Assistant Administrator for Technical Cooperation and Research." Washington: USAID, Technical Cooperation and Research, August 1964. Mimeographed.

Rahim, Syed A. "Collective Adoption of Innovations by Village Cooperatives in Pakistan: Diffusion of Innovations in a Development System." Ph.D. dissertation, Michigan State University, May 1968.

Ramon Magsaysay Award Foundation. "Background Statement on Akhter Hameed Khan, 1963 Ramon Magsaysay Awardee for Government Service." (East Lansing: Michigan State University, Pakistan Project files, August 1963).

Raper, Arthur F. "Some Reflections Upon Leaving Comilla," *Journal* (Pakistan Academy for Rural Development), Vol. V, No. 2, October 1964; reprinted by the Asian Studies Center, Michigan State University, in its *Asian Studies Papers*, Reprint Series, No. 1, 1965–1966, Fall 1965.

———. *The Contribution of Village Development to the Modernization of Nations*. East Lansing: Michigan State University, Papers in International and World Affairs, 1966 Series, No. 1, January 1966.

Raper, Martha J. "An Island of Progress Emerges from a Program of Rural Development in Tradition-bound Villages," *Randolph-Macon Alumnae Bulletin* (Lynchburg, Va.), Spring 1964.

——. "The Comilla Program," *Format* (Michigan State University), January–February, 1965.

Schuler, Edgar A. "Increasing Competence in Education Institution Building Through Cross-Cultural Cooperation: The Case of MSU and the Pakistan Academies for Village Development." East Lansing: Michigan State University, College of Education, Office of Research and Publications, Educational Proceedings Series, No. 4, August 1963. Mimeographed.

——. "The Origin and Nature of the Pakistan Academies for Village Development," *Rural Sociology*, Vol. XXIX, No. 3, September 1964.

Schuman, Howard. *Economic Development and Individual Change: A Social-Psychological Study of the Comilla Experiment in Pakistan.* Cambridge: Harvard University Center of International Affairs, Occasional Papers in International Affairs, No. 15, February 1967.

Sobhan, Rahman. *Basic Democracies Works Programme and Rural Development in East Pakistan.* Pakistan: Bureau of Economic Research, University of Dacca, 1968.

Stevens, Robert D. "Institutional Change and Agricultural Development: Some Evidence from Comilla, East Pakistan." East Lansing: Michigan State University, Agricultural Economics Reports, No. 64, April 1967. Mimeographed.

Tepper, Elliot. *Changing Pattern of Administration in Rural East Pakistan.* East Lansing: Michigan State University, Asian Studies Center, Occasional Paper No. 5, Fall 1966.

Ulrey, Orion. "Cooperatives and Rural Development in Pakistan," *News for Farmer Cooperatives*, Vol. XXXI, No. 3, June 1964, and No. 4, July 1964.

Index

Absorption test, 136-139, 321
Academies (Comilla and Peshawar): establishment of, 12-13, 21-25; governance of, 32-34; proposed financial support of, 25
Academy (Comilla): assistance received by, 294-297; financial support of, 35-36, 315-317; governance of, 35; philosophy of operation, 37-44
Academy faculty: list of, 289-290; opportunities for advancement, 262-263; selection of, 26-27; training of, 25, 28-32
Academy's laboratory area, see Laboratory area of Academy
Academy's two campuses, 38
Action diary, xii, 315-318
Advisors to Academy, see Michigan State University and Danish experts at Academy
Agricultural Cooperatives Federation (ACF), see Cooperatives
Agricultural Development Corporation, 54, 151, 216, 219, 261
Ahmad, A. Musa S., xiii, 243
Ahmed, Taherunnessa, 289
Ahmed, Taslimuddin, 252, 291
Ali, Quazi Azher, 291
Ancient ruins, 54n
Annual rainfall, see Rainfall
Ara, Begum Hosne, 221n, 338
Asfar, M., 294
Asghar, Ali, 294

Asian Studies Center (at MSU), xiii, 22n, 66, 99, 187n, 245n

Basic Democracies, system of, 98-104
Bell, David E., ix
Bengali language, 5
Berelson, Bernard, 342
Bertocci, Peter J., 342
Betrothal, age of, 158
Bhuiyan, Ali Asgar, 187n, 289, 338
Block farming, 54
Booklets by Imams for neoliterates, 197-198
Brick-burning project, 120-121
British volunteers, 150, 297, 300
Buddhists, 5
Bullocks, 7
Burqua, 3, 333

CARE, 207, 317
Carolus, Robert, 299
Case, Harry L., xiii, 295
Causeway, 1, 122
Change, viii, ix, 1, 12, 15
China, 96-97
Choldin, Harvey M., xii, 177n, 183n, 221n, 300, 337, 338, 342
Choldin, Marianna Tax, 279n
Cholera, 145
Choudhury, Moqbul A., 185n, 290
Christians, 5
Civil Service of Pakistan, 98, 263
Climate, 1-2, 21; see also Storms, Rainfall, Floods

345

346 Index

Cold storage plants, see Cooperatives, agricultural processing enterprises
Colombo Plan, see Japanese experts
Comilla approach, 259; basic results of, 269
Comilla as a problem area, 1, 9-10, 21, 107-111
Comilla cooperatives contrasted with commune system, 96-98, 342
Comilla Mohajir Karkhana Cooperative, Ltd., 81, 328
Comilla's international influence, 257-258
Commercial bank, rural, 76-77
Communications, 101, 228-231
Community development, 20, 28, 30
Contraceptives: Islamic opinion on use of, 178-179; mass distribution of nonmedical types, 179-180; price of, 179; see also Family planning program *and* Intrauterine device
Cooperatives, new rural village-based system of: Agricultural Cooperatives Federation (ACF), 63, 64-65, 308-309, 324; agricultural processing enterprises, 84-87; cash deposits of members, 17, 66-69; characteristics of members, 50; comparative status of agricultural and nonagricultural societies, 308-309; compulsory cooperatives, discussion of, 53-57; evaluation study of sample societies, 88-90; five-year mechanization project, 58-59; Kotwali Thana Central Cooperative Association (KTCCA), 57-58, 60, 61, 65, 69-97, 264, 321, 329; loans, 69-76, 308-309; managers (organizers) of local societies, 49-53; marketing, 83-87; model farmers, 52-53; numbers of societies/members, 63-65; shares purchased by members, 67-68; societies discontinued, 75; societies put on probation, 74-75; Special Cooperatives Societies Federation, 63-65, 323; status of cooperatives in Comilla thana, 308-309, in three scattered thanas, 312-313, in seven thanas in Comilla district, 314; women members, 167, 169; see also Special officer of cooperatives
Credit, see Cooperatives, loans
Crop yields, 8, 94, 326
Cultural factors, use of, 268, 269

Dacca University, 216, 255, 261
Danish experts at Academy, 86, 90, 91-92, 297, 300
Datta-Ray, Sunanda K., 342
Departmental representatives in thana: aloofness of, 104-105; confronted by villagers, 103-104; role as teachers, 127-128; shift to thana headquarters, 127-128
"Development Administration," 27-28, 37; see also Public administration
Diversion canal, fear of, 110, 143-144
Doxiadis Associates, 26
Drainage canals needed, 110-111; see also Public works program
Dupree, Louis, 110

East Pakistan Agricultural University students, 255
East Pakistan Cooperative College, 53n
East Pakistan Water and Power Development Authority (EPWAPDA), 108-109, 135, 138-139, 248
Education: with rural bias, 189-194; with urban bias, 186-187; see also "Feeder schools"
Education as related to the development process, 188-189
Ellickson, Jean, 301
Emancipation of women, 157, 160; see also Women's program
Expansion of Comilla programs, 18-19, 232-242, 248-253; see also Impact of Comilla program

Extension, 16, 41-42, 50-53, 242-246, 266-267

Fairchild, Henry W., xiii, 49, 295, 296, 298, 342
Faith, role of, 45-46, 67, 110
Family planning program: effects of, 184-185; expansion of, to district, 180-253, to province, 253; launching of, 172-176; publicity about, 180-182; reaction of villagers to, 175, 176, 179; relation to Comilla program, 182-183; surgical methods used, 182; women organizers, statements by, 176-177; *see also* Contraceptives
Farm- and home-related projects, 191-193; *see also* Education, with rural bias
Farm families without land, 9
Farm tools and implements, 7-8
Farms, size of: in Comilla area, vi, 9; in East Pakistan, 7
Farouk, A., 216n
"Feeder schools," 194-200; *see also* Imams *and* Jana-o-Jana
Fellows of the Afro-Asian Program of Syracuse University, 300
Fertilizer, commercial, 8, 213
Five-Year Plans of Pakistan, *see* Pakistan, Five-Year Plans of
Flood, annual, 2, 9-10, 107, 110, 135, 138
Folk singers, *see* Zari singers
Ford Foundation, vii, 11, 22, 25, 26, 29, 59, 262, 295, 315-317, 318
Foreign personnel at Academy, 298-301

Gaibandha thana, 132, 235, 238, 312
Gant, George, 27-28, 318
Ghazzali, Al, 177
Gilbert, Richard V., 111, 125n, 294, 342
Goripur thana, 132, 235, 238, 312
Governance of Comilla Academy, *see* Academy, governance of
Gumti river: flash floods of, 110, 138, 145-146; levee system, 9-10, the cutting of the levee, 143-147, 322

Haq, Shamsul, 49, 291, 342
Havener, Robert D., xiii, 90n, 296, 298
Hemjora embankment, 109-110
Hindus, 5, 7, 303
Hossain, Shafique, 290
Huq, Anwarul, 289
Huq, A. B. M. Nurul, 289
Huq, A. H. M. Azizul, 261, 289, 327
Huq, M. Ameerul, 289, 336
Huq, M. Azizul, 152n, 341
Huq, M. Nurul, 289, 336
Hussain, A. F. A., 342
Hussain, M. Zakir, 49n, 88n, 134n, 200n, 289

Illiteracy, 4, 157, 187-189
Imams, 132, 178, 187, 194-200, 323
Impact of the Academy, 232, 245-258; *see also* Expansion of Comilla program
India, 22, 116
Indigenous roots of development procedures, 268-269
Industrial Cooperative Society, 92
Institution building, 263, 274-275
International Rice Research Institute (IRRI), 40, 93, 271, 324
IR-8 (rice), 95, 151, 218-219, 250
Irrigation: acreage covered, 149-150, 251; comparative costs of types, 142-143, 148-149; early projects, 137-140; expenditures for, 122n, 137, 150, 249, 252, 310; province-wide program of, 151, 152, 248-251; pumps, deisel and electric, 148-151, 327; Sonaichuri project, 135, 137, 141, 143, 145-148, 218; tube wells, 139-140, 142, 148, 150
Irrigation and need of land to "rest," 140
Irrigation pumps as organizational catalysts, 50
Islam, annual cycle of, 3
Isolation, physical and psychological, 3

Intrauterine device (IUD), 182, 323, 325, 328; *see also* Family planning

Jamma, 146-147, 334
Jana-o-Jana, 196-197
Japanese farm experts, 47, 140, 297, 300-301, 320
Johannes, Phyllis, 301
"Joint Agricultural Enterprise," 56-57
Jinnah, Mohammad Ali, 98

Kaiyim, Ibn, 117
Kazi, Q. H., 291
Khan, Abdul Aziz, 289
Khan, Akhter Hameed, vii, ix, 18, 21, 22n, 37, 45, 124-125, 274, 289, 319, 327, 342-343; acknowledgments of assistance to Academy, 294-297; curriculum vitae, 292-293; quoted, 43, 54-55, 96, 119, 132-134, 136, 157, 177-178, 186-187, 199-200, 208, 212, 245, 258-259, 279-288; role of, 258-262
Khan, Anwaruzzaman, 213n, 289, 339, 341
Khan, A. Majeed, 177n, 183n, 289, 337, 338, 343
Khan, A. Z. M. Obaidullah, 234n, 291, 343
Khan, I. U., 294, 320
Khan, Miriam, 291
Khan, Mohammed Ayub, 54, 98, 243, 246, 294, 319, 322
Khan, S. R., 291
Khatum, Shafia, 290, 338
Koran, *see* Quran
Kumata, Hideya, 299

Laboratory area of Academy, viii, 14, 16, 17, 37-38, 100, 256-257, 267, 319
Lalmai-Mainamati Hills, 38, 54n
Land reform, 7
Larzelere, Henry E., 299
Latrines for village homes, 324
Lesson sheets and leaflets used, 51-52, 175
Levak, Albert E., xii, 28n
Library, 227-228

Listening, importance of, vii, 267-268
Literacy training for adults, 197, 201-202; *see also* "Feeder schools"
Loans, *see* Cooperatives
Local government, strengthening of, 98, 107
Loomis, Charles P., 299
Luykx, Nicolaas G. M., II, xiii, 59n, 90n, 297, 298, 339

Madrassa schools, 4, 188, 334
Magsaysay, Ramon, Award Foundation, 293, 343
Malik, H. R., 294
Mannan, M. A., 290, 337, 339
Markets, *see* Cooperatives
Marriage, age of, 158, 159
Martens, Delvin W., xiii, 296, 298
Maternal and Child Health Centers: in Comilla town, 164; on the Abhoy Ashram campus, 169, 170
Matsuda, Isao, 339
McCarthy, Florence E., xii, 161n, 166n, 171n, 299, 301, 343
McColly, Howard F., 299, 339
McDonough, Peter, 299, 339
Michigan State University (MSU), vii, xi, 12, 25, 26, 29-33, 93, 114-115, 159, 233, 262-263, 295, 298-299, 318
Michigan State University Graduate Research Students at Comilla, 301
Midwife (*dai*) training, 164-165
Model farmers, *see* Cooperatives
Mohammadullah, 291
Mohsen, A. K. M., 100n, 118n, 290, 337, 338, 342-343
Moneylenders, vi, 8-9, 107, 281
Muslim faith, 59, 133, 285; *see* Quran
Muyeed, Abdul, xiii, 202, 290, 338

National Research Institute for Family Planning, 182
National Seminar on Family Planning, 182-183
Natore thana, 132, 235-238, 313
Neal, Ernest E., 343

Nelson, Layton V., 299
New village-based cooperatives, see Cooperatives
Niehoff, Richard O., xii, 66n, 102n, 295, 298
Nor'westers, see Storms

Organizers, see Cooperatives

Pakistan compared with other countries, 302-303
Pakistan, Five-Year Plans of, 239, 256-257, 318
Pamphlets, use of, 52
PARD, PAVD, change of name, 11n
Partition (of India and Pakistan), 7, 10
Patten, Richard H., xiii, 294
Peace Corps Volunteers, 81, 115, 120, 139, 144, 150, 160, 165, 297, 299-300, 305, 320
Peshawar Academy, see Academies
Physical engineering as related to social engineering, 135, 252
PL-480, see United States Public Law 480
Platt, George M., 102n
Polytechnic School, 54n
Population Council, Inc., see Research
Population density, 5, 9, 302-303
Poultry slaughterhouse, 328
Principles of cooperatives, 285-288
Professors and students, influence of Comilla on, 255, 305
Province-wide irrigation program, see Irrigation
Public administration, 12, 27-28, 30, 37, 266
Public works program: accomplishments of, 118-120, 121-123, 245-246; amount of earth moved, 118, 122; Comilla thana pilot project, 118-123; expenditures for, 114, 120-121, 123, 310; project committees, 114-115, 246; roads and flood control, most popular, 123
Pumps, see Irrigation
Purdah, 3, 178, 221, 273

Qadir, S. A., 339
Quddus, M. A. (educator), 290, 291, 338
Quddus, M. A. (cartographer), 6, 62, 170, 237
Quran, 4, 283, 285; see Muslim faith

Radio Pakistan, 181-182
Rahim, Syed A., xiii, 213n, 216n, 290, 339-340, 343
Rahman, A. T. R., 124n, 290, 337, 340
Rahman, K. M. Shamsur, 261, 289, 322
Rahman, Mahmoodur, 95n, 139n, 216n, 290, 336, 340
Rainfall, annual, 2
Ramadan, 3, 334
Raper, Arthur F., 296, 298, 343
Raper, Martha J., xiii, 161n, 166n, 296, 298, 344
Reeves, Floyd W., xii, 25, 318
Refugee problems, 107n
"Rehearsal," the role of, 225
Research, 14, 17-18, 43-44, 210-212; by Japanese experts, 215, 339; by Population Council, Inc., 175-176, 183-185, 218; in cooperation with Institute of Development Economics, 217, with Bureau of Economic Research, Dacca University, 216; MSU advisors in relation to, 226; problems of, 219-226; subjects of, 212-216; use of documents for, 121, 210; use of field enumerators, 211-212
Rickshawpullers, see Cooperatives, SCSF
Rivers, 2, 9-10, 107-108, 110, 138, 145-147, 322
Roads, 10; see also Public works program
Ross, William T., xii, 298
Rouf, A. S. M. A., 291
Rural development, test of soundness of, 269-272
Rural electrification, Comilla thana pilot project, 11, 137, 153-156

Sabuj Sangha, 190-192, 335
Saffiullah, M., 94n, 341
Sahban, Rahman, 344
School libraries, 192
School works program, 202-206; accomplishments of, 206-209
Schools, village, 4; see also Education
Schuler, Edgar A., xii, 295, 298, 336, 344
Schuman, Howard, 344
Smuggling, border, 107n
Singh, Raghu, 336
Sonaichuri project, see Irrigation
Special officer of cooperatives, 47-48, 66; see also Cooperatives
Standard of living, 10-11, 157-159
Stevens, Robert D., xii, 296, 298, 344
Stoeckel, John E., 165n, 185n, 300
Storms, 2, 9, 21, 108-109
Sultan, K. M. Tipu, 290, 337

Taggart, Glenn, 296
Tank (pond), 2, 138
Tax, Sol, xiii
Teachers' College, 54n
Technical advances, 269-270
Tehsil, 23; see also Thana
Tenure of farm operators, 7, 303
Tepper, Elliot, 99n, 344
Terrain, 1, 2, 7-9, 143-145
Thakurgaon tube well project, 251-253
Thana council, 14, 101-106, 109, 115-116, 119-120, 125-126, 130, 134, 144, 239, 250, 251, 274-275
Thana officials as teachers, 127-128, 273
Thana training and development centers (TTDC), 14, 19, 100-101, 128-134, 257
Tractors, 65, 78-82, 150-151; see also Cooperatives, five-year mechanization project
Transportation, importance of, to marketing, 87
Trial and error procedures, viii, 104
Training at Academy, 23-24, 266; for province-wide irrigation program, 251; for province-wide works program, 39-41, 123-125; for village women, 162-164, 169, 311; for villagers, 51-52, 65, 78-80, 102, 106, 113, 116-117, 122, 124, 126, 130-134, 138, 147, 151, 162-166, 190-193, 196, 211, 235, 246, 251, 306-307; types of training, 304-307
Training of women in the villages, 165-166, 306-307
Tube ligations, 328; see also Family planning
Tube wells, see Irrigation

Ulrey, Orion, 344
Unemployment, 110, 113
UNICEF, 165, 317
Union agricultural assistants, 105, 127
Union councils, 101-106, 119, 306
United Bank, Ltd., 76-77, 121
United States Agency for International Development (AID), 137, 322; see also United States Public Law 480
United States International Cooperation Administration (ICA), 10, 22, 29, 36, 318
United States Land-Grant Universities, 17-18
United States Public Law 480 (PL-480), 114, 242

Vasectomies, 328; see also Family planning
Village Agricultural and Industrial Development (V-AID), 11, 16, 22n, 23, 29, 37, 99-100, 106, 132, 160, 318
Village conditions, study of, 13, 18, 43, 45, 104-106, 136, 140, 144, 203, 266-267, 319
Village roads, see Public works program
Villager participation in program development, 15-16, 41, 45-53, 67, 78-79, 89, 103-118, 132-134, 137-148, 154, 156, 160-172, 195-198, 245, 250-251, 253-254, 260, 267-269

Villagers trained at the Academy, *see* Training at the Academy

Wajihullah, A. B. M., 291
Wealth, source of, in East Pakistan, 280
Weekly meetings in villages, 16, 49, 50-51; *see also* Cooperatives *and* Women's program
Wharton, Clifton R., Jr., 250n
Wheat: used in public works program, 111, 113-114, 117; used in schools, 168; wheat use demonstrations, 168
Women: as innovators, 171; diffidence of, 221-222; status of, 157-158, 189
Women in the cooperatives, *see* Cooperatives
Women interviewers, *see* Research, use of field enumerators
Women schoolteachers, 199-201
Women's program: ambivalent attitude of men toward, 165-166; annual rallies of, 169, 329; expansion of, 172n; launching of, 160-161; number of women taught at Academy, 164; number taught in villages, 165-166; orientation of village women, 162-163; Pakistani staff for, 170; place of women in development process, 166

Yahya, A. F. M., 291
Youth rallies, annual, *see* Education, with rural bias
Yugoslavia team visit, 56, 320

Zaidi, S. M. Hafeez, 223n, 290, 340
Zaidi, Wiqar H., 175n, 290, 340-341
Zamindari system, 7
Zari singers, used to publicize programs, 180-181, 230-231, 268, 325, 335